The Prose and the Passion

Other titles in the Cassell Education series:

The Prose and the Passion

*Children and
Their Reading*

Edited by
Morag Styles, Eve Bearne and
Victor Watson

CASSELL

Cassell

Villiers House   387 Park Avenue South
41/47 Strand   New York
London WC2N 5JE   NY 10016-8810

First published 1994

British Library Cataloguing-in-Publication Data
A catalogue record for this book is available from the British Library.

Library of Congress Cataloging-in-Publication Data

ISBN 0-304-32772-7 (hardback)
      0-304-32771-9 (paperback)

Typeset by Litho Link Ltd, Welshpool, Powys, Wales
Printed and bound in Great Britain by Redwood Books, Trowbridge, Wiltshire

Contents

List of Contributors

Michael Armstrong, once a teacher at Countesthorpe Comprehensive, is now Headteacher at Harwell Primary School, Oxfordshire. He is the author of the seminal study of children as artists and writers, *Closely Observed Children*. He writes on primary education for the *TES* and other publications and is well known for his belief in children as creative thinkers. He is a robust critic of those whose views on education are materialistic and mechanical. Michael Armstrong is much in demand as an inspirational public speaker.

Helen Arnold is the author of many key books on the teaching and learning of reading, including *Listening to Children Reading*. She is widely in demand as a lecturer and consultant in reading in this country and in many other parts of the world. Her career has spanned teaching, lecturing, running a research project and advisory work. Her current interests include non-fiction reading and writing.

Eve Bearne has taught English and Drama in schools and colleges for twenty-five years. She was a project officer for the National Writing Project and co-editor of a number of their publications. She is co-author of *Writing Policy in Action*, has produced an Open University In-Service Course and is currently working on a book about the relationship between children's reading and their writing. She is a Senior Lecturer in English at Homerton College.

Anthony Browne is one of the finest picture-book makers for children of any time. His work is extremely popular with children, but his adult following is almost as large. Among his most compelling and innovative books are *Zoo*, *Gorilla*, *Willy the Wimp* and *The Tunnel*, as well as an unforgettable illustrated version of *Alice in Wonderland*. Browne is well known for his startling imagery, his visual jokes and surprises, and for humane and challenging texts.

Helen Cook, formerly a teacher and one-time Education Officer of the Poetry Society, now works in Community Arts. She is co-author of *There's a Poet Behind You*, *Inkslinger* and *The Cambridge Poetry Box*. She devised and ran the massively successful project, 'Poets Live', a series of workshops and readings in Cambridge which has become part of the arts calendar in the region. She regularly organizes arts events (especially poetry) in schools and the community. Helen Cook ran the Cambridge Children's Poetry Festival in 1985.

Wendy Cope is the enormously successful author of *Making Cocoa for Kingsley Amis* and *Serious Concerns*. Both her books of poetry for adults have made the best-seller list. For many years a primary teacher, Wendy Cope has written a book of finger rhymes for young children, *Twiddling Your Thumbs*, and an anthology for teenagers entitled *Is That the New Moon?* She is also well known as a journalist and broadcaster.

Jenny Daniels has taught in a variety of contexts including schools, nurseries, further education, special needs, adult literacy and prison education. She is now a Senior Lecturer in English at Homerton College, where she specializes in the Augustan/ Romantic period and language in the primary school. Her recent area of research is gender and reading practices, particularly as they relate to popular culture. She is also continuing to work on an historical analysis of women, representation and literature.

Ben Haggarty is a gifted storyteller based at the Crick-Crack Club in London. He is much in demand all over the country at schools, conferences and a great variety of venues, sometimes working alone, sometimes with The Company of Storytellers. Ben works hard to promote the art of storytelling and help young storytellers. We are lucky to be able to capture in print one of his remarkable tales.

Avril Harpley is currently a primary adviser in Northants and Vice-Chair of the Association of Media Education. She has been running media education courses for teachers and pupils for many years. She is the author of *Bright Ideas: Media Education*, and her articles on this subject have been published widely.

Lesley Hendy, a former first school headteacher, is now Senior Lecturer in Drama and Creative Arts at Homerton College, Cambridge. She has had much experience teaching drama at primary and secondary level, as well as specializing in drama in the early years. She has produced many plays, including a recent success at the Edinburgh Festival Fringe. She is currently working on a book about drama in the primary school.

Mary Hilton is Deputy Headteacher at Great and Little Shelford Primary School in Cambridgeshire. For the last few years, as well as full-time teaching, she has been researching into literacy and popular culture and is now working towards a higher degree in this area. A gifted and indefatigable teacher, she also took part in the writing project which resulted in *Collaboration and Writing*, to which she contributed a wise and enlightened chapter. She recently published an article about historical continuities in popular fiction in the *Cambridge Journal of Education*.

Robert Leeson has written many novels for children, most of them for teenage readers. All his work is characterized by a concern for ordinary people struggling with poverty, deprivation and prejudice. He is particularly well known for his association with the *Grange Hill* and *Tucker* television series and – more recently – for his *Jan Alone* trilogy, a sharply realistic and compassionate narrative concerned with the sexual and social pressures on girls and young women as they move from school to work.

Jill Paton Walsh is a distinguished writer for children and adults. Her range is wide, including some exceptional picture books, but she is, perhaps, best known and loved for novels like *Fireweed, Unleaving* and *Grace*. Her literary prizes include the Whitbread Award, the Universe Literary Prize for *A Parcel of Patterns* and the Smarties Prize Grand Prix for *Gaffer Samson's Luck*.

Fred Sedgwick is a freelance writer and lecturer, who spends much of his time working in schools, teachers' centres and colleges, mainly on children's writing and poetry. He is co-author (with Sandy Brownjohn) of worksheets on teaching poetry for the Poetry Library at the South Bank Centre and a part-time tutor in Independent Studies at the University of East London. His most recent books are *Lies* (a book of poems), *The Expressive Arts in the Primary School*, *Drawing to Learn* (with Dawn Sedgwick) and *Pizza, Curry, Fish and Chips*.

Brigid Smith taught for many years in schools, was Head of Special Needs in a Harlow comprehensive and is now Senior Lecturer in Education at Homerton College. Her recent publications include *Spelling in Context* (with Margaret Peters) and *Through Writing to Reading*, a book about effective approaches to literacy, based on her research into children's dictated stories. She is currently Language Consultant for ODA primary education projects in India and Pakistan.

Morag Styles is Language Co-ordinator at Homerton College, where she teaches literacy and children's literature. She spends a lot of her time running workshops with children and teachers, compiling anthologies and writing books about poetry. Her most recent publications include the *Cambridge Poetry Box*, *The Books for Keeps Guide to Poetry*, *Mother Gave a Shout* (poems by women) and *The Politics of Reading* (with Mary Jane Drummond), a special issue of the *Cambridge Journal of Education*. She is currently working on a book on the history of poetry written for children.

Mike Taylor has taught in schools and colleges and is currently a member of the Policy Development Unit at Anglia Polytechnic University. He was a regional co-ordinator for the Language in the National Curriculum Project and set up many excellent partnerships with local schools and advisory teachers. He was one of the contributors to *The LINC Reader*, edited by Ron Carter, and is one of the editors of *Looking into Language*, a classroom-friendly, well-informed and exciting book which offers evidence about how the knowledge gained through the LINC Project can be used for the benefit of pupils.

Victor Watson is a Principal Lecturer in English and Head of Department at Homerton College. He has a special interest in the history and nature of children's books and their relationship both with adult literature and with changing assumptions about childhood. He has made a close study of books for children in the eighteenth and nineteenth century, and he has a particular interest in William Blake, Lewis Carroll and Arthur Ransome. He regularly shares books with reception children in a local school, and he writes for *Signal*, *TES*, *Cambridge Journal of Education*, *UKRA Journal* and *Books for Keeps*.

Acknowledgements

The editors and publisher wish to thank the following for permission to reprint copyright material.

Wendy Cope, for her poem 'Deterrent'.

Gillian Clarke, 'My Box', from *Selected Poems*, published by Carcanet Press, Manchester (1985). Reprinted by permission of the publisher.

Kit Wright, 'The Magic Box', from *Cat among the Pigeons*, published by Viking Kestrel, London (1987). Reprinted by permission of the publisher.

Preface

This book, a companion volume to *After Alice*, is the result of the second conference on children's literature which was held at Homerton College in September 1992, entitled 'Beyond Words'. All the speakers and most of the seminar leaders have written chapters related to their contributions to the conference. In addition, Jill Paton Walsh, who lectured at Homerton soon after 'Beyond Words' took place, was kind enough to allow us to include her talk. It is most fitting that it is the final chapter in a book we hope will be both provocative and inspiring.

Planning, hosting and running sessions at the conference involved the collaborative energies of the Language Team at Homerton College and behind-the-scenes help from many who work there. We are grateful to all of them and would particularly like to thank Jill Cafferky for her support before the conference and in the compilation of this book.

The ultimate collaboration was with our guest speakers and seminar leaders who made the conference such a success, and with the warm, friendly, stimulating teachers and others who attended. To them we owe appreciation 'beyond words'. *The Prose and the Passion* is an attempt to capture some of the flavour of this event and to share it with a wider readership.

Eve Bearne
Morag Styles
Victor Watson

INTRODUCTION

Singular and Plural

Victor Watson

For anyone concerned with children and their reading, the horizons of understanding are widening all the time. Perspectives shift continually and there is the constant temptation to believe that there is a choice between certainty and uncertainty.

If we choose the conviction of certainty, we can believe that there is a known, loved and approachable literature; that there is correspondingly a known, fixed and achievable literacy; and that the straightforward connection between them is that the one must be achieved so that the other may be approached. Thirty years ago both literature and literacy were referred to in grand – indeed national – terms: the nation's health was believed to be associated with its literature, and anxious talk of the declining state of the nation's literacy was not uncommon. Books might be literary, people might be literate. Together with the overtly national scale upon which literacy and literature were measured, there was a covert religious analogy which assumed processes of initiation, testing, selection and reverence. Come and worship – starting with Beacon Readers.

But how has it happened that those certainties of the past have reappeared today, unashamedly declaring their links with the market-place and political power?

They were not entirely bogus certainties, for in the era of the grammar schools there was considerable idealism associated with them. But those benevolent convictions and good educational intentions became so embedded in the language that their implicit assumptions trouble our discourses now, an encrusting legacy of past vocabularies. But there are also new, current metaphors to mislead us: literacy has to do with letters – and letters, like the curriculum, have to be delivered; but the letter-box model of teaching has to do less with reflective word

1

play than with muddled thinking. Children who read and reread *The Jolly Postman*[1] know nothing about current pedagogical clichés, but they do know that 'delivery' is an unsafe process.

The metaphors of the past have been taken over by the politicians and the press, and the language of educational discourse has to a considerable extent lost its integrity. If we are to think clearly and honestly about children and their reading we have to begin with the language we use. That is partly what *The Prose and the Passion* is concerned with; it seeks to free both language and thought. That is not as pretentious a claim as it may seem, since quite small changes in the way we use words can open up extensive new perspectives of understanding. For example, the contributors talk of *literacies* rather than literacy. At the most obvious level, this use of the plural recognizes the uniqueness of each young reader's developing literacy, and the private and unguessable characteristics of individual learning styles. It also reminds us that children arrive at school happily and confidently possessing many literacies already. But there is more to it than that. No two texts are alike. They employ different modes of representing experience, requiring each reader to become newly literate, and a single text may employ many different modes within it. We now understand that such texts instruct their readers how to read them. Many do this unobtrusively, or only insignificantly, but others simultaneously challenge and help readers to develop radically different literacies. A reader who moves from Ladybird books to the picture books of Anthony Browne *must* read in new ways. It is not a question of compulsion, but a matter of collusion between text and reader. And the differences are not just a matter of style and design: the fictional Peter and Jane[2] smilingly invited readers into a quiet literacy of concurrence and good behaviour; Anthony Browne's picture books invite literacies of subversion, inventiveness and speculation.

Once we appreciate that every textual mode of representing experience can lead to new literacies, it is a short step to realizing that today's young readers are likely to be confidently literate with texts that we know little about, or may even disapprove of. Many of us have in the last decade been through difficult processes of 'emergent word processing', but that achievement seems insignificant when set beside the range of literacies – mostly self-taught – that young readers are acquiring. The range extends far beyond the stories and poems and information books provided in schools – comics and computer games, magazines and newspapers, cartoons and joke books, adverts and graffiti, soaps and sitcoms. In the face of this enormous range, it is not enough to say that tastes have changed. New technologies summon readers into new literacies. When Winsor McCay began the *Little Nemo* series in the *New York Herald* in 1905, the structural language of the comic strip was a development which required new ways of reading.[3] When the first adventure-game book was published, with its instructions upon how to make narrative choices, its readers were taught a literacy that had not existed before. The invention of aerosol spray-paints led to new literacies. So did the video-recorder. Watching *Match of the Day* is not the same as watching the match; this media mode of representing experience enables us to 'read' a version with the boring parts edited out and the highlights replayed three times, with analysis. And young viewers almost certainly know in advance how this narrative will end, because they will have checked the final score hours earlier on Teletext – another, quite different, literacy skill.

When a reader has learned how to read an unfamiliar text (a child reading, say, the Hob Stories;[4] a teenage reader, perhaps, *Breaktime*;[5] an adult, *Beloved*[6]), the newly acquired literacy is felt as an achievement and begins to shape subsequent expectations. It may, however, have neither of these effects, for a text may be so strange to us that the deep literacies we already possess resist our attempts to accommodate the new one. I recall a group of high school teachers in the USA who repeatedly scanned the closing pages of *Kes* for what they believed must be there – the moment of personal illumination, a sudden life-changing flash of self-understanding, or some sign that Billy Caspar will walk out of his story and take his life in his own hands.[7] They did not expect a psychological triumph, with fanfares; a tentative and hesitant hint of hope would have been enough. But there is no such sign at all, and it became clear to me that many American readers do not know how to read a teenage novel of despair. That is probably why Robert Cormier's work has provoked such dismay. *The Chocolate War*[8] requires a literacy which runs counter to the deep optimistic story of the United States. Conversely, many British readers are impatient with American fiction which spells out explicitly an optimistic message of personal assertion and autonomy. *The Pinballs* is one of Betsy Byars' best novels – but British readers may not have a literacy to enable them to accept the ending, which may seem slick and over-optimistic.[9]

Literacies and literatures are cultural. Young American readers are surrounded by discourses of self-analysis. Quality-time family discussions, therapy programmes, and self-knowledge through talk are part of the everyday reality of American children. Schools reinforce this by running book discussions in which children are invited to tell their group what they have recently read and what they learned from it. American culture welcomes and creates *explicit* discourses, and the literacies associated with them are shaped by expectations of hope and reassurance. A literature (from Twain to Salinger, Zindel and Byars) has been born out of such cultural habits of optimistic narrative patterning. British literary culture prefers the *implicit* and the understated, believing that the image, or the episode, always has sufficient potency on its own and that for the author to explain the point is to constrain or paralyse the reader.[10] A literature of the implicit is a literature of ironies, ambivalences and uncertainties. A literature of the explicit is forthright, uncompromising and socially cohesive.

Of course, it is not as straightforward as that. There are many writers on both sides of the Atlantic whose texts challenge the literacy expectations of their culture. In addition, there are the Counterfeiters,[11] whose works conceal their subversiveness by camouflaging themselves in the colours of orthodoxy (Jan Mark in Britain, Cynthia Voigt in the USA). Novels such as *Trouble Half-Way*[12] or *Seventeen Against the Dealer*[13] lead cunningly and comfortably into new literacies, and new cultural perspectives, that a reader is hardly conscious of achieving.

There is a great deal to be said for educational approaches which acknowledge and respect the moment-by-moment literacy-garnering that individual readers are engaged in, and which simultaneously seek ways of enabling young readers to decide for themselves what their own literature is to be. This undertaking needs plurals and pluralities. *Literacy* and *literature* promise initiation and hint at future rewards; *literacies* and *literatures* acknowledge a general entitlement and recognize a multiplicity of individual moments of engagement.

In the concluding chapter of our previous publication, Margaret Meek wrote: 'We need to redescribe both children reading and children's books and to give ourselves reading lessons from both.'[14] The contributors to this book will be pleased if their chapters are seen as carrying forward that process of redescription. The connections between literacies and literatures are complex and there is much that we do not yet understand. In Chapter 4 Helen Arnold suggests that the texts which we identify as deeply satisfying are those which 'connect the passion of the inner world with the prose of events and circumstances.' Her remark has provided us with the title of this book, for it is that connection which we hope to illuminate.

Notes

1 Janet and Allan Ahlberg, *The Jolly Postman or Other People's Letters*, Heinemann, London, 1986 .
2 *The Ladybird Key Words Reading Scheme*, Wills & Hepworth, Loughborough, 1966.
3 Winsor McCay, *Little Nemo*, *New York Herald*, 1905–7.
4 William Mayne, *The Red, Green, Yellow and Blue Books of Hob Stories*, Walker Books, London, 1984.
5 Aidan Chambers, *Breaktime*, Bodley Head, London, 1978.
6 Toni Morrison, *Beloved*, Alfred A. Knopf, New York, 1987.
7 Barry Hines, *Kes*, Michael Joseph, London, 1978.
8 Robert Cormier, *The Chocolate War*, Macmillan, London, 1978.
9 Betsy Byars, *The Pinballs*, Bodley Head, London, 1978.

10 See Ted Hughes, 'The interpretation of parables', *Signal* 69 (1992), pp. 147–52.
11 See Hugh Kenner, *The Counterfeiters*, Indiana University Press, Bloomington and London, 1968.
12 Jan Mark, *Trouble Half-Way*, Viking Kestrel, London, 1985.
13 Cynthia Voigt, *Seventeen Against the Dealer*, Collins, London, 1990.
14 Margaret Meek, 'Children reading – now', in Morag Styles, Eve Bearne and Victor Watson (eds), *After Alice*, Cassell, London, 1992, p. 178.

PART I

Connections and Exclusions

At a time when so many influences in our society and within education seek to emphasize exclusion and exclusiveness of one kind or another, this part of the book emphasizes connections, in particular the often-confusing connections between popular children's literacies and an approved children's literature. Although teachers need to understand and value both, their wish to respect the disparate elements of the everyday cultural lives of children may sometimes seem at odds with their urgent desire to enrich the literacy possibilities of their children's reading.

The first two contributors to this part seek in different ways to connect literacies with literature. Mary Hilton believes that the connections can be formulated and used in classrooms. She argues that implicit within the apparent brutalities of many aspects of popular literacies there are what she calls 'persistent habits of imagination' which literary genres to some extent share. Jenny Daniels shows how comics and magazines read by girls – despite the gender features which make us uneasy about them – make possible for their readers the development of discourses which enable them to engage with the realities of adolescent life. Those for boys, on the other hand, offer only a narrow and disabling range of escapist possibilities.

In the third chapter Morag Styles points out that, when we exclude the texts that children read, we exclude the readers too. She analyses the appeal of popular writers (Enid Blyton, in particular) and reminds us that Shakespeare – the strongest pillar in the literature establishment – was himself once part of the popular culture. She argues that the story of the canon of literature is one of change and fickleness, and teachers must concern themselves with 'a literature for everyone'. Helen Arnold believes that what distinguishes great literature is that it connects the passion of our inner worlds with the prose of the events we are caught up in, and she goes on to demonstrate that, when children themselves seek to make this connection at first in play and later in their writing, they 'live in fragments no longer'. Helen Cook makes the connection between popular literacies and a living literature in an immediate and practical way – by running an annual 'Poetry in the Community' project. Her chapter concludes this part by describing how such projects work and by giving advice to anyone hoping to arrange one.

The part ends – and leads on to the next – with a short, sharp poem. Wendy Cope, using a hardbacked copy of the poetry of Sylvia Plath, warns against simplistic and sentimental connections.

CHAPTER 1

'The Blowing Dust'
Popular Culture and Popular Books for Children

Mary Hilton

The literacy practices that children become familiar with do not exist in a cultural void. They are inseparable from individual and community identities and activities, and they can be used in classrooms to develop children's understanding of the differences between dominant and vernacular forms. Mary Hilton is under no illusions about the crudeness and cruelty of many popular genres, but she believes teachers must understand their power and the nature of their appeal. She suggests a variety of ways in which the often disguised connections and similarities between popular forms and 'great literature' may be used to provide 'pathways into and out of the dominant literacy'.

> All the dust the wind blew high
> Appeared like gold in the sunset sky,
> But I was one of the children told
> Some of the dust was really gold.
>
> *Robert Frost*

Popular culture and literacy work in schools

As children in primary schools grow into literacy they are encouraged in most schools to read a wide range of books. Their early delight in picture books grows rapidly into a love of a range of different adventure stories, funny books, poetry and short stories. Often by the age of 10 or 11, in the last years of primary school, gender differences become apparent in the children's reading choices, and because they are learning to write in a variety of genres alongside learning to read, these preferred differences show up in their writing. Gender differences are not, however, the only ones: class and community preferences in choice of texts begin to surface as children blossom into literacy and puberty. When older children are encouraged to talk about the books and texts that they read outside school, it is no longer relevant to perceive literacy as a 'neutral technology' learnt solely in school and developed by the individual psyche. It becomes obvious that their literacy is a field open to a variety of cultural and ideological texts and interpretations which influence these growing children in their particular material circumstances.

Now, in the 1990s, when many teachers are committed to a variety of ways of teaching children to write in their own voice, and to read autonomously a range of texts they have chosen for themselves, the role of literacy learning in consciousness formation is under academic scrutiny. The picture of young readers and writers seen developing in the context and voices of their own everyday lives, rather than in a strict set of literacy practices at which they either succeed or fail, has opened up a new interest in the literate practices and events of their local communities; there are now studies of children emerging into literacy in the family, as in the work of Denny Taylor,[1] of the voices of neighbourhoods in the USA, as in the work of Shirley Brice Heath,[2] and recently of the local community in the UK, as in David Barton's work in Lancaster.[3] These rich ethnographies can show that the literacy teaching of school can cut across local community purposes and meanings.

But what happens in schools is often simply a mirror of conflicts in the larger world outside. Now that, on the one hand, Conservative politicians are actually specifying which books children should and must read in school, on the other, the new interest in literate practices and events has, ironically, gone alongside a theoretical erosion of high-cultural definitions of literary merit. English literature, as a canon of essential works which form a great tradition, is now perceived by many critics and writers as a monument of exclusion. Ethnic minorities, colonized peoples and women have suffered suppression, ridicule and faint praise. In many quarters, writing and criticism are moving from literary into cultural studies, and how texts *signify* is seen to depend on the cultural field in which they are situated.[4] For children and teachers, new readings and interpretations of popular texts have opened up and sensitized us to new relationships between writers and audiences. Video tapes, story boards, words for songs, magazine stories, soap operas, pulp fiction, literate computer games and news reports are a growing part of adolescent social interaction, of opinion, of comment, and inevitably of classroom language work. It is noticeable too that, as children grow, they begin to sense the ideological baggage that most written texts carry with them. Issues such as gender and class begin to be confronted, or denied. The vernacular constructions of popular culture are contrasted by the adolescent peer group with those of dominant literacy, the literary constructions of school and the 'classics'. Inevitably the preferred and accessible genres are devalued by their teachers and excluded by the élite culture of school, often to remain the only real pleasure but leading slowly nowhere. 'Voice' in literature lessons is often silenced or changed.

Working with older juniors in a Cambridge primary school and trying to understand child readers and writers, I have become excited by this dissolving of the separating wall between literary texts and popular culture. I have spent some time talking to the children in my class about the texts that surround them at home and how they read them and work the different genres and constructions into their own writing. In the summer term of 1992 we submitted a reading questionnaire to about 160 households in the neighbourhood of the primary school, a pleasant post-war council estate. The results showed the range of familiar texts, newspapers, magazines and books which lie around the homes the children live in, play in and visit. Over four-fifths of the adults read a daily newspaper; the *Sun*, *Mirror*, *Star* and *Daily Mail* together make up over three-quarters of these (the *Sun* and the *Mirror* over half). Two-thirds of women regularly buy and read a women's magazine. Over a quarter of women read a romance novel regularly, which makes up half their reading, the other half being from two other popular genres: adventure and biography. Half of the men read adventure, non-fiction, science fiction, horror and biography fairly regularly. Most, but not all, of this fiction is cheap paperbacks – what is called 'pulp' fiction.

These, then, are the familiar newspapers, magazines and popular books, the common texts which are lying around the homes of the children's locality, their neighbourhood community. It is a fair proportion of the common-or-garden adult reading matter, a 'blowing dust' of iconography, texts and messages which surrounds them from birth.

Dominant and vernacular literacies

The legacy of this division between 'high' and 'low' or élite and popular texts is now showing up in detailed ethnographic studies of literate practice. In my own work I have found many people who do not write at all, and who are deeply conscious of reading only 'rubbish'. They often attribute failure to succeed at school as a lack of engagement with 'real' literature, blaming themselves for not reading 'the classics'. There is substantial evidence that thousands of children pass through school without learning to write in their own voice; having spurned the vernacular voices of their neighbourhood communities, they have simultaneously failed to learn to write in the more formal voice of the dominant literacy.

In his work on cross-cultural perspectives on literacy,[5] Brian V. Street points out that the notion of a single autonomous literacy hides the fact that there is one cultural form which asserts its own proper dominance, disguising its own class and cultural basis, and at the same time marginalizing other varieties. Street goes on to argue that identity and personhood are frequently signified through literacy practices:

> Whether we attend a course or school, or become involved in a new institutional set of literacy practices, through work, political activism, personal relationships, etc., we are doing more than simply decoding script, producing essays or writing a proper hand; we are taking on – or resisting – the identities associated with those practices.

He then goes on to consider and describe how different literacy practices in different cultures can sometimes be sites of negotiation and of transformation.

To me, the most interesting and useful feature of Street's work is that the idea of multiple literacies can be used by teachers and children to enable them to become more aware of the differences between dominant and vernacular forms. Furthermore, if Street is right in his claim that identity is constructed through literacy practices, then it is imperative that children, together with writers, master the genres and constructions of the vernacular so that they can develop critical and creative thought in the language of their own communities. It is equally important that they should master the literacy and language constructions of the élite, so that they are empowered to challenge the dominant discourses of society.

The character of vernacular literacy: what makes it popular?

Most analyses of popular texts structure their descriptions in cultural theories which are either ideological or concerned with social psychology. Fred Inglis puts it well: 'We must not, indeed, lose our nerve, or the nervous citizens will be trodden over by the tough eggs who see plainly that information and media are where the great aphrodisiacs, power and money, are boiling and pouring.'[6] The teacher does not have to engage deeply with media theory to obtain a working knowledge of the powerful attractions of the tabloid press, comics, women's magazines or pulp fictions. Only a sense of history, which can yield insights into the length of endurance of popular genres, and perhaps a sense of humour, are required to engage with its sexual stigma and titillation, its violence, lawlessness, cruelty, irony, misinformation, sentimentality and superstition. These are the time-honoured pigments into which popular writers dip their brushes, and their constructions with them are often breathtakingly simple. Working constantly within the parameters of certain 'persistent habits of the imagination', as Fussell[7] calls them, these industrious fiction-makers capture and enrapture with easy and unconscious mastery of the genres.

Stigma and morality

The devices used to create a (usually sexual) stigma are one of the most horrific aspects of the tabloids. In the *Sun* they are used against almost any collective action: unions, protest marches, clubs, etc., and are often alternated with racial taunts for increased effect. The tabloid-style banner I saw in London springs to mind ('HUN SCUM BOO QUEEN MUM'). Used against women and against Labour MPs, this stigma is its major and somewhat overworked weapon of reactionary ideology. The *Mirror* also uses stigmatizing devices against any public figure it considers fair game: Michael Jackson, Sarah Ferguson, etc. Popular texts have a long history of ridiculing and punishing difference, particularly bodily difference. In her fascinating book, *Small Books and Pleasant Histories*,[8] Margaret Spufford writes of the popular cheap chapbooks sold to labouring people in the towns and villages throughout seventeenth-century England. She writes, 'They revel in slapstick and satire and in the misadventures of unfortunates. The quality they lack to the modern reader is compassion.' Not, I would add, to the modern reader of the *Sun*.

Perhaps literary compassion, however, is an overemphasized virtue in the classroom. The immense popularity of the stories by Roald Dahl, with their harsh portraiture and cruel denouements, needs, I feel, some explaining if we are in the business of promoting kindness and humanity as literary merit. Other genuinely popular children's reading matter, from Enid Blyton to action comics, notably lacks compassion. Perhaps the truth is that children are bitterly aware of injustice, cruelty, stigma and death, and that these must be allowed in their writing just as they appear in their preferred reading. To attempt to keep young readers in a cosy world, denying totally the coarse and cruel humour of the popular genres, is to clean away the rich bacteria of dirt and satire which they need to develop as writers. Here too are links with high culture; tragedy, cruelty and violent death in Greek and Shakespearean stories are well appreciated by gritty modern children.

Fiction, belief and the romance of war

Throughout these tabloids, comics and adventure stories runs another strand which has relevance for children, the mythologizing of the past. Margaret Spufford points out that, even in the seventeenth century, 'The English were extremely fond of reading stories set in a vague and idealised version of the past . . . The historical past of the chapbooks was mythical and fantastic.'[9] The light side of this yields some rich historical continuities in subject matter: after the 'Fergie' scandals of August 1992, when the *Daily Mirror* sold out in Cambridge by 9.00 a.m., it is amusing to read in Spufford that:

> stories about kings' mistresses were popular. Both Fair Rosamund, mistress to Henry II, and Jane Shore, mistress to Edward IV, were well-known. The chapbooks about them were simply excuses for a good story of adultery, high-life, rich-living and repentance, in both cases, reinforced with a moral at the end.[10]

The darker side is that, from the seventeenth-century chapbooks onwards, the popular press has presented the people with 'a second-hand chivalric past, full of battles and adventure, signs and wonders . . . astrology and divination were reliable scientific guides to action'.[11] No popular newspaper today would be complete without its astrology column, and the tabloids' manipulation of rumour, legend and fact is often masterly. During the Falklands War, in 1982, and the Gulf War, in 1990, we read clear evidence of journalists using the genres of fantasy and the unconscious, the wish-fulfilment of blood-lust, romance and heroism to capture modern readers: there was the infamous *Sun* 'Gotcha' headline on the sinking of the Argentine ship the *Belgrano*, for example. Again, it is all too easy to understand the reactionary ideology and material purposes of dehistoricizing popular issues of fact with mythical romance and hatred, in directing the mass of people away from notions of structural power and real decisions.

The children in my class were entranced by war – particularly the Second World War. Public hatred, anger and conflict were concepts that they had derived from stories, many of them told and retold in comics, films, adventure books and magazines, and that seemed to exist outside any knowledge of real history. Descriptions of the tawdry, cruel injustice of war seemed to incite the blood-lust of the boys even more. When relics poured in, they were ration books, recipes and diaries from the girls, but medals, shrapnel, army photos and weapon manuals from the boys (often grandparents' special collections). Treasured war books, full of pictures of weapons and destruction, came from *fathers*. These were not ex-soldiers but their children; the 'cult' of war is very strong on the estate, particularly among the males.

Paul Fussell writes in *The Great War and Modern Memory*:[12]

'What we call gross dichotomising is a persisting imaginative habit of
modern times traceable, it would seem, to the actualities of the Great
War. 'We' are all here on this side; 'the enemy' is over there. 'We' are
individuals with names and personal identities; 'he' is a mere collective
entity. We are visible; he is invisible. We are normal; he is grotesque. . . .
Prolonged trench warfare, with its collective isolation, its 'defensiveness'
and its nervous obsession with what the other side is up to, established a
model of modern political, social, artistic, and psychological polarisation.

It is this sense of 'the other' that runs through so much writing that
children have to make imaginative decisions about. An endless array of
monsters as the 'other' can become tedious and overworked, and yet
the evil stereotypes in the surrounding popular literature can caricature
women or men, ethnic minorities or foreign peoples, or overwork that
catch-all collective, 'aliens'.

Fussell also writes of war as the romance quest. The protagonist
moves forward through a series of tests and dangers to win the ultimate
test. '[William] Morris's most popular romance was *The Well at the
World's End* published in 1896. There was hardly a literate man who
fought between 1914 and 1918 who had not read it and been
powerfully excited by it in his youth.'[13] Fussell shows how this
generation, prepared by such popular texts, could go on 'normalising
the unspeakable', using romantic rhetoric to describe a war 'representing
a triumph of modern industrialism, materialism, and mechanism'.

Here we have two major sources of narrative fantasy in the literate
practice, the 'other' and the romance quest, both used ruthlessly and
often crudely in popular fictions. Can these 'persistent imaginative
habits' pointed up by Fussell be reworked sensitively and radically by
children and writers?

I feel much work needs to be done with children before they write
adventure stories – work on the 'other'. The evil stereotypes of popular
culture are unsatisfactory. I forget when I started to feel sorry for the
faceless Indians in westerns but now, in a multicultural classroom,
children are genuinely artistically dissatisfied with racial enemies. On
the other hand, popular texts remind us, living in a tender-hearted
world, of Fred Inglis' point: 'that societies are made and changed by
men [sic] . . . that men have beliefs, that they fight about them, and that
some men dominate other men'.[14] Because of the mixed messages in the
literate practice and the media, 'baddies' are often the least well-
delineated characters in the children's minds, let alone in their writing.
Work on having oppressive tyrants as evil figures is more successful,
but one is up against this central paradox: the imaginative habit of
having the 'other' as a mere collective entity, reserving personal identity
for the protagonist. I would go further back than Fussell and identify
this habit of mind with British imperialism, looking back to the
imperialist 'books for boys' of Kingsley and Henty, where masses of

mindless natives formed the 'other'. How have good writers for children coped with the 'other'? Asimov's 'wheels' in *The Heavenly Host* are the most brilliant and touching example of anti-imperialism that I can think of.[15] But I feel there is little writing which reworks the conventions so convincingly.

Once the problems of the 'other' are solved artistically, the romance quest falls into place. This is one of the oldest and most time-honoured genres of all, and children can use it to produce long stories of delight and interest. The genre maps itself out in familiar syntax, as Fred Inglis puts it:

> Things happen in a given sequence; the movement of time is straight-forwardly linear; the agents in the stories are uninterruptedly free; events are caused and not arbitrary. This structure, what we may call the syntax of experience . . . is what most people in England were taught and learned as children.[16]

Romantic fiction: the romance quest in the personal sphere

One of the most stable genres of both élite and popular culture is romantic fiction. Jane Austen emerged from a host of conservative women writers of the late eighteenth century: 'It can be argued that Jane Austen achieved the classical perfection of her fiction because there was a mass of women's novels, excellent, fair, and wretched, for her to study and improve upon'.[17] What did all these eighteenth-century novels, written for an almost totally female readership, have in common?

> A young woman is to marry . . . and the whole action impels her towards that marriage as apparently the fulfilment of her own desire, certainly the enactment of her social destiny. Wedding bells resolve all the difficulties raised in the plot . . . And yet the long series of obstacles, trials and perhaps terrors the heroine confronts on the road to marriage also suggests contrarily that permanent happiness is not so easily attained.[18]

Jane Austen's achievements within this seemingly simple genre are legendary. So are Mills and Boon's success and longevity in the romantic fiction market. Although before 1950 many publishers, including Collins and Hutchinson, published a romantic list, Mills and Boon's specialization in this genre has been unique. There is no doubt from its extensive publishing success that Mills and Boon have hit upon a successful formula. Each novel, in fact, features the 'bait', an announcement by Mills and Boon that they will read every manuscript submitted for publication. This encourages readers to send in their own drafts, as new authors are always sought and first publications by new authors are given prominence. The formula is spelled out in the two

main company guidelines for writers still in use today; these are
'Lubbock's Law' and the 'Alpha man'. The literary critic Percy
Lubbock argued that stories should be written from the heroine's point
of view; that would promote reader identification and increase
suspense and interest. The 'Alpha man', according to the Boon
brothers, is based upon a 'law of nature', that is, the female of the
species will always be most intensely attracted to the strongest male of
the species, the alpha.[19] The hero must be recognizable for his great
strength, integrity and potential for providing a secure yet exciting
future; two guidelines with which, in spirit, Jane Austen must have
generally agreed.

   This genre, then, maps itself out in the familiar form that has
survived at least two centuries in literate practice. Always it is in the
form of a romance quest, following many of the conventions of the
male adventure story but worked out in a familiar social world and
with the prize of a binding contract (marriage) which alters the
relations of social power for the heroine. The genre thus allows creative
expression of social psychology and a critique of social structures and
relationships. In the same way that great writers use the genre, there is
no reason why teenagers should not also use romance fiction as a
vehicle for irony and satire. Older junior girls can discuss romance as a
literary device with amazing .sophistication once it is 'allowed' as
literary material.

Power and the self

Finally, I would like to consider a fundamental genre for children,
personal narrative. Diary writing in school can be one of the most
tedious and mismanaged writing tasks in the whole language curriculum. Here the young writer is both acutely sensitive to the voices of
community life: ('She puts hers out Friday'; 'I went round my nana's')
and at the same time hopelessly exposed to censure (often for being
boring) and correction (often for lacking in compassion). As a result
children often internalize the verdict from an adult middle-class world:
'My life's rubbish', children have told me. Yet it is a genre where we
find some great 'primitive' writing by adults – working-class people
who, often over years, settled down to write the fascinating details and
development of their own lives.[20] These were lives spent in poverty and
subjection, yet strangely liberated by literacy. Power over the written
word enabled these writers to flourish and develop, sometimes in order
to narrate back to the surrounding community something of its history,
sometimes to explain and describe working-class existence to a middle-
class readership, and more often, and more importantly for our
purposes, to yield an enhanced sense of personal and class collective
worth.

Scanning the popular books, magazines and tabloids, where can we find writing 'in the first person', let alone literary constructions of use to the young writer? Many of the headlines are 'stream-of-consciousness' constructions. First person 'voice-over' techniques are a well-used device for taking up power positions on a range of so-called factual matters. Photos of the speaker are often capped by 'thoughts' in the first person, often leading to some semantic confusion as to who really said what. Here is a new version of an old literary technique where we were told in history books what people thought when involved in action; speech and image knitted together for the meaning purposes of the writer. Young writers can use this, being encouraged to 'see' themselves in a variety of situations in their lives and to write the thought-speech rather than labouring over the narrative connectives of the day. Rosen's *Hypnotiser* has many autobiographical poems in the first person, worked round images in this way.[21]

Another aspect of 'first person' writing is the 'confessional' genre, which overlaps into the problem pages of women's magazines. The major tabloids use this old popular genre to great effect. Possibly dating back to the confessional box itself and its system of sorting sins and punishments, confessional writing is a whole popular genre in America: *True Confessions* has been bought and read by the reading public there for years, seeming to feed and induce an endless appetite for stories of sin, stigma and respectability. Children are aware of and often attempt to use the 'confessional' constructions. Some of the most enjoyable diary writing has been formed around sin, and the extent to which children reject society's system of sins and penalties (and, sadly, internalize others) can be worked out in this speech genre. Wittily handed back to them by a cunning writer, *The Secret Diary of Adrian Mole* is a children's best-seller.[22]

The classroom: a site of challenge and mastery of dominant and vernacular literacies

Street's anthropological work on vernacular and dominant literacies gives us an opportunity to look again at all the written texts that surround the children we teach. In this 'blowing dust' of texts and messages it is possible to see and sift the time-honoured vernacular roots of much 'great' literature. These groups of discourses, or patterned structures, are used intuitively and daily in the soaps, tabloids, pulp fictions, magazine stories, songs and lies with which the culture industry almost swamps us all.

A classroom can be a site of negotiation and challenge, in which the teacher accepts and works with the children and their concerns, their preferred readings, and their writings. The 'persistent habits of the imagination' embedded in the surrounding literate practice can be revealed, analysed and reworked. The lusts and longings and the rude strength of vernacular forms which, for a time, hold and satisfy, reflecting back the haphazard vulgarity of everyday life, can thus provide creative pathways into and out of the dominant literacy.

Notes

I would like to thank the children at The Grove CP School, particularly Craig Becala and Tracy Ashbridge, for their help with the discussion and survey work that this chapter is based upon.

1   D. Taylor, *Family Literacy: Young Children Learning to Read and Write*, Heinemann, London, 1983.
2   S.B. Heath, *Ways with Words*, Cambridge University Press, Cambridge, 1983.
3   D. Barton and R. Ivanic, *Writing in the Community*, Sage, Newbury Park, CA, 1991.
4   A. Easthope, *Literary into Cultural Studies*, Routledge, London, 1991; T. Eagleton, *Literary Theory: An Introduction*, Blackwell, Oxford, 1983.
5   B.V. Street, 'Cross-cultural perspectives on literacy', paper to Conference, University of Tilburg, October 1991, published in *Functional Literacy*, J. Barjames, Amsterdam, 1992.
6   F. Inglis, *Media Theory*, Blackwell, Oxford, 1990.
7   P. Fussell, *The Great War in Modern Memory*, Oxford University Press, New York and London, 1975.
8   M. Spufford, *Small Books and Pleasant Histories*, Methuen, London, 1981.
9   *Ibid.*
10 *Ibid.*
11 *Ibid.*
12 Fussell, *The Great War in Modern Memory*, p. 8.
13 *Ibid.*
14 Inglis, *Media Theory*.
15 I. Asimov, *The Heavenly Host*, Walker, New York, 1975.
16 F. Inglis, *Ideology and the Imagination*, Cambridge University Press, Cambridge, 1975.
17 E. Moers, *Literary Women*, W.H. Allen, London, 1977.
18 M. Butler, *Jane Austen and the War of Ideas*, Oxford University Press, Oxford, 1975.
19 J. McAleer (1990), 'Scenes from love and marriage: Mills and Boon and the popular publishing industry in Britain 1908–1950', *Twentieth Century British History*, 1 (3), 265–88.
20 D. Vincent, *Bread, Knowledge and Freedom*, Europa, London, 1981.
21 M. Rosen, *The Hypnotiser*, André Deutsch, London, 1988.
22 S. Townsend, *The Secret Diary of Adrian Mole*, Methuen, London, 1991.

Some elements of this chapter have already appeared in a review entitled 'Rags and romances', *Cambridge Journal of Education*, 23 (1), 1993.

CHAPTER 2

'Girl Talk'
The Possibilities of Popular Fiction

Jenny Daniels

Many of us feel an affection for popular children's comics, but are uneasily aware of their crudities and stereotypes. In this chapter, Jenny Daniels first analyses these qualities in comics for young readers. After the early years, boys and girls go on to read separate gender-related comics and magazines. There are crudities in these publications too – but Jenny Daniels argues that girls fare better than boys. She believes that boys are led by their magazines into a cultural and literacy cul-de-sac, whereas the magazines for girls, despite their market-oriented consumerism, encourage and develop a 'girl talk' capable of addressing real issues of adolescence, relationships and responsibility.

In this chapter I want to investigate the complex nature of the relationship between popular fiction, reading behaviour and gender orientation. The world of comics and magazines is one which continues to attract a large readership, with new formats offered and an increased assurance from publishers that the market is 'there'. How and why has that market been created? Why do they sell in such large numbers, and what can we learn about our culture and cultural practices from looking at the pictures and narratives presented to us in this popular fiction?

Teachers and parents have a strange and ambivalent attitude to comics and magazines. They are genuinely regarded as 'tawdry', but, while we know that they are there, we do not always feel sufficiently motivated to do something about them – like dust under the carpet.

Comics are regarded as irrelevant to mainstream literature. What they offer is not legitimate in the classroom and generally not to be encouraged as good reading practice. Interestingly, those same parents and teachers may well buy glossy magazines and feel comfortable when reading them.

Judgements about books and reading behaviour are themselves coloured by our own positioning in a cultural context. By examining more closely some of these attitudes, I hope to show how assumptions can often mask reality – we see only what we have been conditioned to see. My argument is that reading behaviour combines a set of cultural and gender practices, providing a discourse which defines and celebrates a form of social cohesion. Understanding this cohesion is central to a view of femininity and notions of being a woman. It carries with it powerful messages of how to be a woman in the real world. Conversely, other popular fiction which is available for boys demands a very different approach from its readers. It is not only the content which contrasts sharply – what boys are asked to 'do' with their reading is particular and restricted. Consequently the reading activities of boys and girls become increasingly polarized as they reach their teenage years.

In this chapter, I want to look closely at the ways in which reading behaviour for boys and girls develops over a period of time, and deconstruct particular examples of popular fiction to demonstrate the argument.

First, I want to examine current preoccupations with popular fiction, particularly as they relate to views of literature and learning. My concern is one which reflects the increasing difficulties for teachers in the 1990s. Government intervention in curriculum content is tightening through the monitoring and testing mechanisms of the National Curriculum. What is to be taught is openly prescriptive – the debate about the Key Stage 3 anthology for English is an obvious example. Teachers have lost much of the autonomy which was once an integral part of the professional role. The culture of the dominant is one which is now legitimized through content and will soon be reinforced through method.

The relationship between the dominant and the dominated is central to my argument of cultural positioning. Harold Rosen puts it like this:

> A thorough attempt to analyse the relationship between class and language would require us to examine the relationship of the dominant culture of our society to the culture of the dominated. This would inevitably involve an examination of the part played by language in the operation of this relationship . . . I believe that one thing which would emerge from such an undertaking would be that the linguistic capital of the dominant culture is persistently over-valued and that of the dominated culture persistently under-valued.[1]

Popular fiction is not only persistently undervalued, it is largely unrecognized. If we substitute literature for language in the above quotation, then it becomes only too apparent what the dominant culture is and how it operates to reinforce and censure, however unconscious the process might be. The dialectic of struggle, according to Marx, suggests that the dominant culture conquers and absorbs the others. The dominant ideology in children's fiction is one in which the protagonists, however well-meaning, responsible and sensitive, are nevertheless not the children themselves. Writers and critics are adults, who have adult preoccupations and, simply through the passing of time, cannot be children again. (The writers and readers of this book will almost certainly be adult.) We care about the possibilities which literature offers to children. We want to promote reading and literature in our schools and homes. We know the pleasure and the 'possible worlds' available to our imaginations through texts and pictures. But we are not children ourselves, and perhaps the hardest part is to accept that children reading today do not read, and never will read, in quite the same way as we do. This is not a matter of style; rather it is a cultural signifier of a world shaped by us and used by children.

A simple example might be the way in which children watch television. The speed of images, especially on satellite and cable TV programmes, is like quicksilver. I find that my brain simply cannot take in all the messages being relayed – but then I was a late developer, not watching a television screen until I was 16. Young children, however, can sit for a long time absorbing the visual information and appreciating the pictorial texts in a way which I find incomprehensible. The temptation is to adopt a dominant position and question the validity of the exercise, given my adult incomprehension. One is tempted to dismiss or belittle the activity. By assuming that it must be poor quality, it is easy to be critical of children's involvement. We accuse them of being 'couch potatoes', but do not take the time to find out what is so desirable in their viewing. From the dominant position, it is easy to ridicule, or alternatively berate, the decline in moral standards associated with too much television.

It is perhaps in reaction to such attitudes that literature is seen as providing a safe and responsible retreat. The availability of quality books for children has resulted in a new area of study, namely that carried out by the critics and devotees who recognize the inherent value of good books for children. They employ the analytic skills from literary criticism to comment on children's fiction. Twenty years ago, very few works were published which directly concerned themselves with an investigation into books for children. Now, a whole new industry has developed and book shops catalogue an area specifically for such criticism. English departments in universities are increasingly offering opinions on the study of childen's fiction, and colleges for teacher education have often addressed the issue of books to use with children – but one suspects this is in order to maximize on the functional use of books, rather than to appreciate their 'literary' quality.

This book is itself a product of such concerns, arising as it does from a group of people who teach on the children and literature course at Homerton. It, too, will hopefully reflect current concerns about books and reading, the promotion of good practice and the necessary reflection on the cultural and political frameworks within which the world of literature operates.

My concern is that the enterprise itself can easily become the linguistic capital of the dominant culture referred to by Rosen. The study of children's literature is exciting and innovative, attracting the interest of those people who themselves are moved by, and engaged with, literature in its different forms and genres. Victor Watson, in *After Alice* puts it clearly:

> It is undeniably true that children's fiction is a territory controlled by adults – *colonized* by them perhaps – and that in that space they indulge all manner of needs not directly related to the interests of child-readers. But it is also true that children are there too; not all of them, unfortunately – but in sufficient numbers for their commitment and engagement to be taken seriously.[2]

In *After Alice*, we wanted to celebrate our new understandings of the relationships which can be formed between writers, texts and readers. We hope that this book will continue to shed light and understanding, and also challenge what might become a new orthodoxy.

Considerable interest over the last decade has concentrated on showing children how to detect racism and sexism. The resulting orthodoxy has been as pervasive and strident as some of the eighteenth-century insistence on moral purity and self-improvement. While some literature was exposed for its crass racism in particular, the same all-seeing eye was turned on to 'popular' fiction, with the result that librarians and teachers righteously flung out, for example, the Famous Five books. Children were, and are, incredulous. The galling fact is that the Famous Five continue to be a constant source of gratification, particularly for girls. As adults concerned with literature for children, we could not question our own assumptions enough to look closely at what children found so desirable in a Famous Five story. Simplistic explanations about gender roles, together with accusations about class and race, had the cumulative effect of enforcing a 'ban' – and the new orthodoxy had started.

Interestingly, much of the material subjected to scrutiny has increasingly been 'quality' fiction. Comics and magazines have to a large extent escaped, because they are not considered worthy enough;

children's television also escaped because, until recently, the producers and controllers have made conscious decisions to listen and 'tune in' to children's concerns. This is an area I want to return to later.

In the new moral purity, comic and teenage magazines are problematic texts. Despite a wider consciousness about race and gender, the popular fiction continues to be even more popular, and has made no moves towards redressing any bias. It is perhaps this uncompromising attitude which has provoked another reaction. For some, the popular fiction represents a decline in moral standards, leading to depravity and decadence. In a 'gender-aware' world, comics continue to be looked down upon, either by women who 'know better' or by men whose curiosity does not admit to knowledge. The 'dismissed' is always safer than the challenged or accepted.

Nevertheless, comics are an important cultural phenomenon and one which deserves closer attention. As Rosen says: 'dominated culture is persistently undervalued'.[3] I want to look at what happens when girls and boys read the popular fiction available today, what their reading behaviour is, and how they find the language to engage with the phenomenon which is so readily ignored or dismissed by the establishment. 'Girl talk' is perhaps a much more subtle, perceptive and powerful discourse than it appears at surface level.

An examination of the comics available for young children, e.g. *Twinkle* or *Postman Pat*, reveals a world which is cosy and controlled, with cultural issues pertinent to an infant's interests. Animals proliferate – totally unreal animals who carry human characteristics and conform to a stereotype formula of 'nice or naughty' behaviour. Domestic crises centre upon objects being broken or mislaid. Many stories carry moral exhortations of one kind or another to keep clean – both morally and physically, one suspects. The endings are predictable – the objects are found, or mended. Chaos is overcome by a combination of hard work and adult supervision. The dirt is removed and the world is restored to cleanliness and order.

A typical example might be a story from *Postman Pat*.[4] 'Tales from Greenland' tells the story of a bespectacled Mrs Goggins who wakes up one morning to find all the house dirty. She sets to, cleaning and polishing, and dealing with the many interruptions which occur to distract her from her quest for cleanliness. The last frame reveals Postman Pat showing her the dirty spectacles and her own silly behaviour in assuming that the house was dirty. 'Chuckling' and 'laughing' are words which are used extensively in these comics. Children are invited to share the joke revealed by Postman Pat's discovery – they too might well chuckle and giggle, active participants through understanding the meaning of the text. Mrs Goggins' statement 'I am silly' is often echoed by the children as part of their enjoyment and appreciation of the joke.

The worlds of young children's comics are highly desirable ones — largely because they allow both the adult reader and the child to feel safe. This has considerable psychological and cultural importance; it is precisely the ultimate safety of these stories which makes them so desirable.

As well as reflecting cosiness, the comics also encourage children to use their literacy. Pictures may be naively simplistic but the accompanying text often carries strange and complex sentence structures. Yet children 'tune in' to the language of comics very quickly and become active readers — often without adult intervention. Many comics link with the bigger literate world, using TV programmes and characters to capture the children's interest. Activity pages encourage literacy skills in particular. Invitations to join clubs, make badges, send letters, etc., are all ways in which literacy is presented as a 'grown-up' activity. The 'fun' makes it even more attractive and desirable.

These comics are read by boys and girls; the nature of the stories has a universal appeal. They are usually bought by a parent and often 'shared' as part of a cuddling, quiet time at home. Feminists have looked with horror at the gender representations which continue to be reproduced in this genre. A typical example might be 'Nurse Susan and

Frame 2 from 'Nurse Susan and Doctor David' from *Jack and Jill*, December 1985. © Fleetway Editions Ltd. Reproduced with permission.

Frame 5 from 'Nurse Susan and Doctor David' from *Jack and Jill*, December 1985. © Fleetway Editions Ltd. Reproduced with permission.

Doctor David', from *Jack and Jill*.[5] Pictures such as the one in frame 2 inevitably lead to accusations of sexism. Clearly Nurse Susan is not a National Health nurse! The length of her skirt, the stilted movement of the limbs are easily recognized as those of a Sindy doll. Doctor David wears the uniform of an American doctor. The heavy spectacles bestow the air of male authority. It is the male doctor who makes the decisions, carries out the operation and gives instructions to the 'helping' woman.

In frame 5, Doctor David actually holds a mop, though one gets the feeling that he has little idea what to do with it! The operating theatre-cum-kitchen is restored to cleanliness and order, and the two girls are suitably grateful and obsequious.

This is still typical of many of the gender relations portrayed in the stories. Girls are quiescent, tentative and 'willing' in order to be feminine. Boys are assertive, decisive and confident in order to be able to intervene and make things happen.

The next range of popular fiction I want to examine is the 7–11 age range. Here a different phenomenon takes place. The readers become the buyers, often using pocket money and being active consumers in an adult world. The nature of the desire to read changes, largely as a result of an ever-increasing cultural awareness from the readers themselves. A definite gender division occurs, with no comic, to my knowledge at least, being without a gender bias. The 'boy' comics are easily identified from the *Beano* tradition. *Buster* and *Dandy* are replicas in format, presentation and intention. Some more recent ventures, such as *Roy of the Rovers*, take the football theme as the basis for stories which depict the moral steadfastness and indomitable courage of the earlier comics. Against impossible odds, individual heroes perform acts of bravery for the team. The serial format acknowledges a more sophisticated reader and ensures purchase of the comics for the following week. When the Melchester Rovers have to face a 'jinx' at their Wembley game against Sebridge United, Andy exhorts his players (and readers) to give of their best. The image of a powerful and aggressive man, fist clenched and face distorted with passion, is familiar to young boys who avidly watch football.

Beano, *Buster* and *Dandy* have continued their time-honoured tradition of raucous, subversive and violent action. 'Dennis the Menace' challenges authority in its very act of handing out retribution. The stories and pictures are one-dimensional – slapstick comedy reduces the real world to one where action carries unreal intention. In good cartoon manner, heads are knocked, figures up-ended, vehicles indiscriminately squash people and animals, etc. The images are not from social realism, but from a history of vaudeville, silent comedies and music-hall appreciation. The pain of the 'ouches' and 'aarhs' is never felt.

To read any of these comics is to adopt a reading behaviour quite unique to printed material. The text and pictures have a relationship which is less symbiotic than, for example, that in picture books. Many words are repeated or printed in a different type-face to give emphasis

'Calamity James', from *Beano*, no. 2524 (December 1990). © D. C. Thomson & Co. Ltd. Reproduced with permission.

at certain parts of the story. Sounds are printed in non-word forms. The first frame below from the *Beano* is an example.[6]

Words such as 'ouch', 'screech', 'oink', 'chomp', 'waah', 'glub' and 'girr' reflect the way in which written language is used to engage the reader actively in the reading process. Combined with the movement exaggerated in the drawings, the words and pictures of these comics confront the reader with an exciting, loud, hilarious and subversive world. We have to 'read' them differently, in order to appreciate them. The fact that word recognition plays little part in the meaning only gives them wider appeal. In *Kes*, the image of Billy Casper sitting on the moors above Barnsley and reading his stolen comics is a poignant reminder of the way in which this happens.[7] Billy can 'mouth' the words of Dennis the Menace and enter the exhilarating world of *Beano* – a brief escape from his otherwise tragic existence.

The ultimate appeal for *Beano* readers, however, is the challenge it offers to authority and establishment figures. Anyone 'up there' is considered 'fair game', although characters such as Grans are given somewhat kinder, if unusual, treatment. Policemen, judges, lawyers, parents and, of course, teachers all suffer at the hands of quick-witted and shrewd children. The 'Bash Street Kids' has such an approach. When Posh Street School invites a famous old boy to a school reunion, Bash Street decides to do the same.[8] They are visited by a heavy-metal pop singer, a pig farmer with his pigs, and an international art thief who donates the Mona Lisa to the school. The teachers, naive and stupid, are implicated in the crime when the policeman comes to arrest him. As they are all marched off to the police station, the Bash Street Kids have a party with their famous old boys.

The energy of the last frame, the sheer wit and exuberance, resonates with echoes of Rowlandson and Gillray prints from the eighteenth century. The reader is invited to participate, as well as observe. The details have been carefully included and the reader looks horizontally into the made events. Unlike those of the earlier comics, readers here

'The Bash Street Kids', from *Beano*, no. 2524 (December 1990). © D. C. Thomson & Co. Ltd. Reproduced with permission.

are accepted on their own terms, invited into the mêlée and not asked to make moral decisions about either themselves or the activities. It is pure escapism – but an escapism which unconsciously allows the reader to challenge authority, to take action and, ultimately, not to be concerned about the consequences.

Perhaps it is not surprising that these are mostly read by boys. 'Minnie the Minx' and other such 'genderless' characters have been introduced, but the appeal is to anarchy and hilarity. Girls do read comics like the *Beano*, and remember them with pleasure. They are a minority, however – the same girls who will probably as adults buy *Viz*, the grown-ups' version. Interestingly, the comics are finding it more difficult to maintain circulation figures at present. The *Victor* ceased publication two years ago. The publishing company D.C. Thompson and Co. blame it on the larger numbers of cartoons, particularly American ones, which are now available on satellite and cable TV. And, as this chapter was being written, *Roy of the Rovers* ceased publication.

While a small number of girls continue to buy and enjoy *Beano*, the majority of girls turn to comics such as *Mandy*, *Judy* or *Bunty*. Boys will continue to read *Beano*, etc., well into puberty, and are happy to acknowledge publicly their reading when they are older. Magazines for girls are likely to be regarded as decadent or trivial. The messages and reading behaviours differ significantly and I want to look at some of the stories in more detail, to see what 'girl talk' actually means.

The narratives in these girls' comics often revolve around houses, ballet schools, animals and boarding schools – although there are a few deviations into, for example, a wild west setting or an historical one, where a particular discourse is developed. This discourse reflects the very concerns which the fiction supposedly offers the escape from. The appeal to girl readers is a cultural 'space' provided by the fantasy, which incorporates concerns from the real world and allows them to 'try out' the emotions and reflect on the decisions. A typical example might be 'Secret Angel' – heralded by 'Emma Kemp's life of secrecy starts today'.[9] Set in a stereotyped Victorian England, it tells the story of Emma, brought up in an orphanage and subjected in domestic service to physical and emotional abuse. The pictures show horrific scenes of violence and pain – the 'ouch'es of the *Beano* have no significance here.

Emma shows some resourcefulness in biting her oppressor and making her escape. After being chased by the Squire, she falls into a river and is swept away, her employers presuming she is dead. Emma has, in fact, managed to hold on to a branch and hauls herself to safety. Her first thought is to return to the orphanage and help others who are less fortunate, displaying a heroism and an altruism which the Victorians themselves might have admired. This is the tone of many of the narratives: girls facing indescribable odds, fighting back and always

'Secret Angel', from *Bunty*, no. 1570 (13 February 1988). © D. C. Thomson & Co. Ltd.
Reproduced with permission.

winning through with the satisfaction of being 'better' people through self-sacrifice and determination.

In the midst of the more violent scenes, a strange comment sits at the top of the page. Totally unrelated to the text, it proclaims: 'There are some beautiful fashions on Page 2.' It is almost as if the writers are trying to reassure their readers even in the act of frightening them. The ambivalence has interesting repercussions for girls. Similar subtitles say: 'Don't forget girls – never accept lifts from strangers', 'Check your bike brakes regularly – your life could depend on them' and 'Always include your name and address when you write to *Bunty*.' Social realism is an integral part of these magazines, both as an obvious intrusion such as these, and also in the implicit behaviour and expectations of the characters and the unfolding of the story. It is as if the girls are being taught, in the very act of reading, the harsh realities of life. There is a subtle but pervasive tutoring, so that girls can recognize quickly the marks which signal 'escape', but have also to learn what is being escaped from. Gill Frith puts it succinctly: 'the pleasure which these stories offer has positive aspects which directly contravene the concept of femininity found in other forms of popular reading available to girls, and this pleasure contains its own limits and contradictions'.[10]

The reading behaviour demanded by these comics contrasts sharply with that demanded by readers of *Beano*. In *Bunty* and *Judy*, etc., the readers are assumed to be literate, the language is specialized, and events are unfolded in such a way that the reader is invited to comment – or at least adopt her own moral position – in the context of personal relationships. Feelings always run high; emotions are the fuse that makes characters behave in either uncaring, cowardly and dominating ways, or courageous, caring and mediating ways. Interestingly, the protagonists are not passive. All the stories show girls to be creatures of sound judgement – able to 'see the other person's point of view', to consider different ways of solving problems, to conciliate warring factions successfully, while always keeping a determinedly brave face. They become expert at understanding motivation, both their own and other people's, at intervening at the right time, and at taking care of weaker and less fortunate creatures, whether they be children or animals. And they always feel better for doing so! It is an intoxicating mixture, understandably highly desirable.

Not surprisingly, it suggests role models which can more easily move into real life than the antics of Dennis the Menace. The girl readers of *Bunty*, *Mandy* and *Judy* will almost certainly become avid consumers of schoolgirl books from writers such as Enid Blyton and Angela Brazil. So much popular fiction now available, in both magazines and novels, allows this to continue.

Part of the 'social realism' in these comics is an acknowledgement of female development and sexuality. In some, the concerns are over-poweringly to do with fashion and presentation. Beauty aids, how to get rid of spots, and cosmetic tips are all strong messages about the importance of the right image, and the implicit need for male attention. One result of this is that girl readers are quickly expected to become consumers. It is not simply the role of the comic to suggest ways of hiding spots; it offers a range of products which assumes that the readers have money and choice in order to combat the problem. Increasingly, and unconsciously, girls are herded into a marketplace where they are at their most vulnerable. Parents of young girls will recognize only too well the phenomenon which I describe. The expertise which girls acquire is one which might keep them as consumers for the rest of their lives. A cultural concern with style and image homes in on them in young adulthood.

Sometimes, the gender difference only serves to reinforce female friendships. 'Boy trouble for Roz and Laura'[11] documents the activities of the two girls and their involvement with boys. Invited out by an American, Terry, Roz has to fight off his amorous advances. He is shown to be big-headed and (because of his Americanism) different to other (presumably English) boys. She leaves him at the cinema to make her own way home alone. Almost accosted by three rough-looking boys, Roz in desperation calls at the house of her friend Laura. She is

'Girl Talk', from *Nikki*, no. 157 (20 February 1988). © D. C. Thomson & Co. Ltd. Reproduced with permission.

taken in, protected and consoled by Laura and her mother. In school the next day friends tell her, 'that Terry sounds a real pain. Don't be put off, not all English boys are like him, Roz.' The episode continues, celebrating the value of female intimacy and support against the marauding males who constantly threaten. It also acknowledges the importance of the 'hunt' – 'Don't be put off . . .'

Nikki's 'Girl Talk' seems worth considering in detail.[12] The language has a strange, American resonance. Although it is set in an English comprehensive, words such as 'gorgeous', 'hi', 'fancies' and 'what a creep' are part of an accepted form of address. Young readers will often use this language in their everyday world, again shifting the boundaries between created and real worlds. The figures are glamorous and have an obvious sense of style. The arena for catching male attention is carefully constructed – girls must 'stay together' and not let jealousy interfere with female solidarity. Even as Liz exclaims 'Huh – what a creep', one feels that exactly the same thing is likely to happen again. It is an admission that the writer and reader are complicit in their knowledge of sexual relationships and the difficulties which can arise.

It is clear that sexuality becomes increasingly important as the readers move from girlhood to womanhood. The cosy and safe world of the earlier comics takes on a different and often contradictory set of messages. As puberty approaches, girls see their sexuality as a source of power and one which carries with it a responsibility and commitment to nurturing and protecting. It is not always passive, as some writers suggest. On the contrary, I think it is a sophisticated awareness of the possibilities – and impossibilities – of being a woman. Gill Frith's comments on school stories would apply equally to comics:

> Located in an impossible time – the age of puberty in which puberty never happens – and an impossible place – the fantastic dream of a school which has no relationship with the world beyond it – the school story offers its young reader the possibility of resolving the contradictions in her life without ever needing to confront them directly.[13]

In other words, the texts have taught their readers how to read them, how to recognize the fantasy, the deferred gratification, the sheer fun of escapism and the acceptance that the real world has to be dealt with.

The worlds offered to boys and girls in the popular fiction of comics are highly segregated by the time they come to leave primary school. Boys have had repeated exposure to what is ultimately a narrow and foreshortening genre. As stated earlier, adult comics such as *Viz* have a cult following, but are not widely read. The antics of Dennis, Minnie, the Bash Street Kids, etc., remain firmly locked in a cartoon tradition. They will probably continue to be firm favourites, producing to exactly the same format in twenty years' time. In Britain, at least, we outgrow the *Beano*. Interestingly, in other European countries, comics and strip cartoons are regularly read by the adult population – usually males. Some are much more sexually explicit, but one conjectures that the real reasons for their popularity are culturally significant ones.

Girls, on the other hand, are encultured through their reading matter of popular fiction to be more conscious of the real world – probably long before they leave primary school. They have a language and set of discourses (sometimes borrowed from popular fiction) which enable them to enter adult concerns in a much smoother and almost playful transition. It is hardly surprising that girl readers 'move on' to the alternative fantasies offered by romantic fiction, *Jackie* (now defunct), *Just Seventeen* and *Mizz*. They provide the largest variety within a similar genre. The young readers have learnt their reading lessons well. They do not necessarily approach as passive, easily influenced, non-critical bimbos. On the contrary, they know what they are looking for, and how that knowledge can be utilized.

Boys leaving primary school and entering the difficult years of puberty may be expert at reading their strip cartoons, but with increasing maturity they are less inclined to associate with what adults regard as childish. While the girls continue their forays into romance, in both magazines and books, what do boys read? The market is surprisingly limited. Comics and magazines are produced, but they usually focus on a particular sport or hobby. Football is the most popular – but much of the narrative found in them is a continuation of *Roy of the Rovers*. The stories take second place to 'club' activities' and information – goals scored, tactics, individual footballers' performances, etc. Other magazines are based on cameras, motorbikes and, increasingly, computers. In other words, the message for young teenage boys is one which firmly rejects the childish world of comics and beckons to the adult world of information and fact finding. There is a strong contrast between the factual, materialist, competitive values in these magazines and the emotional, psychological concerns associated with romantic fiction.

My concern is that boys have equal curiosity about emotional and sexual development, but that they are not encultured into a discourse which allows for it to develop. The need is painfully obvious. All the female students I have spoken to over a number of years are quick to point out that boyfriends, husbands and brothers do read the 'feminine' magazines – not for salacious reasons, but precisely because they too are fascinated by the perplexing adult world of sexuality and development. Boys have to turn to the magazines and 'just happen' to read the problem page because at least some of their worries do find expression, albeit from Miss C. of Camberley. I do not think it is sexual explicitness which is being sought, rather a fumbling towards understanding the same difficulties of growth and sexual development which girls can start to address in their reading material.

To put it simply, 'girl talk' is not a silly, peripheral discourse. On the contrary, it is one which allows for the playing and 'acting out' of desperately serious issues. Society may try and trivialize it, but I would suggest that girls not only become 'better' at girl talk, they also have choice. Girls are happy to be seen walking out of a newsagent's shop with a copy of the *Beano*. A boy would not be seen dead bringing out the latest *Bunty* or *Judy*.

In this chapter I have raised issues of language, class, gender and oppression. As I said earlier, we have been quick to note the racism and sexism in children's fiction over the last twenty years. We must be careful of creating a new orthodoxy which might be equally oppressive. Popular fiction deserves to be taken seriously as fiction for children. Its influence is increasing, and we need to reflect on the processes involved in order to understand what all children are experiencing.

> If texts reflect the partial agenda of discursive practices lived out in real life, contradicting and uncertain, both powerfully and yet fragilely constituted, then there is much to be gained by teachers exploiting that diversity. Rather than offering our pupils a fixed and unaltering position, we should be facilitating the exchange of meanings, and dealing with the difference.[14]

Above all, we must always go back to the children themselves.

Notes

Comics and magazines referred to: *Playhour, Twinkle, Postman Pat, Jack and Jill, Beano, Buster, Dandy, Roy of the Rovers, Viz, Victor, Judy, Bunty, Nikki, Just 17, Mizz.*

1   H. Rosen, *Language and Class*, Falling Wall Press, 1972.
2   V. Watson, 'The possibilities of children's fiction', in M. Styles, E. Bearne and V. Watson (eds), *After Alice*, Cassell, London, 1992.
3   Rosen, *Language and Class*.
4   'Tales from Greenland', *Postman Pat*, no. 74, 1988.
5   'Nurse Susan and Doctor David', *Jack and Jill*, December 1985.
6   'Calamity James', *Beano*, no. 2524.
7   Barry Hines, *Kes*, Michael Joseph, London, 1968.
8   'The Bash Street Kids', *Beano*, no. 2524.
9   'Emma Kemp', *Bunty*, no. 1570, 13 February 1988.
10 G. Frith, 'The time of your life', in C. Steedman, C. Urwin and V. Walkerdine (eds), *Language, Gender and Childhood*, Routledge & Kegan Paul, London, 1985.
11 'The Comp', *Nikki*, no. 157, 20 February 1988.
12 'Girl Talk', *Nikki*, no. 157, 20 February 1988.
13 G. Frith, 'The time of your life'.
14 G. Moss, *Un/Popular Fictions*, Virago, London, 1989.

CHAPTER 3

'Am I That Geezer, Hermia?'
Children and 'Great' Literature

Morag Styles

While The Prose and the Passion *was in preparation, the Key Stage 3 anthology was being hotly debated. Morag Styles in this chapter addresses the issue of 'great literature' and ranges widely, from F.R. Leavis to Charles Sarland, and from William Shakespeare to Enid Blyton. She suggests that the question 'Is this great literature?' is the wrong question. We should, she argues, concern ourselves with understanding what children's books bring to their readers, and what the readers bring to the books. We should also acknowledge that much great literature was once popular literature, and she concludes by describing ways in which Shakespeare can come alive in classrooms − not by presenting his work as great literature, but by using those very features which originally made him popular,*

But what made me read all the Biggles? I had discovered literature, written literature. I had seen a library for the first time in my life. Books. Books everywhere. Book was magic . . . It was a stage in my life when what was most important in literature was the story and the element of what happens next. And this the Biggles books had in plenty. The Biggles series were full of actions, intrigues, thrills, twists, surprises and a very simple morality of right against wrong, angels against devils, with the good always triumphant. It was adventure all the way, on land and in the sky . . . It was the strong action which made one forget or swallow all the racist epithets of the narratives. The books did not invite meditation; just the involvement in the actions of the hero and his band of faithfuls . . . Biggles was a boy, daring to try, never giving up, stretching the boundaries of what was credible, but inviting his boy readers to join in the adventure. (Ngugi wa Thiong'o)[1]

But Shakespeare one gets acquainted with without knowing how. It is part of an Englishman's constitution. (Jane Austen)[2]

- What is great literature? Who decides?
- Is literature that children like great literature? Great to whom?
- Why should children read great literature?
- Can children's literature ever be great literature?

In discussing these issues I intend to be highly controversial: two writers will illustrate my argument, namely Enid Blyton and William Shakespeare. I am not going to define *children's* literature at present, since the no-man's-land between writing for adults and children is a remarkably tricky area. Few, however, will contest Margaret Meek's assertion that 'Children's literature is undeniably the first literary experience, where the reader's experiences of what literature *is* are laid down. Books in childhood initiate children into literature.'[3]

So, what is 'great' children's literature and why should children read it? Members of the tabloid press, Tory MPs, Prince Charles and recent appointees to the National Curriculum Council may be sure they know what great literature is and why children should read it, but those of us who take the subject and young readers seriously realize it is not as simple as it seems. Most of the commentators working themselves into a frenzy about poor spelling, correct grammar and the neglect of great literature, as they see it, are locked into their own childhood experience of English. Memories are notoriously unreliable and often tinged with idealism: it is very easy to believe that things were better in a past where standards were excellent (in prep, public and grammar schools) and forget about the majority of pupils putting in time at the often less than exemplary secondary modern schools. At any rate these commentators want things to stay the same or, better still, to go back to a past they are nostalgic about. But we cannot. New literacies and new technologies proliferate, while the linguistic and cultural possibilities of closer ties with Europe, and, indeed, many parts of the globe, make it our job to equip children for the rapidly changing world we live in now, rather than indulging in looking backwards.

What does this have to do with literature? No one is going to argue that texts are not infinitely various, that some display qualities of moral authority, depth of characterization, profundity of theme, inventive use of language, subtlety and challenge, and others do not. But to concentrate on the matter that some texts clearly exhibit literary excellence (however that is defined) and others do not means that it is not only the majority of writers who are considered second rate, but, by implication, the majority of readers too. If we concentrate on an élite band of 'great' writers, we also exclude all those who do not read them. In schools we care about *all* our pupils including those who cannot, do not or are not able to read such literature. And if we subscribe to a narrow literary canon, we are also in danger of excluding texts that are not Anglo-centric, thereby ignoring most black writers and neglecting literature that does not fall in line with the prevailing orthodoxy.

Louise Rosenblatt forcefully reminds us that the social and intellectual atmosphere that sets up 'good literature as, almost by definition, works accessible only to the élitist critic or literary historian leads the average reader to assume that he is not capable of participating in them'.[4] None the less, most English teachers operate with an implicit hierarchical model of quality literature. Leavis made his reputation by identifying criteria for judging literary merit, notoriously constructing a strict canon of great and lesser writers which even in this postmodernist era continues to be enormously influential. Leavis's values are hard for many of us to reject, unsurprisingly, as his foregrounding of moral resonance is very persuasive. In fact, is that not one of the most significant criteria for judging the value of children's books? Yet returning recently to *The Great Tradition* I was struck by his limitations and inflexibility. What about this?

> The great English novelists are Austen, Eliot, James and Conrad . . . the present vogue of the Victorian age, Trollope, Charlotte Yonge, Mrs Gaskell, Wilkie Collins . . . one after another the minor novelists of that period are being commended to our attention, written up and published by broadcast and there is a noted tendency to suggest that they not only have various kinds of interesting things to offer but that they are living classics.

and later

> The reason for not including Dickens in the line of great novelists . . . [is that] his genius was that of the entertainer . . . The adult mind doesn't as a rule find in Dickens a challenge to an unusual or sustained seriousness.[5]

I wonder what kind of scorn Leavis would have poured on children's literature? Of course, taste changes – Dickens is now uncontestably part of 'great' literature and Leavis himself admitted this fact at a later date. Interestingly, writers who were often radical in their day become part of the 'literary heritage', when they are safely tamed and muzzled with the passing of time. Examples that immediately come to mind are Burns, Blake, Coleridge, Wollstonecraft, Shelley, George Eliot and Lawrence.

Leavis's tone of superiority is not just characteristic criticism of adult literature. Here is Neil Philip praising William Mayne: 'I say if children will not read Mayne, it is not Mayne's fault. Children do not read him not because he's unreadable, but because teachers teach them to read in a way which excludes him.'[6] This is a smear against teachers from someone who does not have to tackle reluctant readers daily.

So I find myself fairly sympathetic to Peter Hunt when he asks in *Criticism, Theory and Children's Literature* 'why should any student – be it a woman or an American or an East African or a child – give any credence to standards established years ago by old, British, upper middle class, white, university-based males?'[7] It is an interesting argument to pose against Leavis's certainties. Or Michael Rosen:

> Greatness [in literature] is largely a conversation between academics . . . statements about greatness are nothing more than personal preferences. In other words, the texts we are compelled to read at school and university are simply the consequence of agreements in that conversation between academics. Nothing more or less. And these agreements may not coincide with the tastes, pleasures and values of millions of other people.[8]

What happens is that English Literature becomes an élitist club excluding so-called minor writers, and certainly children's literature, from serious attention. But then we do it ourselves. The children's literature world also creates an exclusive canon where the great and the good are lauded and others writers marginalized.

It is widely known that the children's writers admired by teachers and critics are *not* those most favoured by their young audience. (This is not the case with picture books, but they are not within the remit of this chapter.) We know that writers like Dahl and Blume win grudging approval in many quarters only because children love their books, not because they are regarded as having literary merit. The poet Michael Rosen, mentioned above, who writes mainly humorous poetry in free verse which is massively popular with children, is frequently sneered at by critics. The fact that his books have always contained serious and challenging poems on themes that strike a chord with young readers is ignored, as is the quality of his language. Try to write a good Rosen-type poem: it is a lot harder than it looks. Children think it is great poetry, but some critics query whether it is poetry at all.

Another way that English teachers operate in terms of 'great' literature is to attempt to make it accessible to young readers by good, enthusiastic teaching. Secondary English teachers employ a wide range of exciting techniques to bring literature of the past, as well as the present, alive to teenagers of the 1990s. Teachers in junior schools recognize the importance of reading regularly to their pupils and are keen to develop the reading habit in their pupils; and early years teachers using real books are people who put literature first. In fact, the whole debate about reading schemes/real books does not hinge on phonics at all, as it is alleged. (And HMI have shown in their recent reports on reading (1990 and 1991) that phonics is taught in most schools, alongside whatever methodology of learning to read is being employed.) Nor is it a question of structure versus open-endedness.

Teachers employing the apprenticeship approach to learning to read have to be extremely disciplined and orderly in the way they support young learners in their freedom to choose the books they want to read and to let them take the time it needs for reading to become fluent. The crucial underpinning of this methodology is a belief by teachers in the fundamental importance of reading in children's lives and a deep knowledge of those texts which teach young readers how to read. The heart of the debate is actually about whether literature is so powerful that children should have the best of it from the start – in this case, picture books by gifted artist–writers like Anthony Browne, John Burningham and Pat Hutchins.

Of course, good teachers can, with patience and inventiveness, teach any text to any age group in an educationally worthwhile manner. Jenny Dunn has written about her use of *The Ancient Mariner* with 10- and 11-year-olds.[9] Rex Gibson's 'Shakespeare in Schools' initiative has sparked off exciting projects with children from 6 to 16, up and down the country. The Greek myths, Beowulf and Chaucer have all been tackled with younger children. We should congratulate ourselves that teachers in the United Kingdom have developed an impressive armoury of approaches to texts that have been remarkably successful with young people.

But it is still the case that some pupils in some classes remain untouched by literature despite the best efforts of teachers. The reasons why are complex and I try to address some of them later in the chapter. It may simply be unrealistic to expect all pupils to read 'great' literature, much as we would like them to. This is a hard one for those of us who share a passion for the texts and the readers. To question the value of 'great' literature seems to question our *raison d'être*. It is not easy to read in Peter Hunt and similar critical theorists that:

> to introduce children to literature in the way it has been defined until now is to narrow, not broaden, his or her life; it is to cut the freedom of the equality of all texts to the acceptance of the codes of *some texts and those of a privileged minority*.[10]

I find myself schizophrenically torn right down the middle of this debate. I love literature myself, Shakespeare is my favourite writer, I am totally committed to fostering and extending the reading of all the children and students with whom I come into contact. Yet I find some of the poststructuralist arguments convincing in many respects. Why should adults who have power over young readers force them to read certain texts even if their motives are benign? And do we not undervalue the texts that are often popular with children because they appear to lack literary merit?

In order to unpack this a little more, I will use a personal anecdote. When I was 6 my parents went back to India with my siblings for three years and left me with several middle-aged, unmarried sisters who lived together in Aberdeen. I did not encounter any child abuse and the 'aunties' (as I called them – they were not family) tried to be kind to me, but they did not understand children. They dressed me in old-fashioned clothes and made all sorts of anxious restrictions on my liberty to behave like a normal child. I became an outsider, isolated from the culture of childhood, despite the fact that in every other period of my life I have found it easy to make friends. I am quite convinced that the reason I stayed sane in that situation was by reading. I quickly became an avid reader and was privileged enough to have the *Dandy*, *Beano*, *Girl*, *School Friend*, *Girl's Crystal* and, later, *Bunty* delivered weekly, as well as having a new book bought for me every week. (Interestingly, although the 'aunties' were strongly traditionalist in their views on education, they did not seem to worry about the number of comics I read.)

I have no doubt that the function reading served was to offer me alternative worlds to inhabit while my own was fractured and confused; it gave me friends when I did not have any; it offered solace and adventure in the safety of my own bedroom. And it gave me a space where I could deal with feelings. One of the hardest things about the aunties was their emotional demands – they wanted love from me and I found all declarations of affection from them (or actors on television or even love songs on the radio) deeply embarrassing. But in books I had an outlet for love, hate, anger, envy and distress.

So what were the books? The ones I remember of forty years ago are *Little Women*, *Black Beauty*, *Puck of Pook's Hill*, *Anne of Green Gables*, *Little Grey Rabbit*, lots by R.L. Stevenson, and *What Katy Did*. I have always assumed that these were the books that saved my life, providing hope and consolation. That is a very important function of reading and one I want to pass on to the children with whom I come into contact. But in that same period I also read every copy I could find of Enid Blyton, from Little Noddy to The Famous Five and *The Naughtiest Girl in the School*. How do I know that Enid Blyton (and the comics) did not nourish and sustain me just as much as the 'great' literature I was reading? Was it the universal themes in *Anne of Green Gables* that fulfilled my emotional needs, or the time out of real life by going on an adventure with the Famous Five? Probably both. I know I am not alone in finding Enid Blyton a very important factor in my childhood, even though I no longer enjoy her books.

It is conventional wisdom that Blyton can be admired as somebody with a sure command of narrative who turns children on to books. She is said to offer easy reading and quick pleasure and to provide an excellent bridge to 'better' texts requiring more of the reader. Certainly Blyton's writing is sloppy, with unintended repetitions and insufficient editing, full of stereotypes and limited in theme and characterization.

But she *could* write a good story and take a reader on an escapist adventure where children did exciting things without adults around. Is it not just a little unsettling that many librarians actually banned her from their libraries in the sixties? Children loved her work, but adults knew better and censored it.

Judy Blume has never been banned, to my knowledge, but many critics disapprove of her books. She gives a lot of readers what they want — lively story-lines with gutsy characters and openness about bodies, sex, divorce, abuse, etc., sympathetically explored with no holds barred: all the stuff of soap operas, indeed, but also affecting the lives of many young people today. One view is that Blume has become a best seller by exploiting young readers; an alternative stance is that she actually listens to what they say (she certainly gets a massive postbag from them) and respects it. Do youngsters like her books because they deal with the emotions, often confused, of that age group in an easily accessible way, taking the young person's point of view in the form of a racy story? There is little literary merit, in Leavis's terms; what children read Blume for is self-indentification and the way she deals with personal and social issues. Like Blyton, she offers a compelling narrative and the resolution of difficulties. As for Dahl, a master storyteller, whereas his fiction seems to many adults nasty, prejudiced, almost sadistic at times, full of the kinds of revolting reference which mature readers like to leave behind, his work is almost universally popular with the young. I certainly do not enjoy Dahl (except for *The B.F.G.*) as I do other children's writers — I read him out of duty.

This leads me to a revelation that felt like a new insight while I was preparing this chapter, but which seems embarrassingly obvious now. Do we admire Pearce, Le Guin, Garner *et al.* because they speak directly to most adults as well as to children? In other words, do we get the same *kinds* of satisfaction reading Phillippa Pearce or Jill Paton Walsh as we get from Charlotte Brontë or George Eliot? Do Dahl, Blyton, Blume and maybe, in a different way, Rosen appeal exclusively to children? In other words, do they share a genuine child-centredness to which adults no longer have access, thereby keeping adults out? Are we benevolent parents, teachers, librarians, with our concern for children's books and young readers, attempting to knock down the nursery door and jump into the play-pen with the children? And, of course, as self-respecting children, are they hanging on to the books *they* like, keeping some of the culture of childhood closed to adults?

I want to look more closely at what Blyton appears to offer young readers. Charles Sarland and Donald Fry supply the evidence. Sarland suggests that part of Blyton's appeal is that her readers enjoy the security of a domestic world where the adults are conventional, predictable and in charge, *and at the same time* the children have the freedom to go off and have adventures, where they have their own rules and where they are resourceful and intrepid. The need to conform is thus reconciled with the need to be daring: 'benevolent paternalism informs the whole [Secret Seven] Series but within this framework Blyton allows the children a considerable measure of autonomy'.[11] And they are easy to read. Karnail, an inexperienced 12-year-old reader (in Fry's book), found the Secret Seven a route into books for him. Asked why he liked them, he replied, 'I like the way they / get on to mysteries / adventures happen / *I'd like to be like that.*'[12] Here is identification with a character again – the first step in hooking a reader. 'I'm Julian', said my son at 7 after reading his first Blyton.

Fry writes:

> The Secret Seven make us wince: the way they speak, the way they eat . . . the way they relate to adults. They often seem pompous, bossy and prejudiced; and they are supported by indulgent adults, not only parents and policemen, but 'Cookie' and 'Gardener' and friendly representatives of the working class . . . Naughtiness is as strange to them as poverty: they are scrupulous about good manners, and never dream of defying the code of conduct their parents have passed on to them. Peter, in particular, often reminds the others what mummy and daddy have said: 'do not carve on trees, do put your coat on if you are going outside'.[13]

The child characters seem a different breed from young readers. Yet Karnail hardly seems to notice this. Fry goes on to suggest that young readers are more attuned to what they have in common with the Secret Seven than the differences. I think he is right and that the continuing popularity of Blyton means that a lot of readers are editing out the bits that do not work for them – the sexism, the stereotypes, the old-fashioned, middle-class, goody-goodyness of it all. In other words they are doing something quite sophisticated – reading against the text, in parts.

But there is more to Blyton than that. Both Sarland and Fry cite a catalogue of devices she uses which teach the rudiments of reading fiction. Sarland writes: 'By the time they have read . . . these books, readers will have been introduced to the basic grammar of narrative stance, narrative function . . . and many of the techniques of handling time.'[14] Books like the Secret Seven offer context support to the inexperienced reader:

- text in manageable chunks;
- narrative voice which is close to that of the child and addresses the reader directly;
- simple plot structure with lots of mini-climaxes;
- description skilfully woven into the action;
- plenty of dialogue, easily tagged;

- reliable plot organized round recurring elements, so the reader does not get lost or confused;
- few demands on memory;
- characters easy to identify with, rooted in action, and so on.

Finally Blyton, like all the 'best' authors, is on the children's side and takes their play seriously. She offers children the chance, in the virtual world she creates, to behave with independence, to have status, to make decisions, to be members of a special group, and the reader is invited to take part in the adventure in the company of the characters. That is a pretty enticing invitation.

In his 'Preface to Shakespeare', Dr Johnson stated firmly that the only test that could be applied to works of literature was 'length of duration and continuance of esteem'.[15] Whether we like it or not, Blyton is still one of the writers most read by children in the 1990s. Margaret Meek writes:

> which books confirm a child's view of himself as a reader by extending into the medium of play what we know to be the rules of the game? You won't thank me for telling you that it could be Enid Blyton ... Any significant theory of children's literature cannot ignore the texts children hold in common for on those is their view of literature founded, and from those are their competencies developed.[16]

We ignore her at our peril.

I spent two weeks last summer in the Costa Blanca – villa, bathing pool, sun, the good life. And books. What did I read? *Cosmopolitan, The Silence of the Lambs*, recent novels by Ian McEwan, Anne Tyler and Jane Gardam, a Michael Dibdin thriller and the new Inspector Morse. You do not need to know any more except that just before the holiday I had reread five Austen novels, when I was between houses, reading to reassure, perhaps. What does this prove? Literary texts and popular fiction can be equally enjoyable to the same reader and seem to mix together pretty well. Both elicited serious and substantial responses from the reader. What seems to be clear is that:

- different texts offer different sorts of reading experiences;
- the reading experiences offered by texts depend on the reading histories of readers and are affected by the particular reading situation;
- popular fiction can elicit sophisticated responses from readers.

Or as Frank Hatt puts it:

> One reader will read different texts in different ways; one text will be read in different ways by different readers. One reader will read the same text differently on different occasions; indeed, he will read different parts

of the same text in different ways during the course of one reading act, as his mood, his purpose and his knowledge change.[17]

Instead of the 'great' literature debate, would it not be more profitable to try to find out more about *how* young readers read and what puts them off reading? Charles Sarland demonstrates convincingly that pulp fiction can generate intelligent responses in young people, in bottom- as well as top-stream classes.[18] He found that low-achieving working-class boys responded positively to *First Blood* (the Rambo novel), because the external fiction matched the internal fictions of pupils who felt cut off from the mainstream of society. They identified with the hero who has to fight his way out of the bottom of the pile, succeeding by actively using male power. If Margaret Meek is right when she says that young readers need to find their interior fiction as part of a writer's intention, what hope have the least experienced readers with the sorts of literary text we are expected to use with them? Sarland's pupils rejected books (i.e. most books) when they did not find themselves in them. Sarland goes on to discuss how the empty categories created by stereotypical characters and situations provided a social construction easily available to readers. It enabled pupils to find their own experience dramatized in fictional terms which they could understand.

Interestingly, the girls of similar age and experience who read *First Blood* had totally opposing reactions to it. They were more concerned with human elements of the plot and were able to exploit the plurality of the text. Sarland describes their ability to read against this ideologically closed text and go in for a bit of what he calls 'phallic deflation'. In other words, the boys saw Rambo and his exploits as heroic, the loner fighting against society and winning through bravery and violence, whereas the girls were more interested in the characters, but at the same time recognized the crude stereotyping of the novel and sent it up.

Sarland also considered texts rejected by pupils ('It's boring, miss'). This is a very important area for those of us in education who need to learn more about what gets between readers and books. Frank Smith writes: 'the more unconventional the reader finds the text, the less the reader is likely to have any relevant expectations about it and the less understandable it is likely to be'.[19] Even avid readers are often aware of a kind of tentativeness when they begin a new book. 'Will this novel please me?', 'Will I stick with it?' If confident readers resist texts, even when they know they should read them and understand the conventions, how much harder must it be for unconfident readers? It was clear that some of the teenagers Sarland talked to found most books part of a powerful and alien culture that seemed to reject them and that they were, in turn, actively rejecting.

Perhaps, instead of concerning ourselves with what is and is not great literature, we might be better employed by giving more emphasis to what *readers bring to texts*. Hugh Crago argues provocatively that 'in itself a book cannot create any feeling in its audience. The locus of feeling is in the reader, not in the book.'[20] The Plowden Report, not much respected of late, states insightfully (in 1967) 'It is through literature that children feel forward to the experiences, hopes, and fears that await them in adult life.'[21] Louise Rosenblatt says that 'literature provides a living-through, not simply knowledge about'.[22] It is this vital, affective role of literature that I want to look at next, because it is the emotional involvement in a book that provides much of its pleasure. Donald Fry's interviews with young readers provide some forceful examples.[23]

Here is 8-year-old Clayton, an inexperienced reader, on *The Snowman*: 'And this is my favourite / the sad bit / when he melts at the end . . . Usually when / when I do it I don't look at the end page . . . / I always turn it over to the white pages and then go back.' Clayton knows that it is too painful for him to look at the picture that deals with the inevitability of loss as part of love. Sharon is a keen reader of 16 discussing why she hates finishing books: 'It's like a death really, isn't it? You've lost them [the characters] and you can't really get in touch again.' And on *Jane Eyre*: 'You imagine yourself being there, being a little girl sitting in the window seat. I'm saying that I actually feel I am the person.' Joanne also knows how it feels to identify with a character: 'I was somebody watching her doing what she was doing / the actual things she did . . . walking behind her . . . You see yourself there / you're like a shadow.' As Robert Protherough says: '*things happen to people when they read* and any theory about the place of fiction in schools has to begin with this fact'.[24]

I have tried to argue that there is real value in popular fiction and that an exclusively élitist model of great literature excludes many of the young readers we care about: that all texts can elicit interesting responses from readers and that readers' own histories affect the nature of their responses. Literary theorists have made us aware of the centrality of the relationship between the reader and the text. Stanley Fish writes: 'meaning, significance and value are not best described as qualities of a text itself but as experiences of readers'.[25] In attempting to understand all young readers we have to distance ourselves from our own experiences, rather than imagine that the bookish child (whom Meek suggests is ourselves when young) is typical.

I have reached a stage in my argument where I must grapple directly with 'great' literature itself. As the recent thrust of the media debate has centred on him, and as my title includes reference to *A Midsummer Night's Dream*, as he can be used successfully with children of all ages and as he is 'top of the pops' in the literary heritage stakes, I suggest we consider William Shakespeare.

Before I do there are a couple of points that need to be made to set the record straight. Only one A-level English exam board did not make Shakespeare compulsory and very few schools took up that option. If they did, they had to choose an alternative literary text from the past. Neither is Shakespeare neglected at GCSE, although approaches to the texts are often imaginative and not particularly academic in the first instance. (In Rex Gibson's new editions of the plays for Cambridge, lively ways to get more involved in the text are offered on every other page.) In the long run, pupils have to master the texts thoroughly and answer questions on them. Surely it does not matter how they come to know the texts and surely they are much more likely to enjoy, understand and, perhaps, *want* to read or watch more Shakespeare if the teachers have made it exciting and relevant.

Shakespeare was recognized as someone suitable to use with children at least as far back as 1760, when the unknown editor of *Mother Goose's Melody* selected the same extracts that anthologists go for now (Ariel's song, 'When icicles hang by the wall', 'Ye spotted snakes' . . .) and described him as 'that sweet songster and nurse of wit and humour, Master William Shakespeare'.[26] But it was not always thus. Shakespeare's reputation went into a slump not long after his death and critical opinion was somewhat divided, as Schoenbaum makes clear in *A Documentary Life*: 'In London, Shakespeare became a common player in plays, then a popular writer of plays – the most popular in his age, although the literati did not universally concur in this evaluation.'[27]

Although Ben Jonson honoured him, he was also a robust critic of the Bard's failings. But his poem 'To the Memory of My Beloved, the Author Mr William Shakespeare; and What He Hath Left Us' is one of the most beautiful in the English language:

> But stay, I see thee in the hemisphere
> Advanced, and made a constellation there!
> Shine forth, thou star of poets, and with rage,
> Or influence, chide, or cheer the drooping stage
> Which, since thy flight from hence, hath mourned like night,
> And despairs day, but for thy volume's light.[28]

A less rarified view is taken by Samuel Pepys, inveterate theatre-goer:

> 1664 . . . and here saw the so much cried-up play of *Henry VIII*, which though I went with resolution to like it, is so simple a thing, made up of a great many patches, that besides the shows and processions in it, there is nothing in the world good or well done.

> 1663 . . . After dinner to the Duke's house and there saw *Twelfth Night* acted well though it be but a silly play and not relating at all to the name or the day.[29]

Dryden admired Shakespeare, but he certainly is not reverent:

> Those who accuse him to have wanted learning give him the greater
> commendation: he was naturally learned; he needed not the spectacles of
> books to read nature . . . He is many times flat, insipid; his comic wit
> degenerating into clenches, his serious swelling into bombast . . . If
> I compare Jonson with Shakespeare, I must acknowledge him the
> more correct poet, but Shakespeare the greater wit. Shakespeare was
> the Homer, or father of our dramatic poets; Jonson was the Virgil, the
> pattern of elaborate writing. I admire him, but I love Shakespeare.[30]

So what of this? Arguably the greatest writer of all time excites
different responses in different readers living at different times.
Contemporary critics are often harder on a writer than posterity proves
to be, but it is refreshing to hear their genuine opinions untinged by the
idolatry of today. It took nearly two hundred years for Shakespeare's
reputation to become unassailable: before that he was seen as gifted but
flawed, and not quite of the top literary flight, by most, but not all, of
the influential critics until the Romantic era, when Coleridge and others
accorded him genius. *But Shakespeare was part of the popular culture
of his day.*
    I must have been prescient a few years ago when I decided to devote
my back-to-the-classroom experience to the teaching of Shakespeare
with a class of 9- to 11-year-olds. The question I set myself was whether
or not a Shakespeare play, *A Midsummer Night's Dream*, had any
relevance to working-class children in the late 1980s. The answer was a
resounding 'yes' and I want to explore why that was. I will not dwell on
the techniques I used, the standard repertoire of English teachers, which
are now so much the subject of criticism – i.e. ways of making the play
meaningful, approachable and enjoyable for *all* the pupils in the class. I
want to analyse whether the reason for the play's success with my
pupils was that it was made available to them by exploring the links
with contemporary popular culture. (I did not set out consciously to do
so, as the article I wrote on the project some years ago will testify – no
mention of popular culture then.)[31]
    The first plank of the children's commitment to the project was in
recognizing that *The Dream* was a really good story. It did not matter
that it was written four hundred years ago – children reared on *Star
Wars*, *Superman* and *Neighbours* found it gripping. They wanted to
explore the world of Oberon and Titania, magic, spells and powerful
goblins, for themselves. I took the precaution of not mentioning fairies
until we were well into the project and, anyway, the children could see
that these fairies were nothing like the insipid creations of Victorian
fiction. I introduced Puck as Superfairy, blending characters of popular
films and comics with their knowledge of elves and goblins from fairy-
tales and Tolkien. (Most children had seen the cartoon version of *The*

Lord of the Rings or read or listened to a fair bit of *The Hobbit*.) I need not have bothered; Robin Goodfellow, as Shakespeare presented him, was quite strong enough. I often heard children chanting his lines to one another: 'I go, I go, look how I go, / swifter than arrow from the Tartar's bow', 'I'll put a girdle round the earth in forty minutes', 'I am that merry wanderer of the night'.

They found the antics of the rude mechanicals deliciously amusing from the start. Bottom's name alone had then sniggering; add to that his cockiness, his overacting, the way he took himself so seriously and poor Peter Quince's attempts to keep him in order, and the children took him to their hearts. They all knew people like Bottom or had seen someone like him on television. We spent time telling tall stories and trying to outboast each other to get under the skin of the character. And they loved lines like 'What sayest thou, bully Bottom?', 'What do you see? You see an ass head of your own, do you?'

The vicissitudes of the lovers worried me: how were the children to understand all that? They had all experienced jealousy: they knew what it was like to compete for the affection of a parent or sister or best friend. Most had tasted the misery of being rejected or left out. So the human emotions in the play were familiar territory for them. They have not experienced sexual love yet, but they know from *Eastenders* and *Neighbours* that parents often disapprove of young lovers and try to drive them apart; that women often compete for a boyfriend or vice versa; and that unrequited passion is commonplace. I used direct parallels from soap operas after setting the children 'homework' of watching *Coronation Street*, etc., for a week. This caused much hilarity, but they did watch the programmes with a new seriousness. It is no good giving the examples I used: the lovers have long since divorced, had children by other men or left the series by now! But there will always be a new set of complex human relationships in television soaps on which to draw, and children do seem to develop a taste for them quite young.

I must explain at last the title of this article. One rather trying afternoon about half-way through the project, I tried to be too ambitious. To give the children more understanding of the lovers' sub-plot, I decided to use a mixture of mime and improvisation. First I divided the children into threes, with one pupil as the outsider trying to persuade a member of the remaining couple to go away with them. Then I suggested they try the same thing in mime, so I numbered each group 1, 2, 3 and called 1 Hermia, 2 Lysander and 3 Helena regardless of gender. It was a daft idea and I realized I had failed when a lad put his hand up and asked, 'Am I that geezer, Hermia?' At that point the teacher fell about laughing. With the distance of hindsight, I feel humbled that children should tolerate such fumbling with good humour and saddened that with all the National Curriculum imperatives and 'three wise men advice', it is unlikely that many teachers will take the risk of teaching the whole curriculum through a project like mine again.

When the children made their programmes for our performance of the play, they turned it into popular culture. 'Pyramus loves Thisbe', proclaimed one, adding a picture of a love heart with an arrow through it. 'A most lamentable comedy', suggested another: the children heartily enjoyed all the punning in *The Dream*. A third illustrated the nursery rhyme 'Hark, hark, the dogs do bark /the beggars are coming to town' on the back cover. (Weeks before we had considered nursery rhymes and the oral tradition and wondered when some of the rhymes had originated: I had also given the children some background on the social status of actors in the late sixteenth century. One pupil made the creative leap that 'one in rags / one in bags / and one in a velvet gown' could be a reference to travelling players.) A fourth featured a picture of that infamous moon with a red heart dripping tears attached and stars twinkling in the background – a perfect visual representation of the irony in the play within the play.

The children paid close attention to bibliographic details: the play was put on 'by kind permission' of the headteacher; they were quite clear that I was the director and their teacher the producer; they gave credit to behind-the-scenes help with music, costumes, props, etc.; cast lists were given in full with characters' names spelled correctly. I suspect that their knowledge of these conventions was more likely to be gleaned from television viewing and the reading of *TV Times* than from familiarity with theatre programmes. The letters the children wrote to the actors who came into school to perform some of the rude mechanical scenes show their grasp of Shakespeare's comedy and their ability to weave it into their everyday lives:

> In a wood near Athens / Thurs 14th May / Dear Snug, / I enjoyed your visit but you are a very lousy lion. I chose to write to you because you are very funny. You act so cool. I like it when you growl so softly. I enjoyed your acting very much. So goodbye for now I hope you come again. / Your most humble servant / Kuong Chu

> Globe Theatre / Dear Snug, / You play a really good part. I was the one who made the lion mask. You could not roar properly and you kept laughing. Yours / humble servant / Aaron

> Kings Hedges Junior School / Dear Nick Bottom, / Thank you for coming to our school today. I liked thou knavery. I liked the bit you played as Pyramus. I thought you were very funny. Thank everyone else who was in it like Tom Snout, Snug, Peter Quince, Starveling, Flute. / Your most humble servant / Lisa

Naturally, I introduced Shakespeare's language gradually – a word or two at first; the class teacher and I hamming up amusing extracts, then children in pairs, improvising dialogue and trying out short speeches. The treat at the end of the third week was a visit from local actors doing the final scene: this was carefully timed so that by then most children had their ears attuned to the language. Before that we watched a bit of the play on video. The children were transfixed. Whereas I thought they would only tolerate a couple of the brief scenes we had already tackled, they were vociferous in demanding the whole thing. None of these children would have watched Shakespeare before the project, I am quite certain, but they were familiar with video and directed me to fast forward or, more often, to rewind a section they wanted to look at more closely, and were scathing in their criticism of the acting. By the end of the project they were experts on the play and were able to make constructive and penetrating comments about interpretation of character, pace, set and so on when they went to a performance of *The Dream* in London. We should not be surprised that working-class children, many with undeveloped literacy skills, were able to watch their first Shakespeare play (the first experience of the theatre for most) mouthing the lines they knew, and complaining afterwards about the inattentiveness of older schoolchildren in the audience.

These children did not just get the edited highlights of *The Dream*: they got the real thing. They acted most of the text, saw three productions of the play, listened to Britten and Mendelssohn's versions of the music, and learned about the history of that period and of the theatre in particular. Because they became imaginatively and emotionally involved in being sixteenth-century players (Shakespeare's company, of course) putting on *The Dream*, they rose to the difficulties involved – unfamiliar language, complicated plot, and challenging demands on acting and memory.

The children were too young to be aware of the cultural baggage involved in doing Shakespeare. They did not know about Shakespeare as high culture; for them it was living drama. It worked because they found enough that related to their own lives, a genuine universality of experience, and because it was fun. It *is* right that all children should have access to Shakespeare and we need to recognize that they *are* capable of taking on demanding texts, as well as *Neighbours* and Blyton. That is not why pupils' knowledge of Shakespeare is about to be compulsorily tested at 14. He is now seen as the flagship of the cultural arm of traditionalist values, a sacred relic, or as Terry Eagleton put it wryly: 'On the one hand, Shakespeare incarnates certain timeless transcendent values which belong to the very language of Man. On the other hand, you can't actually produce his stuff any more without the sponsorship of Prudential Insurance.'[32]

There has never been a time in this country when a political party in government has used its power quite so crudely to pursue extreme policies in education masquerading as defence of standards, including the so-called resurrection of the literary canon. English teachers of 14-year-olds are now faced with an imposed set of texts which are unlikely to motivate large numbers of pupils. I am not simply arguing that they have picked the wrong texts and that youngsters would be more inclined to read a greater number of contemporary authors, including those who specialize in writing for that age group. Nor am I emphasizing the fact that even a life-long avid reader like myself was not ready for some of those texts until I was much older. (You probably need to be fairly mature to pick up the subtle nuances and the quiet delights of Dorothy Wordsworth's journal.) Nor am I reminding the reader that teachers have never neglected the 'great' writers of the past, though in recent years many have broadened the curriculum to include fiction in English from others parts of the world and, perhaps, given more prominence to women writers.

My frustration at such decisions is for those who find reading burdensome, those who need to find themselves in books if they are to muster the stamina to stick with the texts, those who are already turned off, but whose teachers stimulate jaded palates with popular fiction. The less experienced readers are now much more likely to give up on reading altogether. And I believe that the imposition of prescribed texts demonstrates a lack of respect for the professionalism of teachers. As for the pupils, they have been noticeably absent from the rhetoric: giving choice to *parents* is what is being shouted from the rooftops. If this discussion seems political, I would argue that discussing what children read in school is now unavoidably political.

In the last decade of the twentieth century, books have to compete with television, the onset of cable, a thriving video industry, computer games, slick advertising, action-packed films and the like. Those of us who care about children and education have to win the argument about a *literature for everyone* with the aim of empowerment for all our pupils. Surely what we need is explorations of all kinds of text, fostered by real engagement, in ways that attempt to be meaningful for all our pupils. As Margaret Meek writes:

> We are the accomplished readers of our day and we have to know something of our own literate history as well as the sources from which we draw our judgement if we are to act, in any way, on behalf of those who are less than half our age, growing up in a literate community which is completely different from the one we encountered as children.[33]

In this article I have questioned the accepted literary canon and tried to show the fickleness of critical opinion, while suggesting that popular fiction can elicit valuable responses in readers. My Shakespeare project demonstrated how children can take on the literary canon and make it their own by drawing parallels with their own culture. Although I have not gone the whole way down the structuralist road, I have indicated that it is these writers who are asking important questions and offering significant insights about texts and readers at the moment, rather than the backwoodsmen and women who want to turn the clocks back. Most of all, I have tried to explore some of the ambiguities and concerns teachers face in the daily decisions they have to make about presenting books to children. That is what *The Prose and the Passion: Children and their Reading* is all about.

Notes

I have been strongly influenced by the writings of Margaret Meek and Peter Hunt in the composition of this article and drew inspiration from Charles Sarland's *Young People Reading* (Open University Press, Milton Keynes, 1988).

1   Ngugi wa Thiong'o, *Guardian*, 13 August 1992.
2   Jane Austen, *Mansfield Park*, Penguin, Harmondsworth, 1966.
3   Margaret Meek, 'What counts as evidence in theories of children's literature?', in Peter Hunt (ed.), *Children's Literature: The Development of Criticism*, Routledge, London, 1990.
4   Louise Rosenblatt, *The Reader, the Text, the Poem*, Southern Illinois University Press, Carbondale, 1978, quoted in Meek, 'What counts as evidence?'
5   F.R. Leavis, *The Great Tradition*, Chatto & Windus, London, 1948.
6   Neil Philip, 'Children's literature and the oral tradition'; quoted in Peter Hunt (ed.), *Further Approaches to Research in Children's Literature*, Cardiff, 1982.
7   Peter Hunt, *Criticism, Theory and Children's Literature*, Blackwell, Oxford, 1991.
8   Michael Rosen, 'Poetry in all its voices', in Morag Styles, Eve Bearne and Victor Watson (eds), *After Alice*, Cassell, London, 1992.
9   J. Dunn, M. Styles, N. Warburton, *In Tune with Yourself*, Cambridge University Press, Cambridge, 1987.
10   Hunt, *Further Approaches to Research in Children's Literature*.
11   Charles Sarland, 'False premises', *Signal* 37 (1982).
12   Donald Fry, *Children Talk about Books: Seeing Themselves as Readers*, Open University Press, Milton Keynes, 1985.
13   *Ibid.*
14   Sarland, 'False premises'.
15   Dr Johnson, 'Preface to Shakespeare', London, 1778.
16   Margaret Meek, 'Prolegomena for a study of children's literature', in Michael Benton (ed.), *Approaches to Research in Children's Literature*, University of Southampton, Southampton, 1980.
17   Frank Hatt, *The Reading Process*, 1976; quoted in Hunt, *Further Approaches*.
18   Charles Sarland, *Young People Reading: Culture and Response*, Open University Press, Milton Keynes, 1988.

19   Frank Smith, *Reading*, Cambridge University Press, Cambridge, 1985; quoted in Hunt, *Further Approaches*.

20   Hugh Crago, 'Cultural categories and the criticism of children's literature', *Signal*, 30 (1979).

21   Lady Plowden, *Children and Their Primary Schools: A Report for the Central Advisory Committee for Education*, HMSO, London, 1967.

22   Rosenblatt, *The Reader, the Text, the Poem*.

23   Fry, *Children Talk about Books*.

24   Robert Protherough, *Developing Response to Fiction*, Open University Press, Milton Keynes, 1983.

25   Stanley Fish, *Is There a Text in This Class? The Authority of Interpretive Communities*, Harvard University Press, Cambridge, MA; quoted in Protherough, *Developing Response to Fiction*.

26   *Mother Goose's Melody*, Marshall, London, 1760.

27   S. Schoenbaum, *William Shakespeare: A Documentary Life*, Oxford University Press, Oxford, 1987.

28   Ben Jonson, *The Complete Poems*, ed. George Parfitt, Penguin, Harmondsworth, 1975.

29   Samuel Pepys, *The Shorter Pepys*, ed. Robert Latham, Penguin, Harmondsworth, 1987.

30   John Dryden, *An Essay of Dramatic Poesy*, 1684.

31   Morag Styles, '"Pyramus loves Thisbe": a Shakespeare project in a primary school', *Cambridge Journal of Education*, 18(1) (1988).

32   Terry Eagleton, 'The enemy within', *English in Education*, 25(3) (1991).

33   Meek, 'What counts as evidence?'

CHAPTER 4

'I Normally Daydream on Sundays'

Can Children Write Literature?

Helen Arnold

Helen Arnold's chapter has provided (perhaps 'loaned' would be more accurate) the title for this book. She argues that the texts which we identify as our own literature are those which satisfy because they 'connect the passion of the inner world with the prose of events and circumstances'. She goes on to demonstrate how children's play can reveal the ways in which they are seeking to make this connection between their inner and their outer worlds. Then she analyses the writing of several children in order to show how they too have connected the extraordinary passions of their inner lives with the subtle prose of their stories. Sometimes, she believes, we can see in their writing their inner and outer worlds 'laid out side by side'.

Every normal human being is interested in two kinds of world: the Primary, everyday world which he knows through his senses and a Secondary World or worlds which he not only can create in his imagination, but also cannot stop himself creating.[1]

It is probably a mistake to try to prepare a lecture on holiday. But I was away for a month, so I went prepared with paper, some ideas, a very few reference books and fairly low incentive. If I was going to fulfil my intention to explore children's ability to write 'literature', I would have to define literature. I began by dipping into the books to get myself into the mood and rapidly confirmed what I had already suspected, that what I wanted to say had already been said, much better, by other people. I decided to shelve the whole thing temporarily, and turned with guilty relief to the pile of novels I had brought with me.

I never got round to my original intention of defining literature; I doubt whether this can be done, except in so far as one individual sees it; but I became aware in my reading of some of the elements that constituted what literature was for me, which seemed important in both adult and child writing. The idea of the lecture was submerged, and I read no more reference books. Unconsciously, though, my aimless thoughts fulfilled a conscious purpose.

I had brought a lot of thrillers, some acclaimed new modern writers, a blockbuster which weighed more than most of the rest together, and *Howard's End* to reread. I devoured most of them – I could not put the thrillers down, and I thought Jane Gardam's *Queen of the Tambourines* wonderful.[2] The blockbuster I had to discard after a few pages. I tried to analyse why the books had such different effects on me, why some were like a drug, some were deeply satisfying, and one was unreadable. I was working out what was 'literature' for me. One thing which the books that engaged me deeply had in common was that they were about two worlds – the external world of events and people, and the internal world of the mind. For me it was the best way of knowing what other people were thinking, even though they were not real people.

Another difference was in the way the books were written; the styles varied enormously, but the books which really engaged me were ones in which I took pleasure in the fit of the words with the theme, each enhancing the other, sometimes smoothly, sometimes excitingly, but never boringly.

There are no doubt many other features which should contribute to my definition of 'literature', but those are the two I want to concentrate on, and to link with children's writing. The blockbuster was discarded because it fulfilled neither of these criteria. It gave a catalogue of events which held no tension for me, no excitement, because the world of the mind seemed to me entirely absent, and because the language was so banal. Maybe it told a good story, but I never got far enough to find out.

Howard's End helped me even more to fulfil my unconscious purpose. I read it last in my teens; I remembered the enormous effect it had on me then, but no details of plot or characters. I also remembered the famous phrase 'Only connect', which I have quoted to myself at frequent intervals across the years. I had put my own interpretation on it, gradually forgetting its context in the book. I had used it as a sort of mantra for connecting with other people, an urge to make deep and strong relationships through like-mindedness. But when I reread the novel, I found it was not that at all. Margaret was marrying a man who she realized was her complete opposite. She did not hope to reform or change him. She understood that, and exalted Mr Wilcox for his prosaic and practical qualities. 'Only connect! That was the whole of her sermon. Only connect the prose and the passion, and both will be exalted . . . live in fragments no longer.'[3]

So when I came consciously to my lecture I had my text, 'The prose and the passion', which I then proceeded to distort unashamedly for my own purposes. Re-gloss what I have said about inner and outer worlds and form and function. Literature is that which satisfies because it connects the passion of the inner world with the prose of events and circumstances. Or, to twist the analogy again, the 'passion' of ideas is shaped by the 'prose' of an appropriate linguistic framework.

Children, of course, will not consciously analyse the relationship between inner and outer worlds, and we know little about the development of the inner world. But as soon as the self-concept begins to grow, even before it can be expressed in language, I believe that they are experiencing their dual worlds. 'I normally day-dream on Sundays', is one boy's attempt to put it into words (see below). If we are to believe Vygotsky, speech starts in social interaction and is later internalized into inner speech. But I think that something is *in* there even before this happens, and speech does not always mirror this inner consciousness. The nearest we can get to it is perhaps to observe young children at play. What are children thinking as they play? Is play helping their inner consciousness develop? Do we know when and how? Margaret Meek and James Britton, among others, have realized the importance of play, particularly with regard to language development. Britton sees 'a close developmental link between make-believe play in infancy and the practice of the arts at all stages from kindergarten to the grave'.[1]

I watched a group of children playing, not listening to the language they used, but concentrating on what they were doing. Here were 4- to 7-year-olds in a typical 'free activity' session. It was not, of course, really free. The framework for action was set up for them, so that they were likely to be constrained by what was supplied for them to choose from – the 'prose' of construction toys, home corner, shop, railway track, dressing-up gear, etc. It was a microcosm of the world in which we make choices, bound by what is there for us to choose from. How did they make these choices? Why did they choose differently?

One child was making a working model from construction blocks. He was completely absorbed, he concentrated for a very long time, he looked at each stage of his building and seemed to make a mental check, even commenting aloud at times. It does not seem rash to suggest that he had some sort of internal plan. The connection between the inner and outer worlds appeared quite straightforward here; he did not have to collect a lot of different experiences together before he carried out an action, and yet there must have been many similar experiences which had prepared him for this dexterity.

Equally skilful movements were made by the little girl washing up (how I wish it had not been a little girl!). But the inner mind must have been working rather differently here. She was role-playing, and had therefore created a universe within which she imitated what was entirely appropriate with economical dexterity. It was more than just washing up, because she had placed her 'child', her toy dog, on the draining board to watch and be good. Later only the dog remained; the role of housewife was discarded as she moved into another world, less easy to define, as it involved putting on a tall hat. She removed it almost immediately, however, and tidied her hair carefully – back to her embodiment of the efficient housewife?

Some rather odd crocheted balaclava helmets were greatly in evidence, used apparently symbolically, because they never became part of a proper social drama. It was hard to see what they represented for their wearers, who put them on, discarded them, hung them up, washed them – there must have been reasons which came from inside those helmets!

The little boy in the grey track-suit was perhaps the most interesting to watch. It was as if he was turned inside out. His inner self was far more apparent than the objects around him, or the other children. He was not really able to keep a balance between the prose and the passion. It was all passion. He did more than role-play – he used the objects for real. He lay in the centre of the home corner as a baby; other children tried to join in this game, but he rejected them. He found his own bottle to suck. He too had his toy – a comfort toy, not a child. Later he found a more private corner and curled up as if in the womb. Another boy stroked his hair in a (fairly rough) token of, presumably, affection. That was too much for the grey-suited child. He crawled away. He found a cardboard box in which he shut himself up completely. It seemed that he was not connecting with anything but his own inner world.

It seemed that in their play the children were bringing their inner worlds to the surface without verbalization and often without direct communication with anyone else. Each child was already acting as an individual, with actions which were prompted from these inner worlds, although they were relating to the objects and events of the outer world. Each child seemed to have a unique way of responding to the situation. Each child was very serious; there were few moments of real inactivity; what was being done was fulfilling purposes, though these were not always clear to the onlooker. It is surely these inner worlds that we should be aware of, not probing them as voyeurs, but respecting their autonomy. These worlds can never be assessed by any National Curriculum, but we should have time as teachers to appreciate their existence. And this is where we come to reading – and writing – because it is mainly by reading and writing that children come to be aware of their inner worlds.

Here, of course, language has to be the vehicle. When they are introduced to stories, children are given models of secondary worlds in dialogue with outer worlds – most graphically in picture books like John Burningham's *Come Away from the Water, Shirley*. Here they need no words to understand the difference between what is going on in Shirley's inner and outer worlds.[5] *Alice's Adventures in Wonderland* involves a continuous dialogue – here verbal – as Alice unremittingly talks to herself.[6] The development for children would seem to be from inarticulated 'acting out' of what is in the mind, to internal dialogue, to the awareness that that is what one is doing. One knows then that one can deliberately take on the persona of another, and can appreciate through empathy what is going on in another mind.

> The imaginary spectatorship of fantasy and make-believe play has the special feature of allowing us to look on at ourselves, ourselves as participants in the imagined events – the hero in the rescue fantasy, the victim of the assault ... In spite, however, of seeing himself as a participant in the story, the daydreamer or the child engaged in make-believe remains an onlooker, too; in all his waking fantasy he normally fills the dual role of participant and spectator, and as spectator he can when need be turn away from the fantasy events and attend again to the demands of real life.[7]

How far do children transfer this ability to their own writing? In other words, how far do they become real authors who can express both inner and outer worlds in appropriate language? They usually begin writing with straightforward accounts of events, developing perhaps more from the teacher's requests to recount 'news' than any other awareness. They see series of events on television, they read comics which visualize dramatic happenings in the outside world. They do not usually speak of their imaginary worlds to their own friends or to their teachers.

And yet they have to select from their experiences and find ways of expressing them. They do this with great dexterity, for the most part. They learn to imitate different sorts of language and many of them become successful blockbuster writers at an early age. I am not so much interested in that dexterity here as in how far they are able to connect the prose with the passion of their inner worlds. It is difficult to know how to respond to children's writing, and it is very easy to be bowled over by facile skill which expresses little of the inner world. The strange thing, too, is that if we encourage them, as we did in the sixties, to write 'spontaneously of their feelings and reactions', it rarely works. Nor does it seem to help much to give them a vocabulary of grand emotive words. Paradoxically, just as the children were given things to play with in a fairly constrained framework, just as I had a quite limited purpose for writing a lecture, to give frameworks for writing often encourages the connections to be made. In these circumstances one can find the seeds of literature incorporating both the elements I chose to concentrate on.

I can only show you what I mean by illustration; it is significant for me that most of these examples I have had for a long time – some for a very long time. I suppose I have chosen them because I continue to respond to them with pleasure. My response is not so very different from my feeling about *Howard's End* and *Queen of the Tambourines*. In other words, I am reading them as literature. The examples are mainly prose, not even story, quite down-to-earth stuff, written within given frameworks.

Crayden, at 7 years old, writes about his special place:

> My special place is in my garden near lots of stinging nettles. I can climb from the back of the bonfire pile into it and it has got stinging nettles all round it. I keep an old tyre where I sit. The back of the bonfire pile is supported by bricks. There are some dead leaves from the front hedge, and dead plants. It has an escape route. There is a heap of rubbish at the front of my special place. There is quite a lot of room. You could fit three children in it. I normally day-dream on Sundays. Once it got things thrown on it, such as boxes and a tree. One of the dreams was about it getting burned up. Near it there is a pear tree.

He describes it with careful detail, giving an exact visual account. He does not say that the stinging nettles hurt him, or whether the tyre is comfortable to sit on. But he obviously knows every brick, every dead leaf. And then he says, 'There is quite a lot of room', which again, could be a purely factual, prosaic comment. But it is not; it is the beginning of being allowed into his mind, because he continues, 'You could fit three children in it.' Here are imaginary children, from his inner world – he is not just finding a spatially vivid image, because the next sentence is the wonderful 'I normally day-dream on Sundays', ambiguous, personal, haunting. Then there is another sentence of straight description, but the passion will not go away. 'One of the dreams was about it getting burned up.' Then the last sentence takes us right away from what is getting too close for him, perhaps – 'Near it there is a pear tree.'

I believe that in this simple piece we can see the inner and outer worlds laid out side by side, and can almost see the jumps from one to another.

Gideon's piece, at 10 years old, is much more closely fused:

> *The Gargoyle*
> The gargoyle seems engrossed in some endless task of watching us, forever watching through stone eyes that are wise and thoughtful.
> His head buried in his hands, he cries silently. He cries to all the world, but no-one hears him, for he and the rest of his silent brothers are of stone.

Gideon also starts with intense observation of an external object, a stone gargoyle. His third word, 'seems', shows us that he is immediately transforming it into a gargoyle of his mind, and with exemplary economy he builds the picture of utter rejection. He does not mention himself, but there seems no doubt that he is the gargoyle and the silent brothers are the rest of the world.

My next examples all come from a class book made round 'The Christmas Story', a well-organized, tightly controlled collection of stories from different characters in the Christmas Story. I do not know if the children even picked their own characters. It is always interesting to see a collection of writing on the same theme, because of the wide differences which are always evident in the treatment. There are mini-blockbusters in this book – perfectly readable accounts of actions and events – which I shall not quote. The bits I have chosen show, like Crayden's, how these children flicker in and out of their inner worlds, how I think they have connected the prose and the passion, sometimes in apt and accomplished language.

Gabriel's Story

One day Mary was walking in her garden when God saw her. God wanted a respectful lady to give birth to his son. God thought Mary would make the perfect mother for his son.

Casper's Story

One day when Balthazar was looking through the telescope he saw a new star it was big and very bright. Balthazar looked it up. Small? no. Big not bright? no. Big and very bright, yes. Here it is, now let me see . . . Just then the door opened and Melchior and myself came in, 'What's all the noise about?' . . . So we went to the palace. But no baby.

Patel (all the children were about 9) is both Gabriel and Casper. As Gabriel, he starts a straight story, not mentioning himself as 'I' till the second paragraph. Even within this formal framework we seem to see his attitude emerging; he is thinking of this as an awesome occasion, and he is thinking of what God would want. We have the second sentence, 'God wanted a respectful lady to give birth to his son.' Here the language shows the strength of his culture and his internalization of the heavily weighted 'give birth'. He himself is a little awed by the enterprise. The next sentence contains 'Mary would make the perfect mother', a little less formal, but still awe-inspiring. The piece ends with Gabriel telling Joseph, who understandably was 'worried' by all this, to '"go and get married now", and he did so'.

As a wise man, Patel's 'voice' changes. It is a much longer piece, and he introduces himself as Casper in the first sentence. 'I am Casper. I study the Stars with my friends Melchior and Balthazar. We are astrologers.' Straightforward prose, a factual account. But in the next paragraph he describes Balthazar looking through the telescope, and not only do we switch into his mind, but the language becomes beautifully colloquial. The last part of the story goes back to straight account.

Rebecca tells Mary's story, with a first paragraph which tells the facts, and shows that she was the boss! 'I took the donkey and took it to Joseph who was lying down in the grass.' Then she suddenly connects, beginning the next paragraph conventionally with 'I was very tired, so was Joseph', but going on to 'I was uncomfortable.' And now the sentence where the 'prose' of the language fits exactly what is coming from the inner mind – 'It was very, very bumpy, so bumpy that I nearly fell off.' She cannot quite keep this up, because she slides away from her character in the next sentence: 'Joseph nearly fell asleep until I said "Wake up" in a very tired voice.'

Craig, as Joseph, tells a very short story in straight narrative. He does not seem to bring in his own inner world for most of the narrative; both Mary and Joseph remain rather distant figures. There seems to be just one sentence where some connection is made, or rather one word – 'It was uncomfortable and rocky for the donkey.' 'Rocky' encompasses it all.

The Donkey's Story (Amelia)

It was time to go to Bethlehem. Mary and Joseph were packing already . . . We met lots of people. Gradually they overtook us.

   It was a longer journey to Bethlehem than I thought it would be. It gradually got dark and we arrived in Bethlehem. My feet legs and everything else hurt . . . Joseph went to a door and knocked on it. An innkeeper opened it. 'Have you a room for us kind sir,' 'No the beds and rooms have been booked already' and shut the door . . . Joseph went to another door and knocked on it. Another innkeeper opened it, 'have you a room or even a stable for us,' . . . 'I may be able to help you follow me' with that Joseph pulled me to where the man was going. Where was he taking us? Then at last we came to a stable 'this is where you will have to sleep I am afraid' 'It will do' said Mary . . . So Mary and Joseph and I settled down and waited for Baby Jesus.

Amelia's story is longer and more carefully structured than any of the others in the book. She skilfully avoids preamble and launches straight into the action – 'It was time to go to Bethlehem.' Her mental framework seems to be dominated by time, and she has picked up several different ways of expressing it. 'Mary and Joseph were packing already', and 'gradually' used twice. But there are other touches where her feeling comes through; 'My feet legs and everything else hurt.' She is able to suit the language she is using to the character. Joseph is courteous in a true old-world manner; 'Have you a room for us kind sir.' He does not argue against the sharp retort 'No the beds and rooms have been booked already', but goes 'sadly away'. At the second try Joseph modifies his request to 'have you a room or even a stable for us', with the author's technical and appropriate use of 'even'. And when the innkeeper responds favourably with 'I may be able to help you follow me', she goes on 'with that Joseph pulled me . . .'. She keeps to her role of donkey consistently. Like Patel she makes use of the sophisticated rhetorical question mode, 'Where was he taking us?', to build suspense. When they come to the stable the innkeeper says apologetically 'this is where you will have to sleep I am afraid', to which Mary gives the marvellous pragmatic response 'It will do.' Amelia manages to encapsulate the whole of the future in her final sentence, 'So Mary and Joseph and I settled down and waited for Baby Jesus.' This is true literature in the making.

> It was quite late at night, the dog had just got us in. I cuddled up with my mother and sister.
> Suddenly! there was a great light and the dog started barking. The mountains lit up and there were figures in the sky. Then all was dark.
> I wondered what the shepherds would do. One of the shepherds came and got my sister. I couldn't help wondering where they were going but I had a feeling it was something special.
> I looked into the sky it was full of stars. A bird flew past, the wind blew round and I fell asleep.

Sarah, in 'The Lamb's Story', begins by being fairly predictable, using phrases which she has collected to tell her 'proper story'. 'It was quite late at night', 'Suddenly!' (even making full use of punctuation which is not in most of the children's grasp), 'I wondered' 'I couldn't help wondering', 'I had a feeling'. But it seems to me that at the end the passion is connected with the prose, and without any attempt to describe her feeling in the previous rather arch way she ends 'I looked into the sky it was full of stars. A bird flew past, the wind blew round and I fell asleep.'

Finally Douglas, who contributes stories by Joseph and a sheep.

The Sheep's Story

> . . . out of nowhere there came a brilliant light which lit up this dark and dreary night. What was this strange being.
> I was scooped up . . . I was given to a small baby lying in hay and lived happily ever after.

His account as Joseph is short and distanced. He makes no comment when Gabriel tells him 'You must get married and look after her' – the piece is distanced from his inner world. But as a sheep he seems more able to use language which comes to life on the page. 'I was being put [note the use of the passive voice] into a fold when out of nowhere there came a brilliant light which lit up this dark and dreary night' – not *the* night, but *this* night. And then the lovely (still correct use of the passive) 'I was scooped up'. He must be feeling the animal's inability to do anything himself, and his language conveys this admirably. He keeps this up to the end, where he says 'I was given to a small baby lying in hay and lived happily ever after.'

'The Caterpillar' is the only poem I have included, one which I have had for many years, as you will see, but to which I respond continually with real pleasure. This was certainly not written 'spontaneously'. I was not the teacher, but I happened to be in the room when the session was happening, on a very hot afternoon in a Hertfordshire school, in the middle of the 'creative writing to a stimulus' vogue, about which I think we have since all had serious misgivings. The stimulus in this case was an invitation for disaster. Every child was given a small caterpillar and asked to write about it. The children were sitting at single desks in rows; the sun poured in; I stood unseen behind one boy whose name I cannot remember, but who was one of those fair, square, solid-looking chaps who sat stolidly in his white shirt sleeves, elbows on table. How could prose and passion connect here?

But it did! Against all my preconceived notions of the 'right atmosphere' for writing, the mistaken idea that you could ask children to write satisfactorily from a direct sensory stimulus, the encouragement for drafting, etc., etc., he watched the tiny caterpillar crawling up his shirt sleeve, took up his pencil, and wrote – the whole thing at once!

The Caterpillar

The caterpillar races about
Without hesitation,
As he explores my shirt,
But to him it is like Mount Everest,
If he reaches the top it will be
a glorious day for all British Caterpillars,
As he comes down the North Face
Of the mountain he hears enormous cheers,
As Edmund Caterpillar Hillary has reached
the Top and is about to put
The British Flag on the summit.

But this is because he was not really interested in the caterpillar, because his mind was taken up with the great event which had just happened and which had fired his imagination. So the juxtaposition of the ascent of Everest and the struggling caterpillar in his mind allowed the ironic, beautifully composed and wholly literary result.

Finally we come to Stephen, now 20. Stephen has never been a talker, and is still unable to engage in polite conversation. He does not comment on what he sees or likes; an only child used to pursuing his own interests. His inner world was built up round Dunkurk's coaches, which he invented because his uncle was a bus-driver. He told nobody about this world; he internalized his own audience and began to write prolifically about this world. This took the form of notices, forms to be filled in, drivers' badges, etc. He knighted himself, and later became

Lord Stephen Arthur. He incorporated real experiences into this world; for instance, my small cottage became a five-star hotel. After a visit to Felixstowe docks, Dunkurk's extended to ferry haulage, and later to air flights. Across the years the spelling improved and Stepehen's one real ambition grew out of this world – to be a pilot; he is now training as one for Air UK. What Stephen wrote was perhaps not literature, but it fused the passion and the prose more consistently and for a longer period than most children or adults manage. None of this went on in school, where Stephen became an excellent, quiet, undemonstrative pupil.

Dunkurks Coaches Ltd.

Date 31st October 1980   Manager and Chairman   Sir Stephen Arthur

Dear Driver/Conducter
   Hope you are well, & yore job will come in 1981 (summer) yore DRIVER/CONDUCTER job No. and Licance No. will be 196019. Yore licence runs out on the same date as you got it exept 2 years later.

NOW   Dunkurks coaches limmetetd
                 81 offers

You can go to London from Cambridge for only £1 Adult 50p child (25p cheper Retern) If you would like to book your ticket NOW please fill in the form below & send to Stephen Arthur, Dunkurks Travel. Or take to a Dunkurks Agent or Office.

                                                   31st OCT 1980

THE DAILY EXPRESS NEWSPAPER, Cambridge Edishon

COACH FIGHT LOOSES JOBS

Today naional (eastern counties)
had a fight for sivial when dunkurks
international limmited riduced faairs overnight,
makeing naional (ec.) get 90% bankruped.

DUNKURKS started in 1940 carrying English troops across the English Channel & up to Cambridge where they made their base and called themselves DUNKURKS.

I have tried to show how the inner worlds revealed in play are later articulated, albeit spasmodically, through writing. Britton says, 'What I encode will reflect to some degree the biological, psychological and social aspects of my life.'[8] We transform the situations we are placed in through our whole being. We pull in past experiences, consciously or unconsciously, to create new packages, to show ourselves as well as others what we have made of the world. This is the basis of narrative, poetry, role-play, even of non-fictional writing. How do teachers help children to develop their inner 'voices'? We can respond genuinely to writing; we should be able to convey to children, as they get older, why we have liked particular bits so much. Maybe our remarks are sometimes too general – 'A lovely story'. Our first ploy should therefore be to be more particular in our comments. And we can use the same criteria that we use in responding to our 'adult' reading. We need not patronize the children.

Secondly, and paradoxically, I have shown that limiting the frameworks in which writing is carried out can sometimes 'concentrate the mind wonderfully'. Most of the examples I have given came from such constrained situations, with clear purposes for writing. Stephen, of course, set his own clear purposes, as we hope many children will do.

Thirdly, the importance of reading to and with children cannot be exaggerated. I have discussed my own idiosyncratic ways of looking at writing and reading. We must choose carefully in our models and include those which consider the passion as importantly as the prose. Then we may, I hope, be helping children to 'live in fragments no longer'.

Notes

Most of the children's writing quoted is unpublished. Some published work comes from H. Arnold and M. Morgan (eds) *Yes, We Live Here – A Second Anthology from Suffolk Schools*, Suffolk County Council 1981.

1   W.H. Auden, 'The fairy tale: the reader in the Secondary World', in M. Meek, A. Warlow and G. Barton (eds), *The Cool Web*, Bodley Head, London, 1977.
2   J. Gardam, *Queen of the Tambourines*, Sinclair-Stevenson, London, 1991.
3   E.M. Forster, *Howard's End* (first published 1910), Penguin, Harmondsworth, 1968.
4   J. Britton, 'The anatomy of human experience: the role of inner speech', in K. Kimberley, M. Meek and J. Miller (eds), *New Readings – Contributions to an Understanding of Literacy*, A. & C. Black, London, 1992.
5   J. Burningham, *Come Away from the Water, Shirley*, Cape, London, 1977.
6   L. Carroll, *Alice's Adventures in Wonderland* (first published 1865).
7   D.W. Harding, 'What happens when we read?', *The British Journal of Aesthetics*, 2(2) (1962).
8   Britton, *op. cit.*

CHAPTER 5

Thresholds
Organizing Poetry Events in Schools and the Community

Helen Cook

'*Poetry is more a threshold than a path, one constantly departed from, at which readers and writers undergo, in their different ways, the experience of being at the same time summoned and released.*'
(*Seamus Heaney, 'The Government of the Tongue'*)

Helen Cook's choice of this quotation as the epigraph for her chapter is particularly appropriate. She invites us across the threshold of her experience as an organizer of many poetry events and gives clear and practical advice on how they may be planned, paid for, publicized and successfully run. Furthermore, she demonstrates how a poetry event, for adults or children, can become a *threshold* which both summons people to attend and releases them into new feelings of pleasure and personal empowerment.

Throughout my career as a teacher, as an arts administrator and working in the community, I have found that poetry can be a threshold for adults and children alike. In the classroom it stimulates discussion, reading and writing. On a larger scale, through workshops, performances and festivals which involve all sections of the community, poetry can enrich experience, encourage expression and communication, boost confidence, bring people together, and, last but not least, be extremely enjoyable.

Every year I run a poetry in the community project called Poets Live(!), a seven-week series of workshops and performances. Each week the visiting poet gives a workshop to adults or children in the community (groups can be schoolchildren, elderly people, adults with mental health problems, women's groups, youth clubs, etc.). In the evening, the poet gives a public performance in a local pub. It is these readings in the pub which are at the heart of the project. They create the threshold which summons and releases people of all ages, from all walks of life.

What picture does a poetry reading conjure up? A bleak, draughty room which took half an hour to find in some forbidding building in the university. A sea of empty chairs, the audience – perhaps seven or eight people – serious looking, usually wearing glasses, each hunched in an overcoat buttoned up to the chin?

Try again . . . a room packed to bursting with people aged 18–80. They are standing four deep at the back, the audience is laughing, singing jazz rhythms, sighing, stamping, clapping, calling for encores. In the interval, strangers talk and drink together; two young men from a local hostel chat to a teacher and a taxi driver; a middle-aged man who is learning to live independently quietly explains to a man in his late sixties that this is his first visit to a pub for four years. In one corner a crowd of students are arguing passionately about whether or not it is 'poetry'. In another corner, the poet is sitting at a table signing books and chatting to a small group of people. After the reading, the poet stays on. Most people do not leave until closing time. The next day in the local paper the headline is 'Another scramble for tickets at Poets Live(!)'. A member of the audience is quoted as saying 'I don't understand it, I enjoyed myself – at a poetry reading!'

I am not exaggerating; the above is a description of a typical Poets Live(!) performance. It might be a well-known poet like Wendy Cope or James Berry, or a new name such as Lemn Sissay or Sujata Bhatt. We always sell out and the atmosphere is exciting and friendly. With careful thought and the emphasis on accessibility and enjoyment, every poetry event could be like this.

In this chapter I will be offering ideas and advice, based on my own experience, on how to organize and fund *successful* poetry- and literature-based events, from the one-off visit by a poet, to a regional poetry festival. For the purposes of this book I will be concentrating on events for children, but I would like to emphasize that any of the following ideas can be adapted for adults and community groups.

The success and value of any event or project depends on various factors. I would identify the key factors as being:

- choice of poet(s);
- programme for book week/festival;
- finance;
- publicity;
- preliminary and follow-up work.

Choice of poet(s)

Whether you want to arrange a poet's visit, a book week or a festival, you will need suggestions and background information for poets who are suitable, available and affordable. The following people and organizations can offer help and advice (addresses and contact numbers are listed at the end of this chapter):

- the literature officer or education officer of your regional arts board;
- local librarians;
- the Poetry Society, London;
- the South Bank literature department;
- the Poetry Library, South Bank.

Send invitations to poets at the earliest opportunity, as they are often booked up months in advance. Make sure your letter is clear about dates, times, fees, expenses and age group. Follow up the letter with a phone call to confirm details as soon as possible. Lastly, but perhaps most importantly, look after your poets when they arrive. Many of them travel long distances on tight schedules. They need warm hospitality, time to unwind and somewhere quiet and comfortable to prepare for the workshop or performance.

The programme for the event

If you are planning a large-scale event it is essential to have an enthusiastic and reliable team or committee to help run events and activities. Dividing and delegating areas of responsibility such as competitions, publicity, finance, etc., at the beginning ensures that you do not take on too much and that everything runs efficiently and smoothly.

Before planning the programme, ask yourself why your school or region needs a book week or festival. The different answers to this question will often supply you with ideas for the programme. The following list of my own reasons and ideas may help you:

- a celebration to make poetry more accessible and enjoyable, offering new experiences and opportunities;
- attracting children and adults who would not usually be interested or do not have the chance to take part in such an event – for many of them, a live performance or having a 'real' poet in school is a new and stimulating experience;

- bringing together people of all ages, from schools and all sections of the community;
- cross-curricular activities;
- networking with other schools and organizations in the region, finding out what other people are doing, pooling ideas.

A festival can include artists, photographers, illustrators, exhibitions, competitions and lectures for teachers as well as writers' performances and workshops. Poetry can be linked to other subjects, e.g. poetry and photography workshops, a poetry and computers day, or a poetry and music weekend. These activities can also involve other organizations – museums, galleries, colleges and other schools.

As well as offering a taste of many different types of poetry, a good programme where there is something for everyone will offer a mixture of local poets, up and coming poets, poets from other cultures and some big names. It is all too easy to fall into the trap of finding yourself with a programme dominated by white British male poets, targeted at white middle-class children and adults.

Here are two ideas from the Poets Live(!) project which could be used in a festival or book week:

- *Poetry video*   A group of local women on a beginners' video course filmed the seven-week series of poets' performances and workshops with school and community groups. This included interviews and readings by workshop members. At the same time, a group of teenagers, led by a music teacher and based at a community centre, were composing music inspired by the poems written at the workshops. They used simple keyboard and percussion instruments and some computer technology. Our local polytechnic generously allowed the groups to use their editing suite to put the film and music together, and a grant from the Eastern Arts Board enabled us to produce fifty copies of the video, professionally packaged. The video was a document of the project, a useful poetry resource for schools and local groups, and a lasting 'end product' marking the achievement of all those involved in the project.

- *'Stand and deliver' event*   This event can involve everyone in the community. Using the local newspaper and a freesheet we invited schoolchildren and local people to take the stage as part of the seven-week performance series. After an initial selection process, we allotted a three- to five-minute slot to as many performers as we could fit in to the one-hour programme. It sells out every time, brings people together, is a great confidence booster and can be an intimate and moving experience for performers and audience alike.

Competitions

Whatever you think about poetry competitions, if planned carefully they stimulate interest and enthusiasm for poetry and can be a good vehicle for publicizing festival or book week events. Local papers are usually very supportive, providing publicity, printing poems or even sponsoring the competition.

If there is enough time, organizing a 'design a poster for the festival' competition and an 'illustrate a poem' competition, as well as a writing competition, will open up the festival or book week to more people. Anthologies of the winning poems and exhibitions of the illustrated poems are always popular and can tour round libraries and schools in the future. Timing the competitions to end as the festival begins creates interest and publicity for the events; anthologies can be sold and exhibitions can become part of the programme.

Information about rules, age groups, themes for writing and poems to illustrate should be clearly set out and sent to schools and local people through the schools distribution service or the library service and through your local newspaper. You will need to select sifters as well as judges. Sifters can bring an entry of five hundred down to fifty, a more manageable number for the judges to look at. Collecting points for entries and exhibition space for winners should be arranged. Libraries, bookshops, community centres, foyers of theatres and galleries are just a few of the high-profile places for exhibitions.

Prizes should not present a problem. Publishers, bookshops, local businesses and newspapers are usually only too pleased to donate books, tokens and vouchers. One year we even managed to persuade British Rail to donate rail travel vouchers.

Venues

Unless you are arranging a book week specifically for your school, try to avoid the classic poetry audience syndrome of three people and a dog. Arranging a variety of venues will attract a wide-ranging audience. A school hall or university room only attracts the already committed. Community centres and pubs often have private rooms; then there are cafés, foyers of theatres, galleries, libraries – all providing a relaxed and informal setting. Do not forget access to the room. Unfortunately, a venue with disabled access is sometimes hard to find. Make sure that most venues are accessible to everyone.

Finally, an opening parade or celebration to launch your event will involve a large number of people, create good publicity and raise the profile of poetry – and be great fun.

Finance

The following organizations may be able to provide funding for a one-off event, a residency or a festival (see addresses at the end of the chapter):

- regional arts boards;
- the Arts Council of Great Britain;
- the library service;
- W.H. Smith 'Poets in Schools' scheme;
- the Poetry Society;
- university literary funds;
- the Foundation for Sport and the Arts;
- the Calouste Gulbenkian Foundation;
- the British Council;
- the Compton Poetry Fund.

It is also worth approaching local businesses and organizations for sponsorship, e.g. book shops, newspapers, radio stations, printers and publishers, estate agents, building societies, British Rail, national shops (Sainsburys, Marks and Spencer, Mothercare, Tesco, etc.), language schools, universities and colleges, and city, county and district councils.

If you are applying for a grant, you should read the most recent policy document or criteria for funding that the organization has. It is important to write a clear application confined to a maximum of two sides of A4. Briefly outline the the programme and aims of the event, and give a draft budget and expected audience figures (do not be too optimistic!). Tailoring your application to their criteria and requirements obviously gives you a better chance of receiving funding.

A sponsorship letter should be clear, punchy and straight to the point. It should describe the event and audiences it will reach. It will also point out the benefits to a potential sponsor of being associated with the event, e.g. audiences, outreach, high-profile educational event, good public relations with the community. Do not write a general letter asking for money; offer a specific package with the choice of three or four areas to sponsor – the posters, competition, performance, workshop, etc. – and explain where the sponsor would be acknowledged – programmes, posters, press releases.

Always write to the publishers of your performers and ask for promotional material and books. They will often donate prizes and the publicity material is useful for decorating venues. Local book shops will donate books or book-tokens and often agree to set up a book shop at events.

Running costs can be reduced by working in partnership with local authorities, teachers' centres and libraries. They may be able to help with mailing, publicity and distribution, printing and selling tickets or providing venues at a low cost.

Publicity

Whether your event is a modest book week or a two-week festival, publicity is vital. I would recommend designing a logo which can be used on letters, press releases, posters, programmes, etc. It is the most effective way of creating an immediately recognizable identity for the event.

If you are going to produce posters, ask for quotes from three printers and try to persuade the one you choose to part-sponsor the printing. Publicity should be ready to distribute four weeks before the event. Use the school and library systems or your local authority's distribution service. This, combined with leg-work by you and some volunteers, should ensure good coverage of your area. Send press releases in good time (at least two weeks prior to the event). A press release should contain all relevant information in the first paragraph, with a quotation or a lively sentence or two which can be used verbatim in the paper or on the radio. If possible, fax it, as people will always read a fax immediately. Do not forget entertainment listings in papers, magazines and broadsheets. They often give free publicity but will need your copy at least a month before publication.

Finally, check that all the 'right people' know what is happening from the beginning, e.g. other schools, arts and education officers, inspectors, advisers, librarians. Unexpected help and support can come from good networking.

Preliminary and follow-up work

A 'one-off' workshop by a poet can often be a wasted opportunity unless the group has some preparation before the visit and time afterwards to consolidate and continue work and ideas in progress. Obviously, if you are running a regional festival it will not be possible to do this, but on a smaller scale, a warm-up session before the visit can build up the group's confidence and a session afterwards will capitalize on the experience.

The most successful preliminary session I have tried with adults and children lasts approximately one hour and is based on two poems. You will probably have your own ideas, but you may find it useful to use the structure of this session as a starting point. The two poems are 'The Magic Box' by Kit Wright and 'My Box' by Gillian Clarke.

My Box

My box is made of golden oak,
my lover's gift to me.
He fitted hinges and a lock
of brass and a bright key.
He made it out of winter nights,
sanded and oiled and planed,
engraved inside the heavy lid
in brass, a golden tree.

In my box are twelve black books
where I have written down
how we have sanded, oiled and planed,
planted a garden, built a wall,
seen jays and goldcrests, rare red kites,
found the wild heartsease, drilled a well,
harvested apples and words and days
and planted a golden tree.

On an open shelf I keep my box.
Its key is in the lock.
I leave it there for you to read,
or them, when we are dead,
how everything is slowly made,
how slowly things made me,
a tree, a lover, words, a box,
books and a golden tree.

Gillian Clarke

The Magic Box

I will put in the box

the swish of a silk sari on a summer night,
fire from the nostrils of a Chinese dragon,
the tip of a tongue touching a tooth.

I will put in the box

a snowman with a rumbling belly,
a sip of the bluest water from Lake Lucerne,
a leaping spark from an electric fish.

I will put in the box

three violet wishes spoken in Gujarati,
the last joke of an ancient uncle
and the first smile of a baby.

I will put in the box

a fifth season and a black sun,
a cowboy on a broomstick
and a witch on a white horse.

My box is fashioned from ice and gold and steel,
with stars on the lid and secrets in the corners.
Its hinges are the toe joints
of dinosaurs.

I shall surf in my box
on the great high-rolling breakers of the wild Atlantic,
then wash ashore on a yellow beach
the colour of the sun.

Kit Wright

1   Read the poems aloud, then ask the group to read them quietly to
    themselves or to each other. (If possible, everyone should have a
    copy of the poems.)
2   Discuss the poems – subject matter, use of language, rhythm,
    images, etc. Move on to talking about what individuals would put
    in their box and why.
3   Using the structure of Kit Wright's poem, write up the beginning
    line of each new idea on the board, or give out on a duplicated
    sheet. List the subjects for each verse, e.g. 'three verses beginning
    "I will put in the box . . .", then three lines of what would be in your
    box. The penultimate verse would say what the box is made of and
    the last verse would describe what happens to the box or where it
    would be.'

The group now has the recipe for writing their own poem.

4   Allow 15–20 minutes thinking, drafting and writing time.
5   The last 10 minutes can be spent reading out the poems.

I have never known this session to fail. The beauty of it is that it is
simple, it catches everyone's imagination, and it enables them to
complete a poem and feel a real sense of achievement.

Earlier in this chapter I suggested that you ask yourself why you are
organizing a poetry event or festival. For me, all the different answers
are covered by the general title of this chapter: thresholds. The readings
and the workshops create the thresholds which give people of all ages
and from all walks of life that experience Seamus Heaney describes as
'being at the same time summoned and released'. It is perhaps best

summed up by John, an adult member of one of the Poets Live(!) workshops, speaking about the poet's visit to his group:

> It was enlightenment for me because I'd been living in a depressed state and he came along with his ideas and brightened up my life – not in any fantastic way but it gave me ideas to put down on paper and I could continue if I wanted to, if I really wanted to I could continue.

Useful addresses

Books for Keeps – the essential guide to the latest books for children.
6 Brightfield Road
Lee
London SE12 8QF   Tel: 081–852 4953

Children's Book Foundation – information and guidance on children's books with newsletter, Book Week pack, Books of the Year, catalogue.
Book House
45 East Hill
London SW18   Tel: 081–874 2718

Children's Writers and Illustrators Group
Diana Shine
84 Drayton Gardens
London SW19 9SB   Tel: 071–373 6642

Letterbox Library – book club specializing in antisexist and multicultural children's books.
8 Bradbury Street
London N16 8BR   Tel: 071–254 1640

Schools Poetry Association
27 Pennington Close
Colden Common
Winchester
Hampshire SO21 1UR   Tel: 0962 712062

The Poetry Book Society
10 Barley Mow Passage
London W4P 4PH   Tel: 081–994 6477

The Poetry Society – information and advice on all aspects of poetry, a register of poets, administration of the W.H. Smith 'Poets in Schools' scheme, financial assistance, regular tours and events.
22 Betterton Street
London WC2H 9BU   Tel: 071–240 4810

Poems on the Underground – beautifully produced poster poems available quarterly.
London Transport Museum
Covent Garden
London WC2E 7BB   Tel: 071–379 6344

The Poetry Library – comprehensive collection of poetry books, tapes, video. Also disseminates a wide variety of information.
The South Bank Centre
Level 5, Red Side
Royal Festival Hall
London SE1 8XX   Tel: 071–921 0943/0664

Arts Council of Great Britain – literature department organizes writers' tours and produces a quarterly bulletin with schedules of tours and events which is available free on request.
14 Great Peter Street
London SW1P 3NQ   Tel: 071–333 0100

Commonwealth Institute – information, events, workshops, etc., designed to promote a knowledge and appreciation of writing from Commonwealth countries and writers now living in Britain.
Kensington High Street
London W8   Tel: 071–603 4535 ext. 255/263

The British Council
10 Spring Gardens
London SW1A 2BN   Tel: 071–389 4071

Calouste Gulbenkian Foundation
98 Portland Place
London W1N 4ET   Tel: 071–636 5313

Foundation for Sport and the Arts
PO Box 666
Liverpool L69 7JN   Tel: 051–524 0285/6

Deterrent

Wendy Cope

They're rarely poets, the people who tell you, 'Poetry is FUN',
And add an exclamation mark, and sometimes more than
    one,
And little know how lucky it is for them that I've no gun.

One of these days I shall place myself in a poetry-is-fun
    merchant's path
And bash him or her with the hardback edition of the poems
    of Sylvia Plath.

PART II

*The Power
and the Story*

The previous part showed how texts for children are firmly embedded in cultural contexts. This relationship between text and context is a thread which is followed throughout this part of the book. The notion of intertextuality – reflections within texts of other texts – deepens the meaning of context, reminding us that contexts of the mind are as powerful as physical environments. Underlying all the chapters in this part is a strong assertion that children know a lot about texts. Their mental contexts contain knowledge about every different kind of text – spoken, written and visual. A second assumption follows the first: since children come to classrooms with a wealth of such awareness of texts, it is important to help them bring this knowledge to the surface, to examine what they do know in order to take their knowledge further. The classroom context, then, must be a forum for establishing and extending what children know – and can come to know – about texts. This continues the challenging view of just what 'reading' means and follows the theme introduced in Part I, which offers a wider view of literacy. It is all a matter of power, and how children can be empowered. This part of the book brings together the important threads of principle outlined in Part I with practical classroom suggestions. In helping children to see beyond words and images, often by making their own texts, teachers help them to take charge of their own literacy – to make texts their own.

Children's story-making can reveal a great deal about the texts they have already made their own. Eve Bearne's chapter explores not only what children know, but why it is important for them to have a chance to take their knowledge of texts further. In their everyday narratives lie the seeds of future knowledge; narrative is a powerhouse of future possibilities. Avril Harpley takes the theme of power further by suggesting ways in which teachers can help children take media images and presentations apart, remake them and so come to see just how they operate. She points out that the world is changing fast and that through their toys and leisure pursuits children are on the receiving end of some powerful forces. If they can take a look behind the images and hear beyond the words, then they will be more informed, more critical and more able to make choices.

Going beyond what is known is Lesley Hendy's starting point for using drama to understand stories. Through a range of drama strategies she shows how children's implicit knowledge of story structure, character and theme can be brought to the surface. Starting with already known stories, active involvement in a range of different approaches can not only emphasize what children already know about texts, but allow them to discover what was unknown. Mike Taylor echoes the importance of children 'developing an ear for the rich varieties of language and an awareness of how these varieties work'. This can best come about when children have opportunities to delve into texts, to excavate the 'rich seams of tacit learning about language' in the reading material teachers present to them and the strategies offered for digging deeper. Michael Armstrong's chapter presents three caught moments in the development of children's narrative voices as they echo the 'rich varieties' of texts. As he points out, making stories helps children both to discover and to invent their worlds. 'The ordinary and the magical are inseparable' in children's narratives as they give shape to their inner knowledge. But for Brigid Smith there remains a problem. What can be done for those children who are not in a position to lose themselves in satisfying reading or make their own statements through engaged writing? She points out that in the world of school 'some children's voices are difficult to hear', particularly the voices of girls. In describing some dictated stories by girls for whom literacy is a struggle, Brigid Smith gives a sharp focus to the importance and power of story.

Finally, moving out of the classroom context, this part comes full circle – back to the texts themselves and the writers who make them. If teachers have a responsibility to help children get to grips with texts and how they are made, then, argues Robert Leeson, writers also bear an important responsibility. He reminds us that the process of learning goes on beyond the classroom walls through the crucial role of 'education by the book'. Underlining the theme of power, we are reminded why texts, literacy and story-making are often the sites for struggles between those who want to know and those who try to suppress their knowing. That is why it is so important for teachers to help children develop the power of narrative and their powers as story-makers.

CHAPTER 6

Where Do Stories Come From?

Eve Bearne

*Classrooms are complex communities. All those who enter the classroom
contribute unique expectations, experience and knowledge, flavoured
and textured by the cultures of the home, as they combine to form that
community. In the following chapter, Eve Bearne argues that this rich
cultural mixture, seen through the narratives that enter the classroom, is
a crucial element in developing confident literacy. The future repertoire
of texts available to children is embedded in their cultural awareness of
spoken and written language. Rather than try to prise children away
from these culturally developed texts, she sketches out the dynamic
potential in working through and out of children's own language and
literacy experiences. If classrooms are genuinely to acknowledge and
value diversity, then the cadences, rhythms and truths of home narratives
are powerful starting points.*

It was Harold Rosen who said that narrative is 'ordinary, everyday and
ubiquitous'; he also pointed out its value and centrality to learning.[1] In
order to reach a narrative we select events, interpreting them as having
certain relationships, motives or consequences. And through spoken or
written narratives we make sense of what events mean *to us*. Even the
storytelling of a small child creates meaning out of the daily muddle and
rush of actions and events. In this chapter I want to look at the
ordinariness of story. I want to look at how children *use* everyday
experience to forge narrative, how they combine different kinds of
'ordinary' text as they make stories their own and make their own

stories. This means taking a rather broader view of 'text' than might be usual. It is now an accepted idea that television or video can be described as text; pictorial texts and spoken texts are equally being recognized as part of the fabric (or 'texture') of children's cultural and literacy experience. I would like to push these definitions a little wider in thinking about the texts which children draw on for their own narratives. One of the ways in which I want to use 'text' is to do with the cultural settings which children encounter at home and at school. In other words, I want to look at how cultural contexts generate or encourage particular kinds of text.

Culture is a difficult and elusive concept, so I shall try to be clear just what I mean in relation to cultural texts. All elements of a culture have their own specialized texts. In the United Kingdom, examples might be the highly formalized legal documents and language of parliamentary statutes or the ways in which doctors speak with patients. Culture operates through these developed and organized kinds of language in interactions which make (more or less, perhaps) meaning for those involved. But it is not these more formal elements of cultural text I want to look at. I am interested in the informal kind of cultural language practice – the kind that operates in the home; that everyday kind of text which surrounds children in their homes as they learn about life as it is perceived in *their* family's cultural practice. This includes, of course, elements of literacy. The print and visual experiences of homes have their impact on children's developing literacy. All I want to suggest is that there may be another kind of text which should be included in our growing understanding of the importance of home language and literacy for children's future learning, and to relate that to children's story-making.

Margaret Meek Spencer gave us the phrase 'the music on the page' as a helpful way of understanding how children come to be satisfied readers.[2] The significant moment at which any child takes on literacy is when he or she makes the connection between what is spoken and heard and what can be read off a page, and the cadences of previously heard readings will feed into that moment of enlightenment. Similarly, the repeated patterings of anecdotes, warnings, word play, and conversations about hopes, intentions and daily actions seem to me to be significant texts which children draw on. Both in the rhythms and syntax which offer possible ways of saying things and in the content of what is said, these culturally developed language practices give children a strong base for story. In other words I want to offer a small (but, to me, significant) extra element to the idea of intertextuality and children's narrative. After that, I want to follow the implications of 'where children's stories come from' towards an idea of where they might lead.

There is a growing body of evidence about relationships between the cultures of home and of school. Particularly influential has been the work of Shirley Brice Heath. Her studies alert us to the implicit assumptions it is all too easy to make about how children take on schooled literacy.[3] In an impressively detailed set of case studies, Hilary Minns takes up the notion of the importance of the link between home and school versions of literacy when she tracks the course of young readers entering her school. Her insights illuminate the range of possible texts – spoken, visual and written – which children may have encountered before reaching formal schooling, and the ways in which they build on these in extending their literacy. In reflecting on her findings she explains the value of the case studies:

> I never paid much attention to the kinds of knowledge and experiences of reading that were part of the life of the community beyond the school gates; not because I wanted to hold myself away from it, but because I had no idea that by listening to and observing the way these families used a rich living language I would have a firmer base on which to begin to build a theory about children's reading, a theory whose foundations were set in an understanding of their own real world of experience, their own lived lives.[4]

The detailed information which Hilary Minns describes allows a teacher not only to see the breadth of experience a child may be bringing to school, but also to create opportunities for home cultural experience to be valued and built on in the culture of the classroom.

Minns' work bears out Bruner's view that 'most learning in most settings is a communal activity, a sharing of the culture'.[5] But Bruner takes his view of culture further, referring to it as 'an ambiguous text that is constantly in need of interpretation by those who participate in it'. He goes on: 'a culture is as much a *forum* for negotiating and renegotiating meaning . . . as it is a set of rules or specifications for action. . . . Education is (or should be) one of the principal forums for performing this function.' In placing side by side the essential negotiatory aspect of culture and the role which education plays, he sees the participants as having an active role in 'constantly making and remaking the culture'. In terms of classroom practice this offers a powerful – but flexible – way of looking at children's home cultural experiences and what they can mean for learning. It not only has implications for processes of enculturation into learning, but suggests a wider view of what we consider valid content for learning, too. It lends new possibilities to the idea of intertexuality through Bruner's view of how narrative offers 'landscapes of consciousness' as well as 'landscapes of action'.[6] Stories may contain events, but those events are shaped by cultural knowledge and consciousness.

On the track of intertextuality

I want to start the hunt for different kinds of text in quite a traditional way – the 'serendipitous approach', or 'I just happened to be there at the time when . . .'.

Gary and Michael were 8 when they collaborated on this story:

Michael the Avenger and the Three Beasts

One day in New York maze something was changing. The hedgerows were changing to grass snakes, the ground broke and the pavement cracked and out came a swapper with two heads.

Then another one came out so he started to fight and chopped off its tail. But as soon as he chopped it off another two heads grew on the other side, and he killed the two swappers.

He went a bit further, there was a massive lake he gathered up all the sticks he could find, and he made a raft, he went across the lake and then out came a sting ray. The giant sting ray had six heads, two stings, two glue guns, he fought the sting ray he got his dagger out threw it at it and it died.

Then he saw the treasure but guarding it there was the Lambton, it was worm-like. He bought a flute and played a tune and it went to sleep, he grabbed the treasure he went back to the king with the king's treasure and he gave him half of the kingdom and he lived happily ever after.

Their teacher had read them myths and legends and they had been asked to make up collaborative stories about finding treasure. Most of these were drafted and then word processed before being made into illustrated books, though some children chose to make their books with handwritten pages. Gary and Michael put theirs on the word processor and added authors' descriptions:

My name is Mike my hobbies are football, and writing and netball, tennis.

Hello my name is Gary. My hobbies are football, riding my bike and writing.

Both of them, like most of the other children in the class, were quite confident in asserting themselves as authors. Their tale bears all the rhythms and cadences of traditional quest stories, including a resolution depending on trickery and ending in reward.

But it was not the writing achievements that drew my attention to their book in particular so much as the variety of sources they seemed to have drawn on, and the mixture of home and school experience. I was hot on the trail of intertextuality! I was intrigued by the setting of the story in 'New York maze' and impressed by the inclusion of elements from traditional story – three incidents; overcoming the beast by lulling it to sleep with music; the reward of half the kingdom and, of course, the ending tag. When I talked to the two boys about their story I became even more impressed:

EB   The story started 'One day in New York maze something was changing'. What gave you that idea?

G   Oh, that was my idea . . . um . . . the rest of it says, um, 'the hedgerows were changing into grass snakes and out came a swapper with two heads'. The idea of a swapper was because I go to my uncle's every so and again and we play on my cousin's computer which has got a swapper, that's what I think . . .

M   (pointing to the illustration) this is the swapper and that's the pavement . . .

G   I did that when Michael was away ill . . .

EB   Oh, right . . . then you went a bit further and there was a massive lake and this is where the sting ray comes in. What gave you the idea of a sting ray?

M   I been to water . . . in . . . um . . .

G   Was it Great Yarmouth?

M   Yea . . . Water World I think it's called . . . and I've been there twice and, um, I watched sting rays because they're nice animals . . .

G   . . . and dangerous . . .

M   Yea . . .

EB   Hadn't you seen them on the television as well . . .?

M   Yea . . . Sea Trek . . .

G   Oh yea . . .

EB   What programme's that?

G   It's the one on BBC 2. In the night around eight, isn't it?

M   Mmm

EB   So it's a wild life programme . . .? a sea programme . . .?

G   . . . animals in the sea . . .

M   And last night they showed you um er a tortoise on the beach and eggs, dropped their eggs in a hole . . .

G   Not tortoises, turtles . . .

M   This is um . . .

G   That's photographs from a book . . .

M   This is the one what I was coming . . .

EB   It's a worm called . . .

G   Lambton . . .

EB   And you found that in a book, didn't you, and we were saying that there was a song about the Lambton Worm . . .

Apart from the picture book with the Lambton worm and a previous conversation where they told me they had read Anthony Browne's *Changes*, the main inspirations for the content of their story do not come from the kinds of text which we would generally identify when noting intertextuality in narratives. Gary drew on his knowledge of computer games, Michael on his personal experience of visiting an aquarium twice and his interest in nature programmes, and both referred to photographs of lakes and castles. Just as an aside, it seems, too, that they are drawing on a kind of subtext of comic-book humour in their illustrations and the use of glue guns rather than real weaponry.

The range of sources which these two were aware of drawing on is very wide indeed, including not only narratives which could be expected to feed into children's own story-making – traditional story, heard and read, classroom picture books and songs. These two writers also give us an insight into much wider intertextual sources – factual television programmes, visits to places of interest, computer games and photographs, as well as the traditional written and spoken texts which might be expected. This rich mixture combines the ordinary and everyday stuff of young people's home culture and experience with what they can learn from books. It is an awesome and powerful mix, but what are we to make of it?

A now commonly accepted view of narrative is, in the words of Gordon Wells, that 'stories provide a major route to understanding'.[7] They provide mental frameworks for other kinds of learning: 'Constructing stories in the mind . . . is one of the most fundamental means of making meaning; as such it is an activity that pervades all aspects of learning', and through hearing stories children: 'begin to assimilate the more powerful and more abstract mode of representing experience that is made available by written language.'[8] Harold Rosen's view that 'narrative is an explicit resource in all intellectual activity' echoes these points: 'Inside every narrative there stalk the ghosts of non-narrative discourse . . . inside every non-narrative discourse there stalk the ghosts of narrative.'[9] Gary and Michael gave us a glimpse of some non-narrative 'ghosts' and some of their origins. When Gary talked about going down to his uncle's and Michael told of his trips to the aquarium, they were not only reflecting non-narrative sources but pointing towards the kinds of cultural text which shimmer through children's story-making. Before I go on to consider what teachers might be able to do with this kind of ghostly information, I want to look at the idea of cultural texts and narrative a little more closely.

What we tell, who we tell and how we tell it

In our thought patterns narrative is pervasive, helping us to develop ways of ordering ideas which in the future will be the basis for constructing more formal kinds of learning. The nitrogen cycle is, after all, a narrative, as is the process of geomorphic change. This bears out Harold Rosen's view of the ubiquity of narrative and suggests its importance in an individual's cognitive development. But narrative also plays a part in our emotional development. We do not just organize ideas, we also organize our feelings through narrative. Aspirations, disappointments, joys and fears are rehearsed and replayed in the stories we tell ourselves and in the stories we tell others. Since language is itself impregnated with social qualities, stories necessarily reflect the social world in which they are told. Narrative begins in our social and cultural experience of language, and in putting that experience into words, even very young children reveal the depth and importance of cultural texts.

Thanks to Sarah Trinder from Aberbargoed Nursery in Mid Glamorgan, we have a brief 'Portrait of Natasha' who was 3 years 8 months old when she told this story. Sarah had started off a discussion as part of her planned language development activities. It was all about a trip to Cardiff to buy brushes. As the children told their stories (with help) Sarah wrote them on a flipchart so that they could be read again. Natasha's story began:

N   I found little brushes on the floor, the ball showed me where they are.
S   That's a nice ball.
N   Yea and I found them on the floor.
S   Did the ball play with you?
N   Then he said I can paint and he said I can go over his house and I said 'I'm not allowed am I?' I'm not allowed to go up Ball's house, am I?
S   Oh, you're not allowed to go to the Ball's house are you?
N   Only after.
S   Oh, I see. Did you talk to the Ball for a long time?
N   He didn't have a mouth, but he could talk.

When Sarah read this story to a group of children, Natasha wanted to illustrate it. As she drew she added more to her story, bringing it to a conclusion:

N   This is the bouncing ball and he's only small, he's a baby ball and that's why he wanted me to go up his house 'cause he didn't know the way.

Because Sarah had acted as her scribe and had reread the exchange so that Natasha could hear her story, she was able to supply a reason for events which were unexplained in the first version. She was also quite clear about what she wanted to include in *her* story, resisting and ignoring Sarah's prompts where they did not fit with her own ideas. She drew on the conventions of other narratives for her original piece, giving character to an inanimate object and holding together the paradox of such an object talking even though it has no mouth. But into the story she wove texts drawn from her own everyday experience, when she said, 'I'm not allowed to go up Ball's house, am I?' and gave the explanation that a baby ball might not know his own way home. These are things which she would have learned from home conversations about her own safety, and often those conversations would have included anecdotes about other children and other experiences.

But children do not just draw on these cultural texts and leave them there. Natasha uses her knowledge of what adults say about safety to

Daniel

The wolf
once upon a time there was
a wolf and He wanted to
play with a boy but the boys Dad
told him not to talk to strangers so

He ran off and the wolf came
to a bird but it Just fleow off
as well then He came to another
wolf and they Made freinds
and they Lived together happily ever
after

construct a satisfying resolution to an event in her story – she wants to give a reason for Ball asking her to go to his house. She knows that adults want – and give – reasons for doing things which may seem to run against the text of what is expected. In a similar way, Daniel weaves one significant moral warning into his story about a wolf while at the same time finding a resolution to the narrative which satisfies him.

At its most everyday and ordinary, narrative exists in anecdote, gossip and what is often called 'social chat' – what children hear from adults as warnings, jokes and everyday conversation. But even these forms presuppose a certain ordering and selection of experience, to fulfil specific intentions: for example, when we have to 'own up' to something we tell a story where the selection and highlighting of events is likely to minimize the parts which show just how much *we* were at fault. When we tell anecdotes about any incident, we necessarily select – we do not just rerun what happened like an unedited tape or video-recording. In these selections we begin to categorize experience, a cognitive operation which sets mental frameworks for later, more complex forms of categorizing, selecting and generalizing of experience or facts. These orderings of cultural telling give a rhythm and pattern to everyday exchanges which children use as a basis for an increasingly complex set of textual possibilities. Natasha shows that she knows quite a bit about selecting, ordering and explaining experience, and ably combines conventional and everyday narrative to make her own story. Daniel's fable, perfectly formed, reflects a delightful combination of ideas drawn from sources spanning centuries of experience. Both of them suggest the story-maker's capacity to use narrative to express lived cultural realities.

In recent investigations into children's narratives, student teachers have found a rich array of cultural detail in children's oral, written and pictorial narratives. Two examples parallel some of the points made by Carolyn Steedman in her study of working-class girls, *The Tidy House*, where she points to the relationship between children's writing and imaginative play that helps them to see things from different perspectives. 'But writing, unlike play, lets children watch from two perspectives simultaneously.'[10] Text can serve children both to articulate certain values and norms and as a way of questioning those values.

The first example, from 7-year-old Gary (partly scribed, partly written by him; presented here in standard spelling) has within it motifs which are repeated in his other stories – raves and microwaves:

> One day a big gang was playing baseball and a big boy said, 'I am going to beat you up' and the gang beat he up and a dog camed and it was hungry and it was a pit bull terrier. And they kept him. A bunch of kids camed and said 'I want that dog'. The gang got hold of the kids and threw them in a ditch. Then their cousins came to a rave party and brought the gang a bunch of motorbikes and a bunch of electric guitars. They had some new jeans and even more food and a microwave. And their names were . . .

In commenting on this piece, Alice MacFarlane writes:

> it would probably be more accurate to say that Gary is asserting values rather than questioning them, but I don't think the idea of exploration should be entirely dismissed. For example, Gary's view on raves seems undecided – they appear to hold an attraction for him yet in a second story the characters end up in prison as a result of taking drugs at a rave, therefore they are obviously seen as being somewhat risky too.

Gary's story is certainly rich in cultural symbols of power and ownership. Endearingly, and bafflingly, the microwave figures in a lot of his talk and writing at the time. But its presence suggests once again the interweaving of home-spoken texts into stories. And these stories allow Gary the chance to be both actor and director in his narratives of life. In the story above he names himself as one of the gang, but not until he has told the story from an outsider's point of view.

In a similar study, Alex Hughes found that children's pictorial narratives carried powerful cultural assertions. She was at first rather concerned that in talking to three children aged between 6 and 7 they seemed not to read very much. She had taken them *The Enchanted Garden*[11] to look at – a book which is almost entirely pictorial text – and after they had read it together, she invited them to make up their own picture stories. These showed evidence of sustained setting and characterization, drawing richly on television and cartoon forms. All were enthusiastic assertions of what these children knew about and could do with pictorial narrative. But, in wanting to take forward Cary Bazalgette's plea for an understanding of a new kind of literacy, since visual literacy is not recognized as 'school knowledge',[12] Alex suggests that rather than seeing home and school literacy as separate, they could usefully be seen together:

> Could the knowledge not be *combined* with what children learn at school, and the literacy they are developing there – why must the two be regarded as different targets? . . . A most valuable asset to a child's education is recognition by a teacher of the knowledge that they have gained to date, and this needs to be developed, not ignored.

It certainly seems wise to take some account of the varied textual knowledge which children bring from their home cultures, giving it value *as text* rather than using the information as 'background' to help us see what their home lives are like. If we use children's narratives as spyholes into their lives, we are in danger of forgetting just what making stories is all about.

From everyday forms and functions of narrative spring the more formalized and consciously shaped stories, accounts and explanations which we recognize in printed books, demonstrations of how to do or make something, films, lectures and newspapers. Told (or made) stories offer the chance to 'be scientists' – to wonder about the world, to hypothesize, predict, confirm or unconfirm, and to explore all sorts of possibility in the safe knowledge that we are exploring a world of imaginative ideas. But they also offer tellers the chance to express and examine their knowledge of their own social worlds. In extending the idea of 'text' to take into account culturally shaped and shared meanings which adults transmit to children, the importance of narrative as a possible site for negotiation between the cultures of home and school emerges. The narrative possibilities open to children and their culturally developed 'ways of taking' narratives will make differences to the choices they operate in their 'ways of making' narratives.[13] Since narrative is such a demonstrably powerful means of learning – about things, about ourselves, about others and about our emotional worlds – it is important to look carefully at how narrative enters the educational process in the classroom. The variations of 'what, who and how' are critical elements in children's developing language and literacy.

Considerations of genre(s)

Recently there has been criticism of the use of narrative as the main form of writing experience offered to children in schools. Text linguists argue that young children are asked too often to use 'recount' forms of writing in the primary school. While there may be a ritual of 'do it then write about it' which permeates (and stultifies) much that goes on in primary classrooms, this narrow view of narrative needs to be looked at carefully before teachers start to feel guilty. The linguists use their evidence of recount/narrative as the most common form of writing experienced in primary classrooms to argue that children should be *taught* to write in other forms/genres – for example, explanation, instruction and argument. There is no controversy about the importance of introducing developing writers to a wider repertoire of possible forms of writing. It is true that in the early years narrative often takes the form of the daily 'news' writing, or teachers use the word 'story' to mean any kind of writing, and the suggestion is that teachers should be more conscious of different kinds of text and actively create chances for children to work with a variety of structures. The criticism is not just that narrative is all-pervasive, but that it is not taught properly anyway. J.R. Martin, writing about Australian schools, claims:

> In spite of the fact that Narrative is the main type of writing encouraged by schools, and that the vast majority of writing in primary school tends in this direction, only a minority of children learn to write successful narrative by the end of Year 6. Poor writers make use of Observation/ (Comment) or Recount genres; and average writers often produce Narratives lacking in the development of crucial stages. Teachers do not really understand what is wrong and so cannot help.[14]

In suggesting a more explicit teaching of genres, Martin and his colleague Joan Rothery use the idea of genre in a rather wider sense than we may expect. It is intended to include not only those literary uses of 'genre' – for example, mystery stories, narrative poetry, soap operas – but the 'staged purposeful processes through which a culture is realized in language'.[15]

One important difficulty with this view, however, is that it does not seem to take into account the plurality of cultures which enter the educational process; so that first of all, it lacks an examination of what 'culture' might mean and imply for classrooms. It assumes that there *is* just one culture – the one which children are to be inducted into for school success. While it is certainly true that teachers have a responsibility to children to provide access to established forms of education, it seems equally true that providing children with the means to make choices and decisions within school learning is crucial to their gaining power over their lives.

Another problem about the notion of teaching generic forms is that there seems equally to be no interrogation of just what can be defined as a genre. In his book *The Double Perspective*, David Bleich outlines the view that 'any one genre has been made up of a variety of others'.[16] He gives as examples the television spot, women's magazines, and slave narratives as texts which are made up of a combination of a general category and a particular, historically developed form. Quoting Ralph Cohen, he points out that 'genre-naming fixes what is necessarily unfixable', warning of the dangers of too inflexible a view of generic categories. However, since some kind of naming is necessary if we are to be able to talk sensibly about different kinds of text, Bleich points out that it is as well to remember that 'genre naming or grouping is both necessary and loose'. Rather than discussing how many generic forms will fit on the head of a pin, I think a more fruitful pursuit might be to see how narrative and other forms of telling and writing relate to what children know and need to know, in terms of formal and informal learning, and of acknowledgement of formal and informal texts.

Recently I had a great treat: I was asked to tell stories with some children in a story-telling week. It was, on the day, a delightful experience, and as a starting point I told the children an anecdote/story from my own childhood about when I was naughty. The children then had the chance to tell each other about 'naughty' stories. A few weeks after the session, I received a bound book of letters from every child in the class, some in languages other than English. But to make the point about genre: these were letters, but they were also stories. The storying grew naturally out of shared reminiscence of a cultural event and was being refracted through another culturally developed practice – the thank-you letter. It already takes on some gleams of intertext!

Aimee thanks me, then goes on: 'My brothers been naughty too he found a box of paints and he painted on his wall and that was really naughty.' Her gloss on the story, 'and that was really naughty', already shows a sense of 'rounding off' as well as echoing all those familiar and familial stories told to visitors, which take on a more crafted form as they are retold.

Matthew is already a teller:

> Thank you for coming into school during storytelling week and telling us about when you were naughty. I thought it was very funny. It was very good when we told our own stories. We eventually finished telling the rest of our stories. I really enjoyed it. In my story my mum went out and bought four choclate bars. I was about four years old. I took the choclate bars out of the cupboard and put them in my wardrobe. When I went to bed I got the choclate bars out of my wardrobe and got under the quilt and started eating them then my mum came in to say goodnight so I stuffed the choclate bars between the bed and the wall in my draw. The next day my mum got some clothes from under my bed, and found a half-eaten choclate bar. I didn't think it was funny at the time, but it is quite funny.

Shades of Michael Rosen? Completely true story? Who knows? And it does not really matter. What is clear is that Matthew has a good sense of writing for a reader or telling for an audience; he introduces his story as a developed text; he gives me the kind of detail I need to understand the whole episode – his age, where the chocolate came from and where it went. He uses the language of more formed storytelling when he 'stuffed the choclate bars between the bed and the wall' and his mum found a 'half-eaten choclate bar'. His final gloss is a mature reflection on a childhood escapade.

Lisa took the opportunity of letter-writing and storytelling to deal with something rather more frightening. At the risk of appearing immodest, I include the whole of her letter, the opening of which says less about me than it does about Lisa as someone who has an ear for the cadences of story:

> Dear Eve
>
> Thankyou for coming in and sharing your story with us I enjoyed it very much it was funny excellent exciting and fabulous. As you shared your story with us I would like to share my story that relley happend but the problem is its not about me being nortey its something that was bad. One morning last summer holiday my frends came round for me and asked me if I wanted to go to great Yarmouth. I asked my mum and my mum said I could go so I told my friends Kerry and Joanne I could go then they whent home to tell there mum that I could go then they came back for me I took a ponud then we got on the coch when we got there we whent to the indoor swimming pool Kerrys mum paid for me. When I had my costume on I went in the swimming pool as I wasnt very good at swimming I yosed arm bands so I could get down the other end. It was deep very deep down the other end. Then I went to the watershoot that was fun but then as my friend Kerry went down the other end with a grown up that i know I chased her then thats where its bad I nearly dront. Thats my story Thank you again.
>
> From Lisa

The detail of events, the deliberate repetitions and the tag 'thats where its bad' are all part of the growing ability of this young narrator. Built into a story about an event which was naturally very significant for her are other hints of her cultural understandings 'As you shared . . . I would like to share' – the expected and equivalent exchange of story; 'The problem is . . .' – a concern about genre. But the object of my hunt for other cultural texts is evident in her knowledge of what adults say about safety, reminiscent of Natasha and Daniel; she is careful to tell me 'I yosed arm bands' and 'with a grown up', interweaving home-learned language practices with the school-requested task of a letter to a visitor.

Rachel reflects the same kind of family discourse when she tells me: 'When I was a naughty girl I went outside with my friend at 7.00 and went over the school. We were meant to come home at 8.00 but we got home at 8.30.' And as a final example of how genres can mix through narrative, Hugo's letter says:

> we've made you a rap:
>
>> Thanks for coming to our school,
>> The stories you told were really cool,
>> When we were young we were really bad,
>> When we get caught were really sad.

That is a powerful combination of cultures generally found outside the classroom and schooled literacy.

Where stories go to

What is crucial is a teacher's awareness of the value of what children bring from their home cultures, their own language and their literacy experiences – the texts which they draw from their cultural experience. Building on that awareness by creating structures which will lead to progress, intermingling these experiences and the new learning opportunities offered in the classroom, make the dynamic which moves literacy – and learning – on. Both teachers and children need to pay attention to just how texts have been put together; how they can be reorganized, if necessary, to do the job better; what other models and examples are available for a developing understanding of genre. All of these mean a growing knowledge about texts.

Since narrative is culturally developed, our perceptions of what it is and how we might use it will be affected by the experiences we bring with us and the environments we inhabit. In other words, to any context we bring our own texts, shaped and understood by the cultures in which we have learned to use them. The ways in which our cultural worlds operate influence the roles which we use as models; developed practices in relation to gender or class will be reflected in the texts – spoken, visual and written – which the predominant culture makes available to be used as models. And these available forms are often those which have permeated the expectations of a school curriculum. As teachers, we cannot afford to ignore the importance of the range of available models and the ways in which some become recognized as valuable in the education process while others are seen as having lower status. It is certainly worth discovering just how powerfully young people understand and use (and subvert) 'popular' and 'accepted' forms and the ways in which these are constructed. But beyond that, it is important to see in narrative the possibilities for using and making another kind of text – the text of cultural knowing.

In an article describing the experience of secondary students using writing to 'manipulate and rearrange the symbols of their social realities', John Hardcastle emphasizes the importance of narratives – those read, those heard and those written: 'To deny children the symbols which have the capacity to represent their own and their communities' past and current experience is to deny them the opportunity of understanding their lives and the possibility of changing them.'[17] Through the mixture of texts which make narratives, and given the chance, children will be able to use this opportunity.

Notes

Thanks are due to Michael and Gary from the Spinney School, Cambridge; Sarah Trinder and Natasha of Aberbargoed Nursery School, Mid Glamorgan; Daniel from St Nicholas C of E JMI, Harpenden, Hertfordshire, and Louise Enstone, a student teacher; Alex Hughes, Alice MacFarlane and children from Priory Junior School, Cambridge; children from St Luke's School, Cambridge, and Emma Munn.

1   H. Rosen, 'Making it tell', lecture to the Conference 'A Telling Exchange' at the University of London Institute of Education, July 1984.
2   M. Meek, 'Play and paradoxes: some considerations of imagination and language', in G. Wells and J. Nicholls (eds), *Language and Learning: An Interactional Perspective*, Falmer Press, London, 1985.
3   H. Minns, *Read It to Me Now! Learning at Home and School*, Virago Press, London, 1990.
4   *Ibid.*
5   J. Bruner, *Actual Minds, Possible Worlds*, Harvard University Press, Cambridge, MA, 1986.
6   J. Bruner, 'Life as narrative', *Social Research*, 54 (1987), pp. 11–23.
7   G. Wells, *The Meaning Makers: Children Learning Language and Using Language to Learn*, Hodder & Stoughton, Portsmouth, NH, 1986.
8   *Ibid.*
9   H. Rosen, *Stories and Meanings*, NATE, Sheffield, 1985.
10 C. Steedman, *The Tidy House: Little Girls Writing*, Virago Press, London, 1982.
11 S. Jenkin Pearce, *The Enchanted Garden*, Oxford University Press, Oxford, 1988.
12 C. Bazalgette, 'They changed the picture in the middle of the fight – new kinds of literacy', in M. Meek and C. Mills (eds), *Language and Literacy in the Primary School*, Falmer Press, London, 1988.
13 S. Brice Heath, 'What no bedtime story means: narrative skills at home and school', in N. Mercer (ed.), *Language and Literacy: Vol. II*, Open University Press, Milton Keynes, 1982.
14 J.R. Martin, 'Types of writing in infant and primary school', in *Proceedings of Macarthur Institute of Higher Education Reading Language Symposium 5: Reading, Writing and Spelling – 1984* (unpublished).

15 J.R. Martin and J. Rothery, 'What a functional approach to the writing task can show teachers about "good writing"', in B. Couture (ed.), *Functional Approaches to Writing: Research Perspectives*, Frances Pinter, London, 1986.

16 D. Bleich, *The Double Perspective: Language, Literacy, and Social Relations*, Oxford University Press, Oxford, 1988.

17 J. Hardcastle, 'What was necessary to explain', in K. Kimberley, M. Meek and J. Miller (eds), *New Readings: Contributions to an Understanding of Literacy*, A. & C. Black, London, 1992.

CHAPTER 7

Unpackaged Text
Learning to Read the Media

Avril Harpley

Avril Harpley follows the theme of children's knowledge of texts, offering a warning and a challenge. Since children are already familiar with media texts and new technology in a way which few adults can match, teachers have to take that level of expertise into account in the classroom. At the same time, however, the increase in media exposure calls for a response in terms of media awareness. How can children be encouraged to develop a discriminating approach to their media images which make up such a significant part of their everyday lives? There would be little opposition to the idea that a teacher's job includes promoting literacy. Now that there are new elements of literacy – or new literacies – the challenge is for teachers to find ways of including those, too, in approaches to critical awareness of texts. Children need to be able to take charge of their own knowledge. This chapter offers practical suggestions for 'unpackaging' media texts so that familiar and taken-for-granted media artefacts can be examined critically.

Jason made a final study of his reflection in the mirror . . . his hair fashionably short, sleeked at the edges and shaved in the middle. His nostrils sported four broad green bands, painfully inserted but precisely equidistanced. He smoothed his green fitted one-piece and adjusted the two superb peacock feathers attached to his left shoulder. He sighed and smiled, knowing he looked good, then went to join his group. As his eyes swept the room, he felt his stomach churn. Nose bands were out; long hair was in; blue was the colour. No one rushed to greet him. Eyes avoided his. He felt embarrassed and outcast. He was no longer one of the 'in' crowd. (Avril Harpley)

Children do not like to feel different. They need to feel accepted by their peers, to be able to talk about the same things, share jokes, swap the latest collectables, wear the right make of trainers. New fads and fashions spread like forest fire, ideas cross continents at the flick of a switch. With today's technology we have instant mass communication through a wide range of media, each giving us covert messages along with its facility.

Communication is the key word. How do you communicate your needs, ideas, emotions, dreams and fears? It can be in ways beyond words – visual, using gestures, movements, painting, music, photographs, film making; you can communicate to an individual, a small group or world-wide through the medium of film and video. In media education we hope to develop children's knowledge and understanding of communication and the media themselves. Children can become media literate, able to analyse and interpret the world as it is presented to them, sorting out fantasy from reality.

Newspaper reports about the standard of children's English fail to take into account that a child of 4 years upwards can use a keyboard, a tape-recorder and have knowledge of how to use a VCR. Older children acquire editing skills and understanding of production techniques. They are sophisticated users of today's technology, yet they could be ignorant of media messages. A 5-year-old will have seen more drama than my grandmother did during her lifetime, yet may not be able to tell the difference between an advert and a sitcom. Once upon a time, before widespread media communication, parents were able to act as filters of information from the outside world; now children are exposed to events and situations that can be confusing, conflicting, or even disturbing to a young child. Many people do not realize that we need to be taught how to understand media communications, yet those same people would be outraged if teaching reading were abolished.

The media influence us all; we are vulnerable to the seductive image of a perfect life-style as portrayed in visual and printed texts. Children can be at the mercy of big business – advertisers are aware of their needs and recognize the potential market. Children are big business. A great deal of time, talent and money is employed to seduce them into purchases. Skilful teams convince them of their needs and shopping can become a nightmare. Young children happily, eagerly, desperately reach out for the merchandise, unaware that they have been made to want it. They are customers today and for the future, as well as having a strong influence on what their parents buy. We may not realize just how powerful advertising can be. We surround ourselves, our bodies, our homes with desirable objects. We pursue the latest leisure activity stimulated through a kind of osmosis of the airwaves and printed media.

The facts speak for themselves: although products are manufactured in massive quantities they enter our homes, and our heads, controlled by a few:

- In America the film industry is beginning to be controlled by Japanese owners.

- Supermarkets have reduced our choice of certain goods to what is convenient for them in packaging and price. Apples, once available in dozens of varieties, now reduced to a handful and half of those grown abroad, are equal in shape and size and sit on a polysterene tray.

- Soap operas churn out similarly banal story-lines on a factory-style production line. In America there are 500 sitcoms a week on television. Rosanne has 80 million viewers world-wide.

- During the summer of 1992, popular newspapers fed us pages of the Royal Family marriage speculation at the time the Maastricht Treaty was under discussion, without giving us details of this important event.

- In 1989, Nintendo type games and related material turned over $3.4 billion. Schools in the USA are offered up to $50,000 to include adverts on their schools television.[1]

- The wonder of television – we accept it, without assessment, a form of leisure and entertainment, as its influence steadily percolates our life.

Media text

Every form of media is a text with its own language, signs and codes. When we think of media we tend to think television or news, yet media texts engulf us, surround us with silent messages to read. We read these, often unconsciously and sometimes unaware of the complexity of the communication. We need to learn how to read the text in order to understand the message fully. Everything we purchase carries a message indicating to others how we see ourselves and how we wish to be seen, and we are educated by the image the advertiser gives us. Even the logo on a carrier bag becomes an icon, telling the world that you are a well-travelled cosmopolitan picking up duty frees at the world's airports, or that you are concerned about the environment and so reuse and recycle, or that you buy designer clothes.[2] Large stores sell their carrier bags, complete with distinctive colour or logo, knowing that customers are willing to parade the promotional material in the streets to show they shop at that store, which in turn conveys their own desire for the image wrapped in the understanding of the logo.

The well-known advert for the *Yellow Pages* portrays a man trying to find a book about fishing: J.R. Hartley's *Flyfishing*. This book has now become a reality.

We learn to form opinions based on what we believe we see. We may judge people on their dress style, the car they choose to drive, the area where they live, but are we really influenced by the coffee they drink? Advertisers believe we are: 'The beliefs you hold affect the way you see the world and the way you relate to it. Seeing is believing or believing is seeing.'[3]

Effective communication means you are able to express yourself and understand others. A media text is constructed with codes and signifiers to communicate a meaning. These signs can be visual, verbal, aural. A picture going out of focus may be signifying a dream, an action happening simultaneously, a flashback to past events, or a wish, whereas a cut from colour to black and white may be used to suggest a different genre or an historical viewpoint. Some images can be ambiguous and misleading; many are stereotypes and gender biased. For instance, a picture of a strong young man riding a horse through a rocky mountain pass will represent the strong, hard and healthy life, yet the manufacturer's logo will tell us that a cigarette company is the media agency that has commissioned the advert. Coca Cola used a television advertisement, approximately 22 seconds in length, with each scene lasting barely one second, the visual images linked to the words of the jingle, making possible several quite different readings of the meanings of the words. Despite the short length of time on screen young viewers were able to recall the main events of each scene, and the whole advert reinforced the image and life-style described as those of a Coca Cola drinker.[4]

Consumers succumb to these persuasive communications, buy the goods together with the implied message, and thereby create their own self-image. We buy, therefore we are. And so we define ourselves through a mixture of visual and verbal messages transmitted to others, signalling our attitudes, desires and innermost feelings. Meaning is created by interaction with the reader/audience: we all have different backgrounds and experiences, different knowledge and understanding, therefore no two people have exactly the same interpretation of a media text.

Children have to try to make sense of the world they live in; they have to interpret and understand communications, making deductions based on their previous knowledge. This makes it all the more important to educate children into reading the media.

Don't lose touch with the real world

What is real? How can we tell? A camera never lies, but the picture is constructed, a setting chosen, lighting perfected, objects arranged, some discarded – a series of carefully considered choices. It is a 'mediation

... an assembly of objects that have themselves been through mediation along the way'.[5] In the real world cars get dirty, bumped and dented, and break down; people eat their sandwiches, argue and sing in them. But in the world of adverts cars are sleek, powerful, sexy, giving a message to the world about your status and worth. In the world of adverts women are young, slender, smooth, their hair shining and perfect, their clothes elegant, with expensive accessories. A quick look along the local High Street confirms that real people come in all shapes and sizes, dress often for warmth or comfort, and carry shopping bags rather than designer holdalls. In the world of photographs the people always smile: it is a happy place where even mishaps are recorded with a grin. Examine your own snapshot album. Photographs record many different family occasions, but no matter how awful they really were we remember them with smiles. The television show *You've Been Framed* claims huge audiences by showing people's home videos, sharing and celebrating their own misfortunes with laughter.

How can we help children to learn to unpackage media text?

First of all, we need to get behind the text. In 1948, Harrold Lasswell described this process as finding out 'who says what in which channel to whom and with what effect'.[6] In 1989, the BFI defined five signpost questions for primary media education.[7]

Aspects of media education help to interpret the meaning of visual language. We need to learn how to deconstruct, unpick, pull apart the image in order to understand it and use it for mutual benefit. Yvonne

Signpost Questions

WHO is communicating and why?	MEDIA AGENCIES
WHAT TYPE of text is it?	MEDIA CATEGORIES
HOW is it produced?	MEDIA TECHNOLOGIES
HOW do we know what it means?	MEDIA LANGUAGES
WHO receives it, and what sense do they make of it?	MEDIA AUDIENCES
How does it PRESENT its subject?	MEDIA REPRESENTATIONS

I use strategies for encouraging children to become media literate similar to those that help children to read books:

- Link with their own experiences – start with what is there, what they know about – Turtles, Bart Simpson, Nintendo, etc.

- Make connections with what they know – is the family depicted in the soap like their own? If not, how not? Are they allowed to behave like the children on TV? If not, why not?

- Value their contributions – they have had a lot of experience viewing television and videos, being exposed to advertisements, and listening to jingles.

- Acknowledge their expertise and maximize their interests and motivation. Look around your class to see what is 'in' and what is 'hot' at the moment.

- Create opportunities – allow their current fad into the classroom, promote discussion and questions.

Do not ban television – use it

- Develop activities – there is material available for use in the classroom that provides starting points for media education for all ages and across the curriculum.

- Share prime time with them – let the children know you value their interests.

- Do not make value judgements about interests – provide quality examples to discuss.

- Provide resources – you can tape adverts from the television; and 20 seconds provides a wealth of discussion. Have available audio tapes and comic magazines, as well as examples of the latest collectables.

Join in and enjoy yourself!

- Let the children become producers; this is the best way to understand how meaning is made.

- Use media techniques to record their work – photos, audio tape, advertisements and posters.

- Recognize the stages, like emergent writing, when it is necessary to scribble, jot and redraft.

- Don't expect a seamless product the first time. Look at mistakes and learn from them.

Doing it and experiencing first-hand is crucial. Children learn how it has been done and why it has been done.

Davis, speaking at a media conference, likened television viewing to jelly.[8] At home, jelly is special – it is for parties; at school, jelly is a science activity. Much the same thing may be true of our use of television in school. Focusing on an area that is familiar and taken for granted, but with sound learning objectives, media education can improve children's understanding and enjoyment.

Media artefacts surround us, engulf our lives. The moment we switch on the television we are involved. When we walk down the street every item we see, from the billboards to the litter bin, has been mediated. Each one is the result of people's choices and decisions.

> The media are not a separate part of our experiences . . . they are inextricably bound up with the whole complex web of ways in which we share understanding about the world, a web which includes gestures, jokes and hairstyles as well as news bulletins, opera and architecture: books as well as television.[9]

Media = text

A book waits for us to open it before we engage with the text. The cover tells us what to expect, attracts us. We might recognize the author or the publisher, having enjoyed their previous work. There may be some blurb summarizing the story, or quotations from reviews. The style of fonts used may indicate the content – letters dripping blood indicating horror, or a plain, straight type-face. The artwork, commissioned, designed and produced specially for this book, will tell us what to expect from the story. There will be hard information about price and circulation, bar codes and ISBN. For a young reader, one who is not able to skim and scan the pages to sample the text, covers and illustrations are very important, giving immediate attraction.

You can discover clues with children before you open the book. Use the signpost questions to ask:

- Whom is the book written for?
- How can you tell?
- What information is available?
- Why do we need the information?
- Who made it?
- Why was it made?
- How was it made?
- Whose name is written on the front?
- What did you think about it?

After reading a book, each child can make his or her own cover for the book, perhaps for a different audience, and they can all discuss the reasons for the different interpretations.

The same discussion points can be used with a cereal packet or a toy package. Even at a simple level, children will be learning to look more critically. They will be learning to use technically appropriate language: front, circulation, producer, frame, shot, focus, close-up. Older children are able to transmute the text of a story into a visual medium. Some of the skills require the ability to recognize significant action, develop the atmosphere of a setting, highlight body language and gesture. Children used to watching television are familiar with the conventions and learn how to recreate the language of close-ups, cuts and pace. They can mix their knowledge of behaviour signals with visual messages to transmit their ideas to others.

Children are living in a rapidly changing, high-tech world exposed to powerful advertising forces. As educators we dissect the curriculum minutely, painstakingly ensuring that we are covering content and attainments. Yet children's toys and leisure pursuits emit powerful messages about values and attitudes which are taken in without question. Media education helps children to discriminate, become more critical, better equipped to make informed judgements and able to communicate in a variety of ways with a range of audiences. They will be able to choose.

> Jason picked up his mobile phone and dialled. A fax had arrived that evening whilst he had been on his personal virtual reality machine. He had left a search function on the phone for a blue one-piece suit. He had already secured hair extensions and removed his nose bands. A store in New York had a consignment. With luck he could arrange to have one by the weekend. He placed his order, using the multi national credit card linked to the phone. Satisfied, he adjusted the volume of his implanted stereo earpiece and relaxed to the sound of the latest music. (Avril Harpley)

Notes

1 *Media Values Magazine*, 52/53 (1990/91).
2 Geoff Dean, Adviser for English, Oxfordshire, speaking at a TVEI media conference at How Hill, Norfolk, November 1991.
3 Anthony Bethell, *Eyeopeners One and Two*, Cambridge University Press, Cambridge, 1981.
4 BFI Education, *Primary Media Education: A Curriculum Statement*, British Film Institute, London, 1989.
5 Richard Dimbleby and Graeme Burton, *More Than Words: An Introduction to Communication* (first published 1985), Routledge, London, 1989.
6 Harold Lasswell, in Dimbleby and Burton, *op. cit.*

7   BFI Education, *Primary Media Education*: A Curriculum Statement, British Film Institute, London, 1989.
8   Yvonne Davies, Community Education Officer for Central Television, speaking at a TVEI media conference at How Hill, Norfolk, November 1991.
9   Cary Bazalgette, *Media Education*, Hodder & Stoughton, London, 1991.

Further reading

For good background reading and knowledge about advertising: Judith Williamson, *Decoding Advertisements*, Marion Boyars, London, 1978.

For an excellent, easy-to-understand and practical guide to media education: Carol E. Craggs, *Media Education in the Primary School*, Routledge, London and New York, 1992.

For classroom activities: Avril Harpley, *Bright Ideas: Media Education*, Scholastic, Leamington Spa, 1990.

For classroom activities on image analysis: *Reading Pictures*, BFI Education, London, 1991.

Further material may be found by contacting: BFI Education, 21 Stephen Street, London W1P 1PL.

CHAPTER 8

From Drama into Story
Strategies for Investigating Texts

Lesley Hendy

Stories are like doors and windows; you can enter places and leave by them, hide behind them or see through them. When children use stories as starting points for drama, they can enter unexplored places and learn from the previously unknown. Lesley Hendy combines the imaginative world of story with a range of practical strategies which can be used to deepen children's understanding of the story itself. Character, motive, story structure and themes all become more readily understood when children step through the story into drama. Even the most challenging of texts can be the entry point for exploring the unknown, an adventure for teachers and children making drama together, and a chance to bring back new and invigorating knowledge.

Drama is not simply a subject but also a method . . . a learning tool. Furthermore, it is one of the key ways in which children can gain an understanding of themselves and others.

Good drama is about discovering what is unknown rather than re-enacting what is known already.

(National Curriculum English Non-Statutory Guidance)

Primary teachers at Key Stages 1 and 2 have always found drama a useful learning tool to help pupils experiment with the 'as if'. Exciting and well-written stories are an established source for this drama making. Teachers, working in and out of role, have used drama devices called 'drama strategies' to help children engage in living language. Using story as a springboard, the learning tool supplied by drama strategies gives children a variety of contexts in which they can use language to find the appropriate registers to deal with a range of different oral situations and, as the non-statutory guidance suggests, to discover what is 'unknown'. From a whole range of different texts, children from Key Stage 1 onwards can make new and exciting stories from old, often-told legends, myths and fairy-tales. The story provides an outline from which the drama is made with only passing reference to the original. The pupils can take the story in a completely unexplored direction, with new learning coming from the investigation of the 'unknown'.

This chapter aims to call attention to the possibilities of using drama strategies to look more closely at a written text, its language, its structure and its content. Such a method of looking at stories seeks to be not a replacement for other, more established ways of making drama from stories, but a complement to them. It offers an alternative way of stepping inside another world.

Understanding and using drama strategies

Drama strategies (see Table 8.1 on page 108) are structuring or framing devices which can be employed by a teacher to focus children's attention on the variety of questions, events, issues and concepts that arise within a drama. When the drama is being made from the unknown, such strategies are initially used as what might be called *macro-framing* devices, to establish the larger structural elements of content and form. Such terms as 'teacher-in-role', 'mantle of the expert', 'forum theatre' and 'investigative drama' may be familiar from the National Curriculum English 'Aspects of Programmes of Study' as techniques suggested as starting points. In the early stages of drama making, these strategies help to build aspects of plot, character, issues and events which will become the focus as the work develops. As the major elements of content and form emerge, drama strategies are subsequently employed as *micro-framing* devices to focus more specifically, and so deepen understanding of the drama and commitment to it. A strategy known as 'hot-seating' is a popular method of building information about characters, while 'thought-tracking' allows pupils in role to reveal their private thoughts in a public way. Through such devices, information about an individual's feelings towards another person or an event in the drama can be revealed, deepening commitment and understanding.

When starting from an existing story, the content and form are already present within the text, so macro-framing devices are not needed. Micro-framing strategies, on the other hand, can be used immediately to focus on specific questions, issues and concepts provoked by the story.

Table 8.1   Some drama strategies used in the activities

Strategy	Description
Still image (freeze frame)	The group, using themselves in different poses, construct a frozen picture to describe what they want to say.
Captions	Often used with a still image: each group, or another group, is asked to put a caption or title to what they have made or what they see.
Trailer	The group make a series of scenes, with or without dialogue, leaving the audience in suspense as to what will happen next.
Montage	A series of quick images that will tell the whole story or important moments of the story.
Voice-over	A voice is used to link scenes through either narration or explanation of events.
Hot-seating	A role or character is adopted by the teacher or a pupil, who is questioned by the group. This strategy can be used to explore the background, thoughts, ideas, etc., of the role or character.
Thought-tracking	Individuals, in role, are asked to speak aloud their private thoughts and reactions to events.
Prepared scenes	Small groups are asked to prepare the content and form of a scene to reveal ideas, events, etc. These are then shown to other groups.
Collective role-play	The group or the whole class take on the responsibility of playing a key character in the drama.
Interviews	Some individuals take on roles of characters within a drama, others act as interviewers, to discover information about events, relationships, etc.
Documentary	In role as historians or investigative reporters, the group creates a documentary programme based on the events in the story or drama.

The range of activities and the drama strategies suggested in the following sections can be used with any story of the teacher's choice. If the pupils are not familiar with drama work it might be more productive to choose a story that is complete, not too long, and of literary merit. Anthologies of stories with short, well-written texts would be suitable for this approach.

Active involvement with a text

Many teachers not familiar with the regular use of drama as a teaching tool can find the thought of active learning very daunting. The approach suggested here may be a useful starting point for teachers who have such reservations. All the activities are based on small-group work and none requires the teacher to be actively involved unless she or he chooses to be so. The activities are set out as a series of tasks, which can be employed as part of a lesson or taken as a whole lesson, depending on the requirements and timetabling of individual classes.

The programmes of study for English encourage active involvement with 'memorable language and interesting content'. In this first series of activities, pupils are asked to look closely at the written text. The tasks are put in the context of film and film advertising. Such a theme will be familiar to most pupils and a setting in which they should feel secure. It is important that pupils are able to relate to the context of the drama. The opening exercise involves the use of 'still image' where the group, using all the members in different poses, creates a still or frozen picture to describe what they want to say. (See Table 8.1.)

Film still

Each group is asked to look carefully at the story and to choose three moments they think are important. They are then asked to create three still photographs that might be put outside a cinema to publicize the film of the story.

After a prescribed length of time (certainly no longer than 10 minutes), each group in turn is asked to show the finished 'photographs' to the other groups. The audience is then asked to decide whether the pictures they are being shown represent the same three moments as those of the group they worked in themselves. If so, they can discuss and assess whether the presenting group have chosen to portray them in the same way. On the other hand, if the 'photographs' are of different moments, the observers can be asked how clear it is which parts of the story are being shown. Giving the audience a task of this kind helps them to focus in a more detailed way and serves to prevent the more self-conscious aspects of 'showing'.

On the whole, groups engaged in this activity do *not* choose the same three moments. Working on a fairy-story such as 'Little Red Riding Hood' might produce a variety of important moments. Some groups may choose the scenes where Little Red Riding Hood is given the basket by her mother, where she meets the wolf in the forest, and where she encounters the wolf dressed as her grandmother. Another may choose the meeting with the wolf as their first moment, followed by Red Riding Hood's discussion with the disguised wolf, and end with the rescue of Red Riding Hood and her grandmother. This can lead to some very interesting discussion about story structure, and to reflection on the forms of criteria being employed by groups when they made their choices.

Film still with caption

Each group is asked to choose the one of their three 'photographs' which they felt was the most effective. They then choose a caption taken from the text. The 'photographs' are shown again. As each picture is made, the audience is asked to find a caption for it, using phrases or sentences from the written text.

To complete this the pupils have to involve themselves quite closely with the text. Groups can become quite specific about the phrase or sentence that they will allow to describe their tableau. Such activities can help pupils build their visual response to the written word.

Film trailers

By creating prepared scenes the groups are asked to make a trailer for the film to be used either in the cinema or on television. Using dialogue from the text or making up their own, pupils show incidents from the story, but leave each one on a cliff-hanger. The scenes are connected by a voice-over. Pupils should be encouraged to capture the feeling of the story.

Activities such as this help pupils build their understanding of tension and suspense, important elements in the art of storytelling. They can be asked to reflect upon the nature of the tension: whether it was caused by the relationship between characters, was the result of actions and the motivation behind them, or was brought about by the use of mystery and surprise. Discussion could then follow on how groups captured the tension successfully.

Fast forward

The groups are asked to prepare the story as a montage without sound, depicting as much of the story as they can in the shortest possible time, like fast forward in a video. They should be encouraged to make clear distinctions between scenes and to show where characters enter and exit from the story.

This is another exercise that helps to develop pupils' understanding of story structure. It can also be a useful evaluation exercise for the teacher. Groups that have difficulty may be unsure of the development of the story and the role of the characters within it.

Role-play to examine plot and character

When pupils are challenged by a complex text, they can be supported by work in role-play which will help them to examine their understanding of plot and character. The following section uses hot-seating, collective role-play, prepared scenes and thought-tracking as framing strategies to help pupils uncover aspects of a story.

Invent a scene

Using prepared scenes, groups are asked either to create an incident that the story does not tell or to invent some dialogue between characters in the style of the original narrative.

An exercise such as this requires the pupils to explore the style of a text and examine the language structure. Goldilocks never speaks to the three bears, but it might be interesting if she did. What did happen to Kay after he was captured by the Snow Queen and before Gerda found him?

Many are one

A small group of pupils are chosen to play some key characters in the story as a collective role-play. The teacher or other pupils can question the 'characters' about events, issues and relationships, either as part of the drama in role or out of the drama as themselves.

Collective role-play is a productive strategy. It allows more than one person to play the main role and it helps pupils to build a collective picture of central characters. By reflecting in this way the group can establish a deeper understanding of the people they meet in stories. A collective role-play of the Snow Queen meeting a collective role-play of Gerda could be a very effective way of examining their motives and circumstances.

Speaking to a character

One of the group is chosen to be in role as a character from the story and is hot-seated.[1] The remainder of the group can ask questions of them: about their former life, their feelings about their situation, or their feelings about other characters in the story.

Hot-seating offers pupils a forum to discover information about characters, their ideas, their feelings and their viewpoint. Teachers who take on a character in the hot-seat have a powerful means of feeding information about the story into the drama.

What are you thinking?

Groups are asked to form a still image depicting an important moment in the story, and while in their image, individuals are asked to thought-track[2] by speaking aloud their private thoughts or feelings about the event.

This strategy gives the pupils the opportunity of providing the story with a subtext and can provide a useful entry into discussion about motive and purpose. Hearing the thoughts from the crowd witnessing the emperor in his new clothes could be a useful introduction to the motives and behaviour of groups.

Using a modern version of the text

When pupils are introduced to texts that are written in language distant from their own experience, they can sometimes be helped by using strategies that bring the writing into a style more immediate to their environment. Television and television formats are very accessible to modern pupils, and the activities suggested in this section use this context.

The six o'clock news

The groups are asked to retell the story as if it were an item on the six o'clock news. There is a newsreader who is in the studio, and an outside reporter who interviews the different characters from the story.

By employing this device, pupils are able to access the basic ideas and structure of a story or part of a story. When they return to the original text they will have points of identification which will allow them to approach the story with more understanding. Teachers often use this exercise in a written form. Children are asked to rewrite a well-known story as if it were an item in the newspaper. This is the same task but in an active form. An interview with the victorious Beowulf after his defeat of Grendal could make compelling viewing.

Drama documentary

The groups devise a format in which they can show the story as an historical investigation using documentary techniques. There will be a presenter who takes on the role of narrator and investigator. Experts, historians, distant relatives, etc., can be interviewed and reconstructions of events can be shown.

This activity is a longer project and could take some time to prepare. The final results could be video-recorded and the presentations shown to other groups in the form of a television 'programme'.

A difficult text such as *Beowulf* would be an excellent story to investigate in the ways described, as a close examination of this story can provide a deeper understanding of its complexities. Pupils can be encouraged to include passages from the text itself, making use of one of the excellent modern translations.

This series of activities is not exhaustive, but it can provide a starting point from which to explore and investigate texts with children in a more active way. By using such a structured approach, teachers who have not attempted drama in the past may feel able to launch out into the 'unknown' territory of drama-making through story.

Notes

1 If the teacher has not chosen to be in role for the hot-seating, it is important that the pupil volunteer is chosen with care. If the class is not accustomed to this kind of work, several pupils can be chosen to play the role collectively.

2 The teacher may ask 'How do you feel about this incident?' 'What are you thinking as you see the emperor with no clothes?', 'What would you like to call out but daren't?,' etc.

CHAPTER 9

What Children's Books Tell Us about Teaching Language

Mike Taylor

This chapter rings with different voices. First of all, Mike Taylor reminds us of the variety of tones and resonances in much-loved stories. Humour, gravity and mystery echo from the extracts which he uses to show just what knowledge about language these texts offer readers. The 'rigour and elasticity of language' as shown in just a few examples is present in many of the texts which children encounter, making those texts 'tacit teachers' of the structures and variety of language. Using a three-tier model, Mike Taylor outlines how culture, system *and* situation, *although a simplified framework, can be used to explore the texts which children encounter and the texts they make. The chapter ends with the children's voices, confidently and powerfully demonstrating the range of their knowledge about language.*

Twenty years or so ago I was a young English teacher at a grammar school in the north of England. One morning, a colleague came into work with this story. His 6-year-old son, Mark, went to a formal primary school in another town which prided itself on the percentage of pupils it got through the 11-plus. The lad was not a very fluent reader and had hitherto shown little interest in books. That night my friend had gone into his bedroom to kiss him goodnight and had been delighted to find Mark curled up in a bedside pool of light absorbed in Paddington Bear. 'My goodness, it's lovely to see you enjoying a nice read,' he ventured. The 6-year-old rolled his eyes. 'Literature exam tomorrow,' he groaned. In our subsequent chat about the enormity of the educational crime being perpetuated at this Dickensian institution, further horrors were revealed. When he was not doing literature, the young man was subjected to an enforced linguistic safari through a patchwork tundra of partial texts, shooting down nouns, adverbs, gerunds, similes and the like. This of course was his language work, the necessary antidote to reading books.

Now I have just left a children's literature conference at Cambridge. The conference has been an outstanding success. Teachers have come from across the country and, over the two or three days, faces drained by the enforced labour of the National Curriculum have returned to life. Authors have shared their thinking processes with readers; readers have been reconfirmed in their knowledge that the writing and reading of literature are richly intuitive processes. We return to school high on adrenalin, transformed, empowered. But in the classrooms we return to, the wedges that prise apart 'language' and 'literature' are once again cracking the ceiling. We face once again all the old 'ills' of a hermetic approach to English teaching – reading through skills, language through drills, and, with the imminent publication of prescribed texts, literature that kills.

It is still possible, however, to hang on to our belief, as lovers of children's literature, that sharing books in the classroom is a central resource not only for learning to be a responsive reader of significant texts, but for developing an ear for rich varieties of language and a more conscious awareness of how these varieties of language work. In other words, however much government imperatives drive us back to basics (or 'forward to fundamentals', as one educational publisher has stirringly put it), we should continue to regard rich and varied book provision as a key resource for language teaching. This is because 90 per cent of what children need to know about language (including spoken language) is being engagingly presented to them through stories and poems by writers whose skills as tacit teachers far outweigh anything the earnest toil of textbook writers can dig up.

A few brief extracts from some much-loved books illustrate the access they give to wide-ranging 'knowledge about language':

The bear stared, the cat sat, the mole rolled, and the dove shoved the grumpalump. The lump still grumped.[1]

While they were gone, Somebody came to the door. Somebody knocked and, when no one answered, Somebody tiptoed in . . . 'This food is too dry,' said Somebody. 'This food is too noisy,' said Somebody. 'But this food is just right.'[2]

'I've been waiting for some time now,' said George, 'to speak to you on your own. This is the first proper chance I've had, what with feeding and bathing and nappy changing and people coming to see me all the time. And talk about making noises – that's all some of them do. They bend over me with silly grins on their faces and then they come out with a load of rubbish. "Who's booful den?" "Who's a gorgeous Georgeous Porgeous?" "Diddums wassums Granny's ickle treasure?" It's an insult to the English language.'[3]

A daring armed robbery on a grocery shop was foiled today by the single-handed bravery of the shopkeeper Miss Elsie Podmore. Miss Podmore, past president of the Huddersgate and District Cheese Girdlers Association, denied that she was a very brave lady. 'There was really nothing to it,' she said. 'In fact you could say it was child's play!'[4]

I'm the Wolf. Alexander T. Wolf. You can call me Al. I don't know how this whole Big Bad Wolf thing got started, but it's all wrong. Maybe its because of our diet. Hey it's not my fault wolves eat cute little animals like bunnies and sheep and pigs. That's just the way we are. If cheeseburgers were cute, folks would probably think you were big and bad, too.[5]

In the first extract, rhymes illustrate relationships between the sound system and associated letter strings in English. Invented words conform to morphological rules, e.g. verbs (grump) formed from nouns (grumpalump) and vice versa. Cumulative repetitions of rhythmic syntax underline basic sentence structure. Again, in the second, basic sentence patterns are repeated but with variations. Any young reader/ listener who has internalized the musical syntax of this story 'knows' how to use subordinate clauses and how to create textual cohesion without using 'and'. Young readers will also recognize the gentle parody of Goldilocks – the collusion between reader and writer of a shared culture informing and enriching the reading. Extract three relies on the reader's understanding that language varies and is adjusted for an appropriate audience. George's formal spoken register, 'I've been waiting for some time now . . .' with its amusing role reversal (this after all is the language used by Victorian fathers as a prelude to a rehearsed 'birds and bees' speech), poses questions about the kind of baby talk that follows. Is it comfortingly musical or patronizingly inappropriate? In the last two extracts, the writing again echoes speech patterns. In the fourth, the convention of radio-style reporting assumes no prior knowledge on the part of the reader. Packed noun phrases compress the necessary(?) information into memorable 'sound bites'. Journalistic vocabulary comes close to cliché. On the other hand, the last extract invites the reader into an immediate dialogue where a background of shared information is essential. Even this short extract draws on the reader's knowledge of the Chandleresque monologues of gangster stories (movies); of American English – 'Hey'; 'cute'; fairy-tale language – 'big and bad'; and of an 'original' version of the tale told from the conventional point of view.

A recent national project on language involving many thousands of teachers throughout England and Wales[6] made a brave, last-ditch attempt to establish at the centre of public consciousness about English a clear and comprehensive 'model' of language; i.e. a description of those working assumptions about language shared by professional linguists and teachers which underpin their practice. This model (essentially the same one which guided practice at my direct grant grammar school in 1972) is based on the following assumptions:

- The making of meaning is the reason for the invention, existence and development of language.

- All meanings exist within the context of culture. Cultural values and beliefs determine the purposes, audiences, settings and topics of language.

- Texts, spoken and written, are created and interpreted by making appropriate choices from the language system according to specific purposes, audiences, settings and topics.[7]

These assumptions differ from prescriptive notions of 'basic grammar' and 'correctness' in their recognition that language is both highly flexible and complexly rule-governed. While the same underlying structures of English inform its wide-ranging uses in our varied lives, all sorts of fine tuning occurs at all levels of the system – sound, vocabulary, syntax, discourse structures, etc. – as producers and receivers adjust the subliminal language choices they make to suit a wide variety of social contexts. This idea of rules of appropriateness as opposed to a grammar of immutable correctness acknowledges, for instance, that during the course of a day, speakers and writers will switch and slide along a fretboard of grammatical rules as they modulate their language to the expectations of a variety of changing audiences. While Standard English is a key aspect of such a language repertoire, the capacity to handle a spectrum of functional variation is the key to true language competence. The model of course also accepts that linguistic appropriateness is itself culturally determined and that groups in different speech communities may share different rules. As we have seen from the brief examples above, these working assumptions about language are those that writers themselves rely upon as they use the rigour and elasticity of language both to mirror nature and to create new experiences for us to live and grow through.

Returning now in more detail to the part that children's books can play in celebrating and highlighting children's knowledge about language, we can expand our three-tier model – culture, situation, system – as follows, pausing only to note that like all models it simplifies the truth. Many books will share characteristics from all of these levels; indeed, features of one level will be realized through others. For the present, however, readers might like to check any small selection of children's books they are familiar with against this list of criteria.

Culture

Some books may focus particularly on who we are and where we come from. Some may tell us about experiences from the different points of view of gender, class or ethnicity. Anne Fine's *Bill's New Frock*,[8] for instance, explores what it may feel like to be a girl in school. Others, like *Ten in a Bed* by Ahlberg and Amstautz,[9] show authors drawing on a common culture shared by many of their readers. Others still may highlight linguistic diversity and the rich resources of spoken and written variation in our regional cultures. In particular we might find writers foregrounding:

- *regional, historical, social and individual* uses of language shaped by such determinants as gender, class, age, and ethnicity, and including representations of accent and dialect;
- *other Englishes*, e.g. Australian, Caribbean, American;
- *attitudes* to other people's language;
- events reported from *different points of view*: change of narrator, villain as hero or heroine, parallel stories or pictures telling a different story;
- *characteristics (and stereotypes)*, e.g. Stickly-prickly, Mr Plod;
- the *reader's knowledge of other books* (and other kinds of writing).

Situation

Within this broad area some books will focus on the way language varies according to where we are and what we are doing. Some of these may explore the possibilities of different purposes and audiences, for instance the American gangster retelling of *The True Story of the Three Little Pigs* by Jon Scieszka. Some, like Keith Brumpton's *A Dinosaur's Book of Dinosaurs*,[10] look at the ways in which fiction can incorporate different kinds of writing – diary entries, lists, notices, labels – or how it can parody their conventions. Some explore the differences between spoken and written language and how the spoken voice is represented in writing. In particular we might find writers foregrounding:

- *language appropriate*
    - to *purpose*, e.g. to persuade, amuse, present facts, parody;
    - to *topic*, e.g. tall story, how to look after a pet, business letter;
    - to *reader or listener*, e.g. younger child, teacher, parent (e.g. terms of address according to relationship, status, etc.);
    - to *situation*, e.g. use of slang, jargon, technical language, formal/informal uses;

- language use in *different types of writing*, e.g. story, diary, instructions, letter, labels, lists, captions, language of information books;
- *spoken language represented in writing*, e.g. speech balloons, dialogue, speaker tags like 'he riposted smartly'.

System

Language is shaped by these two aspects – cultural background and context of situation – but meaning is expressed through choices from the language system. A third way in which writers may front-up language is through such choices, foregrounding for readers ways in which language is patterned and organized. This organization may be chronological or non-chronological; it may focus our attention onto sentence structures which are marked by variation or repetition or on imaginative uses of words. Some writers may even show us the ways in which individual letter forms and fonts can be varied for effect, e.g. Graeme Base's *Animalia*.[11] In particular, writers may be drawing our attentions to:

- *organization of text* – chronological/non-chronological;
- *story structure*, including cumulative story, flashback, first or third person narration, description, explanation, argument;
- *how ideas are linked together* in texts – meanwhile, finally, however;
- *sentence patterns* – repetition and variation, question and answer, listing, simple or complex sentence patterns;
- *words as parts of speech*, e.g. emphasis on adjectives or verbs in alphabet books, word play, imagery, metaphor;
- *sounds and letters*, e.g. rhyme, rhythm, alliteration, use of typographical features to represent sounds or loudness, conventions used in print – italic or bold print, use of upper case, use of different type-faces for different purposes.

Teachers on many INSET courses throughout East Anglia[12] who have looked at familiar children's books together in the light of the above model have found it helpful in two complementary ways. Firstly, identifying language features within the familiar context of stories has helped them to conceptualize their implicit linguistic understanding and assimilate a more precise language for describing and identifying language structures, variations and development. Secondly, teachers can see the rich seams of tacit learning about language which writers are making available to children, not of course as their focal point of concern but as an integral part of the pleasure principle afforded by the very vigour and individuality of their writing. There is no reason why

Tony Ross: **Dr Xargle's Book of Earth Hounds**

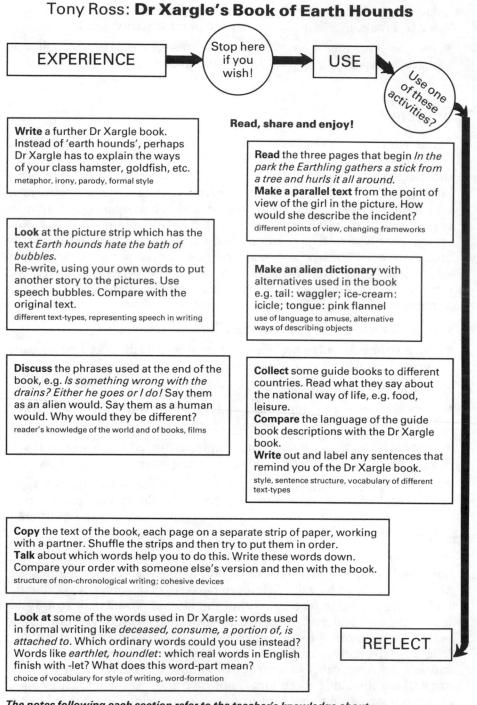

EXPERIENCE → Stop here if you wish! → USE

Use one of these activities?

Write a further Dr Xargle book. Instead of 'earth hounds', perhaps Dr Xargle has to explain the ways of your class hamster, goldfish, etc.
metaphor, irony, parody, formal style

Look at the picture strip which has the text *Earth hounds hate the bath of bubbles.*
Re-write, using your own words to put another story to the pictures. Use speech bubbles. Compare with the original text.
different text-types, representing speech in writing

Discuss the phrases used at the end of the book, e.g. *Is something wrong with the drains? Either he goes or I do!* Say them as an alien would. Say them as a human would. Why would they be different?
reader's knowledge of the world and of books, films

Read, share and enjoy!

Read the three pages that begin *In the park the Earthling gathers a stick from a tree and hurls it all around.*
Make a parallel text from the point of view of the girl in the picture. How would she describe the incident?
different points of view, changing frameworks

Make an alien dictionary with alternatives used in the book e.g. tail: waggler; ice-cream: icicle; tongue: pink flannel
use of language to amuse, alternative ways of describing objects

Collect some guide books to different countries. Read what they say about the national way of life, e.g. food, leisure.
Compare the language of the guide book descriptions with the Dr Xargle book.
Write out and label any sentences that remind you of the Dr Xargle book.
style, sentence structure, vocabulary of different text-types

Copy the text of the book, each page on a separate strip of paper, working with a partner. Shuffle the strips and then try to put them in order.
Talk about which words help you to do this. Write these words down.
Compare your order with someone else's version and then with the book.
structure of non-chronological writing; cohesive devices

Look at some of the words used in Dr Xargle: words used in formal writing like *deceased, consume, a portion of, is attached to*. Which ordinary words could you use instead? Words like *earthlet, houndlet*: which real words in English finish with -let? What does this word-part mean?
choice of vocabulary for style of writing, word-formation

REFLECT

The notes following each section refer to the teacher's knowledge about language. He or she will judge how far this can be made explicit to children.

any teacher who is committed to sharing books in the classroom need feel ashamed about neglecting 'language' or 'basic grammar' since the books will be highlighting a wide range of linguistic features so successfully. What we need is to be aware of what we are doing, and to give children the chance to reflect from time to time more consciously upon the language options taken up by some of the writers they read. Shown opposite is an extract taken from a recent EastLINC booklet[13] which includes ideas based on twenty books that might help us to encourage such reflection. Each page is framed with the words 'experience', 'use' and 'reflect', to emphasize that children may learn from all three ways of encountering books – through a wide experience of language in a rich learning environment, through opportunities to use their knowledge, and, later, by reflecting on what they have learned.

Finally, here are some examples of children's own writing which hint at the benefits to be derived from looking more closely at the language of books. The young writers have used the kinds of activity suggested above to focus on the language of three books.[14] Sharing this reflection has helped them to broaden their own repertoires, to bring their writing under more conscious control, and to extend the range of choices they are making from a shared grammatical system.

Hi, the names Volfe, B.B. Volfe Private Eye. This is the true story of Red Riding Hood and the Wolf!
The Wolf and Miss Hood
One dark night, I was just packing up when there was a 'knock' at the door. I was really cross, that stupid 'knock' was always at my door! Anyway, I sent him packing. A few minutes later a beautiful dame walked in! 'Hello, my name's Miss Hood!' said Miss Hood. 'I, err, I'm in a spot of bother!' she said.
'My incredibly wealthy, stinking rich, leaving-a-fortune to me! Dear old old granmamma has disappeared.'

4S wants / the story tape / a bucket of balls / a box of chalk / the sports cupboard key / and don't forget the / PRINTER!
4S wants / the cuddly ape / a bucket of balls / a box of chalk / the sports cupboard key / and don't forget the / PRINTER!
4S wants / the cuddly ape / the Niagra Falls / a box of chalk / the sports cupboard key / and don't forget the / PRINTER!
4S wants / the cuddly ape / the Niagra Falls / a teacher that talks / the sports cupboard key / and don't forget the / PRINTER!
4S wants / the cuddly ape / the Niagra Falls / a teacher that talks / a cup of hot tea / and don't forget the / PRINTER!

Good morning class today we are going to learn about earth nibblers and nibblets.
Nibblers eat earth scholars' morning grub
They eat greens from the growing patch
They jog to the loft gym every Saturday morning

The nibblets have an automatic fur coat. When 5 days old they press a button and it gradually starts to grow. Instead of shoes nibblets wear sponges on their feet.
When grown up they have open blinds and long pieces of thread attached to their sniffers. They have different coloured coats and a stump wag at the back
The earth scholars stroke the nibblers with their wrigglers.
Don't hold tight with your wrigglers or else you will splatter your nibbler.[15]

Through the vitality and precision of their writing, authors expose children to the word patterns, cadences and rhetorical structures which will help them to shape their own significant experience, and which extend the linguistic options already available to them as speakers and listeners. Talking about the language of books can give children additional insights into the way grammar works in a context that makes such learning both memorable and enduring. As teachers we must recognize this as *real* grammar 'knotted together deep down in the gut',[16] and resist those pressures trying to impose upon us the linguistic etiquettes of the prep school.

Notes

This chapter draws heavily upon professional development material written by Pat Baldry and Frances Smith, with contributions from Brigidin Crowther, Diana Fogg, Pauline Minnis, Liz Slater and Mike O'Reilly (EastLINC advisory teachers 1989–92).

1 Sarah Hayes and Barbara Firth, *The Grumpalump*, Walker Books, London, 1992.
2 Marilyn Tolhurst, *Somebody and the Three Blairs*, ABC Books, London, 1992.
3 Dick King-Smith, *George Speaks*, Puffin, Harmondsworth, 1992.
4 Bob Wilson, *Stanley Bagshaw and the Mafeking Square Cheese Robbery*, Puffin, Harmondsworth, 1990.
5 Jon Scieszka, *The True Story of the Three Little Pigs*, Puffin, Harmondsworth, 1989.
6 The Language in the National Curriculum Project (LINC), 1989–92. This £21-million, government-funded project to update teachers' knowledge about language was condemned by ministers for insufficient attention to the basics – 'grammar, spelling and Standard English'.
7 Ronald Carter, Introduction to R. Carter (ed.), *Knowledge about Language and the Curriculum*, Hodder & Stoughton, London, 1990.
8 Anne Fine, *Bill's New Frock*, Metheun, London, 1989.
9 Allan Ahlberg and Andre Amstutz, *Ten in a Bed*, Granada, St Albans, 1983.
10 Keith Brumpton, *A Dinosaur's Book of Dinosaurs*, Orchard Books, London, 1991.

11 Graeme Base, *Animalia*, Puffin, Harmondsworth, 1990.
12 The activities summarized here were among many resources developed by the regional LINC advisory team to support the professional development of primary language coordinators between 1990 and 1992.
13 Language in the National Curriculum Project: Eastern Region, *Looking at the Language of Fiction*, Cambridge, 1991.
14 Scieszka, *The True Story of the Three Little Pigs*; Pat Hutchins, *Don't Forget the Bacon*, Bodley Head, London, 1976; Jeanne Willis, *Dr Xargle's Book of Earth Hounds*, Anderson Press, London, 1989.
15 With thanks to the teachers and children at Sutton CE School, Cambs; John Paxton CP School, Cambs; and Elsenham County Primary School, Essex.
16 Tony Harrison, 'Fireater', in his *Selected Poems*, Penguin, Harmondsworth, 1984.

CHAPTER 10

Three Moments in the History of Narrative

Michael Armstrong

As a fine counterpoint to the previous chapter, Michael Armstrong looks in some detail at three young storytellers. Underlying his careful exploration of the children's texts is a view of story-making as critical practice. Earlier chapters have commented on cultural aspects of story from different angles. Michael Armstrong argues that entering a cultural tradition need not be simply initiation to new mysteries. Entering the cultural tradition of storytelling necessarily involves innovation as well as imitation; and children are as powerfully placed to enter the critical practice of storytelling as adults. Once teachers are in a position to recognize children's artistry, then they can 'provoke, sustain and challenge' that critical practice.

For several years I have been preparing to write a natural history of narrative. Let me explain.

I take it that storytelling is a critical practice, in the course of which, through our engagement with a particular form of expression, we both discover the world and invent it. In the preface to his great work *Time and Narrative*, the French philosopher Paul Ricoeur pus it like this: 'I see in the plots we invent the privileged means by which we reconfigure our confused, unformed and at the limit mute temporal experience.'[1]

It is commonly thought that critical practices are accessible only to those who have undergone a lengthy apprenticeship. The ancient metaphor of initiation dies hard. First we must master a skill; then we may hope to practise an art. But that is not, I think, how we enter into a cultural tradition. Innovation and derivation are inextricable in every act of invention, at any age, at any moment of experience. To quote from Ricoeur once more:

> [Every] work of art . . . is an original production, a new existence in the linguistic kingdom. Yet the reverse is no less true . . . The labour of imagination is not born from nothing . . . It is bound in one way or another to the tradition's paradigms.[2]

The fascinating thing about narrative, as perhaps about every kind of critical practice, is the way in which, from the outset, it obliges us to innovate even as we try to imitate. What is true of storytellers at the height of their maturity is equally true of young children composing their earliest tales. Vivien Paley puts it best, at the beginning of her account of storytelling in a pre-school classroom in Chicago, *The Boy Who Would Be a Helicopter*: 'Remarkably, each child's first story is a unique event in the history of the world.'[3] And yet, for all that, we never start from scratch.[4]

Some day I hope to trace the tortuous line that runs from the infant's opening achievement in the linguistic kingdom of narrative to the adult's mature accomplishment. I would like to explore the conditions that make for success and failure, including those that might depend upon teaching. I would like, that is, to write a natural history of narrative. But at present all I can describe are moments, points along a line that is still to be drawn. Hence my title: three moments in the history of narrative.

Narrative in the early world

> Once there was a man and a mother and two sisters and a brother. First the oldest sister ran away. Then the second sister decided to stay home with the father but he ran away too. So the little brother and the sister were left and she learned how to cook. One day a lion came because she wished for a lion and also they lived in the jungle. He said 'Can I be your pet?' She said 'I was just wishing for a lion pet. You can carry us wherever you want.' So they lived happily ever after.

The storyteller is a 5-year-old African American called Wally. Wally is the hero of Vivian Paley's remarkable book *Wally's Stories*,[5] a disruptive member of Paley's kindergarten class in Chicago. Before he came into her class, Wally had never tried to write a story, as Paley explains.

> The first time I asked Wally if he wanted to write a story he looked surprised.
> 'You didn't teach me how to write yet,' he said.
> 'You just tell *me* the story Wally. I'll write the words.'
> 'What should I tell about?'
> 'You like dinosaurs. You could tell about dinosaurs.'
> He dictated this story.
> The dinosaur smashed down the city and the people got mad and put him in jail.

'Is that the end?' I asked. 'Did he get out?'

He promised he would be good so they let him go and his mother was waiting.

We acted out this story immediately, for one reason – I felt sorry for Wally. He had been on the time-out chair twice that day, and his sadness stayed with me. I wanted to do something nice for him, and I was sure it would please him if we acted out his story.

It made Wally very happy, and a flurry of story writing began that continued and grew all year.[6]

Twenty-one of Wally's stories are reproduced in Paley's book. They form a fascinating archive. Here is a child engaged in the practice of narrative for the very first time. In the plots that he invents we glimpse the privileged means by which Wally reconfigures his own world and ours.

The story which I have chosen to discuss is one of Wally's earliest. Like most of his stories it is set in the jungle, sometimes described simply as the forest or the woods. This is the realm of narrative, the confused, uncertain world that must be reconfigured by means of the plot. The jungle represents adventure, which holds the risk of injury or death but also the promise of new acquaintance and companionship. Every encounter in the jungle is poised between loss and recompense. In most of Wally's stories it is the protagonists who leave home and must negotiate their own return. But on this occasion the heroine and her brother confront the jungle from within their home, victims at first of the jungle's fatal attraction and recipients at last of its favour.

Wally's characters, too, change little: mothers and fathers, sisters and brothers, and everywhere, lions. Paley tells us that Wally's lions are usually 'aggressive beasts', but this is an exaggeration. In at least half of the stories the lion is a helper or, as here, a guardian. Our story opens with a family that is on the point of disintegration. We never find out what happens, or may have happened already, to the mother; she seems to have left the scene before the plot gets under way. As for the other, older, more experienced, more responsible members of the family, they both desert, first the older sister, then the father, for reasons which are neither given nor required. Theirs are stories yet to be told; Wally's concern is with the children left behind.

The father's desertion is especially cruel since it was for his sake that the younger sister chose to stay at home rather than follow her sister into the jungle. In recognizing this we experience for the first time the precision of Wally's language. '*Then* the second sister *decided* to stay home with the father.' It is not by chance that she stays, but by choice. Throughout the story it is this second sister who carries the power and demonstrates resolve. At first to no avail – '*but* he ran away too'. Once again it is the apparently insignificant word, 'but', like the earlier 'then', that carries the greatest force, in signalling the fruitlessness of the second sister's resolve and the perilous situation of the two younger children. And now, immediately, there is a third significant connective, emphasizing the consequence of a conjuncture. '*So* the little brother and the sister were left *and* she learned how to cook.' Desertion is followed by new resolve; 'so', followed by 'and', fixes the meaning as directly as any storyteller might wish.

'She learned how to cook'; that is to say, she learned how to cope, to look after her brother as well as herself. We are not altogether surprised. The second sister's autonomy has already been recognized in her decision to stay at home. Now that the father too has deserted it seems natural for her to fend for herself. But it is not, after all, so easy to replace the protection and the companionship that a parent might have offered. Enter, then, the lion. 'One day a lion came because she wished for a lion and also they lived in the jungle.' The lion enters in response to the sister's wish, confirming her power. But Wally, who is consistently ingenious in his explanations, is careful to ally the magical to the plausible: 'and also they lived in the jungle'. Accident and sagacity are inseparable in almost all these stories.

The surprising fact about this lion is not that he talks but that he wants to be a pet. A lion that is yet a pet: guardian, friend and servant. But even that is not all, for this pet has his own autonomy. The sister confirms it in her final speech: 'I was just wishing for a lion pet. You can carry us wherever *you* want.' The choice of 'you' where we might have expected 'we' shows that the lion can be trusted to know what is best and is therefore a fitting replacement for the lost father, or even representative of the father's return, transformed. 'So they lived happily ever after.' Was ever a 'so' more exact?

Walter Benjamin, in his essay 'The Storyteller', celebrates 'the liberating magic' of the fairy-tale, which, he suggests, 'does not bring nature into play in a mythical way, but points to its complicity with liberated man'. 'The wisest thing', so the fairy-tale teaches us, 'is to meet the forces of the mythical world with cunning and with high spirits.'[7] Wally at the age of 5 is a young storyteller who has already appropriated the fairy-tale as Benjamin describes it. He has entered the world of narrative and at once made it his own. The story which he tells is also the story of himself.

At ease in the early world

I Found It in My Bowl of Cereal

One day I was eating a bowl of cereal when I looked and saw something in my cereal. It was a bit of chewing gum. It was the colour pink. I picked it up and put it into my mouth and it was strawberry flavour. It was yum. Whenever I eat something I always swallow it even if it is some bubble gum. You get all of the flavour out that way. So I swallowed it. For a moment I had a tummy ache. I then felt as if I was being blown up into a balloon. I looked at myself. I was blowing up and I started to float. !OH NO! The window was open and I was heading straight for it. I tried to hold onto the edge of the window but it did not do any good at all. I just hurt my finger. As soon as I got outside I got higher and higher and suddenly I was sitting on top of a cloud. I sat down and I started to cry. Then a little cloud went flying towards me, it was going to crash into me. I jumped up and I started to go higher and even higher. I was going so high that I was going up into space. I could stand it no more, I tried to stop myself. I still did not get anywhere. I was so fed up I did not want to be alive any more. So I tried to choke myself and suddenly I felt something in my mouth. I took it out and I saw it was the chewing gum. I threw it into space and as soon as it was out of my mouth I suddenly popped and shoooow I was falling down and down. Boomth I had landed. I looked around and I saw that I was sitting on a cloud – shoooow – I had fallen straight through the cloud and I was falling again. Boomth I landed again. This time when I looked around I saw that I was on a double decker bus! I also had a ticket in my hand. Suddenly I saw my house through the window. I pressed the special button and gave the driver the ticket. I got off and went inside. My mum was up now and she said 'Did you have a nice time at the cinema?' I said 'What cinema?' 'The cinema you went to today to watch the film called The Girl Who Blew Up Like A Balloon,' she said. Then I said 'Oh, yer, now I remember.' I thought to myself 'I don't remember.'

'I Found It in My Bowl of Cereal' was written by 9-year-old Lydia, a member of my own class at Harwell Primary School in 1988. Lydia, like Wally, was an enthusiastic storyteller. Among the twenty-two stories of hers which I transcribed at the end of the year, this was the eighteenth. It had been written in late spring, towards the end of the school year, almost exactly a term after she had decisively found her form as a storyteller with a story entitled 'The Magic Stone'. Magic is at the centre of many of Lydia's stories, but her use of it is more self-conscious than Wally's. In particular she is fascinated by the distance between parents and children in their appreciation of the power and reality of magic, as we shall see.

The opening of the story presents to us a narrator for whom experience and exploration – the world made up of hypothesis, test and speculation – are the very conditions of her existence. (I would not wish to identify narrator and author. There is a good deal of Lydia herself in her narrator, of course, but there are also significant differences.) In an early aside, marked by a shift of tense, the narrator establishes at once her self-consciousness and her eagerness for experience: 'Whenever I eat something I always swallow it even if it is some bubble gum. You get all of the flavour out that way.' 'So I swallowed it.' This is the first of two critical actions that determine the story's plot, but Lydia seems anxious to play down its significance by presenting it as a simple consequence of her narrator's point of view. It is characteristic of magic, as Lydia presents it in her narratives, that it exploits experience and reason in this way. The ordinary and the magical are inseparable; it takes adults to prise them apart. (Our next story, however, will exhibit a rather different understanding of the bond between the magical and the everyday.)

As magic takes hold, the narrator never ceases to keep her wits about her. She examines herself, observes what is happening, attempts to prevent it. But magic is not to be denied, as the narrator ironically observes. 'I tried to hold onto the edge of the window but it did not do any good at all. I just hurt my finger.' Eventually it is her inquisitiveness that will save her, but not before magic has come close to overwhelming her. As the world recedes, magic grows hostile and alien. 'I was so fed up I did not want to be alive any more.' If this sentence seems melodramatic, it should perhaps be read as the melodrama of a fairground attraction – the octopus, big wheel or whizzer – which makes us feel we would, as we say, do anything to stop it. It is the moment at which for once the narrator loses confidence in experience and at the same time it is the moment that saves her. 'So I tried to choke myself and suddenly I felt something in my mouth.' By now we know that this particular narrator is bound to discover what it is. By testing experience, even at the limit, control is regained.

Or is it control? Here we confront the interrogative ending of Lydia's story. The narrator is returned home by a carefully controlled sequence of descents, from space to cloud, to top deck of a passing bus, to kitchen, to mum. Back home it seems at first that magic is to be discounted. As the mother reads it, the narrator has simply returned from the cinema where she has seen a film that has overstimulated her imagination. But Lydia is not content with the well tried formula of waking as from a dream. As so often in her stories, she offers the familiar ending only to withdraw it: 'Then I said "Oh yer, now I remember." I thought to myself "I don't remember."'

In story after story that year, Lydia played with the differences between the adult's and the child's perception of magic. Magic is inaccessible to adults. Their explanations exclude it. There has to be a reason for everything and of the most matter-of-fact kind. Common sense rules. But Lydia's narrators are never convinced. The world which they experience is beyond the grasp of adult thought. It is outrageous, wonderfully strange, often inexplicable. Yet Lydia at the age of 9 never stops searching for explanation even as she welcomes magic. At the heart of disorder her narrators discover their own kind of order, one which does not eliminate magic in favour of logic but looks for ways of accommodating both.

Even so there is a terror in magic which Lydia cannot fully absorb. It is present in her narrator's sudden wish to end it all, and in the interrogative ending itself with its half-suppressed anxiety that no companionship is complete and no explanation satisfying. And this leads me to my final narrative moment.

On the threshold

Girl Today, Hare Tomorrow

Saturday, June the 13th. The time was 7.00pm. Rachel Slatter was going to be in a play called Alice. She got in the car with her father. He started the engine of their big Citroen Family Estate. It shuddered. 'Got everything?' said Mr Slatter. 'All my costume is in the hall apart from my ears,' Rachel replied stiffly. She was a bit nervous. 'Right', said her dad. He let the Citroen roll slowly down the drive. He swung it round and drove to the junction. Then he sped past the White Hart and up the Grove Road. He accelerated all the way up to Rowstock. They went round the roundabout and headed for Wantage. They were nearly at Wantage when the car started hiccuping. 'She's got the hiccups again,' said Mr Slatter. Suddenly a great spurt of steam came up from the car bonnet. 'What is it?' Rachel cried. 'I can't be late!' She fingered her felt ears nervously. 'It's not much,' said her father. 'But I'll have to phone up Pete to tow us back'. 'Where's a telephone?' Rachel said. 'I can't see one.' 'There'll be one in Ardington,' Mr Slatter replied. 'But Ardington's four miles back!' Rachel shouted. 'And I've got a play to put on.' Her father thought for a moment. Five minutes later he had gone to find a telephone. Rachel began to walk to Wantage. She put on her felt ears. She sucked a travelling sweet hungrily. 'I wonder if they'll miss me,' Rachel thought. 'After all, I am only the March Hare.' Her nose began to itch. She twitched it. Her hands and feet tingled slightly, probably with cold. Rachel was still hungry. She picked some grass and chewed it thoughtfully. Her glassy eyes shone with the moon reflection. Her furry paws glistened with the dew of evening. Far away Mr Slatter returned. In the light of the moon, he saw a hare jumping away on the grassy bank. It leaped over the hedge and scampered on the corn field. Mr Slatter shook his head, and smiled. 'As mad as a march hare.' He thought.

Rebecca wrote 'Girl Today, Hare Tomorrow' when she was 11, during the last term she spent at Harwell Primary School. She had become an exceptionally fluent writer, at ease in many different genres, technically accomplished and rarely at a loss for ideas. The story was composed in a single session and never revised. The title seems to have been invented before the story itself. It derived from no particular stimulus as far as I could tell at the time. When Rebecca handed me her page-long manuscript its appearance was flawless. There were no afterthoughts and no corrections. Down at the bottom of the page there was just enough space to sign the story with her full name and a perfunctory flourish.

For some time the themes which dominated Rebecca's writing had been darkening. Her last poem of the year was a meditation on the colour black; her most ambitious story had been a terrifying tale of a small boy sucked below the waves into an alien underwater world. Yet she was neither an anxious child nor unduly introspective. Her favourite reading was Enid Blyton.

At first glance Rebecca's story seems to push to the limit that estrangement of children and parents which Lydia toys with at the conclusion of her own study of magic. Moreover, on this occasion, a much closer correspondence exists between the fictional family of the Slatters and the author's own real family. The fictional father bears more than a passing resemblance to Rebecca's own father; the car is her own family estate; the village is Harwell; Grove Road, Rowstock and Ardington are real places, Pete a real family friend. Even the forthcoming performance of *Alice* recalls the part that Rebecca had taken in a school play some years earlier, although in reality she had been the Mad Hatter rather than the March Hare. But while it is important to the author to establish these particularities of place and family setting, the issue of family conflict is in the end subordinate in this story to an exploration of identity, on the threshold between childhood and adolescence, and to a vision of the precariousness of a youthful imagination. Lydia's stories, for all their acceptance of magic, never lose sight of the productive interplay between magic and the real. By contrast, in Rebecca's narrative we are forced to contemplate the possibility of an enchantment that is without redress, a fracture in that complicity between nature and liberated man which Walter Benjamin discovers within the genre of fairy-tale.

The most immediately striking feature of Rebecca's story is the extraordinary degree of control which the author exercises over her material. In language notable for its economy and precision, the narrative systematically unravels the significance of its flamboyant and distinctly literary title. From the moment that Rachel Slatter gets into her father's car, clutching her felt ears and feeling nervous, every step in her metamorphosis is simultaneously foretold and disguised. It is not until the words 'she picked some grass and chewed it thoughtfully' that we know for sure what is happening to her, and by then, as listeners or readers, we are already as exhilarated by the escalation of the narrative as we are unnerved by its direction. This is not a story that leads its teller along unexpected paths. It has none of the open-endedness that is so characteristic of Wally's stories, or even of Lydia's. Rebecca lays claim to an authority which the younger narrators do not seek. Her narrative imposes itself upon the reader; it is irresistible.

For Rebecca's purpose the anonymity of 'Once upon a time' would be ineffective. Nothing is more controlled than the precision of the story's opening sentences. In order to expose the shocking rift between magic and reality it is necessary to insist on the matter of fact: 'Saturday, June the 13th. The time was 7.00pm. Rachel Slatter was going to be in a play called Alice.' But the last of these sentences is less matter-of-fact than it appears. It foreshadows all that follows. For this is a story in which the heroine disappears into her own narrative, and no one notices, neither her father nor even, she speculates, the rest of the cast. It is as if, for Rachel Slatter, the linguistic kingdom is all there is. The fascination of art becomes a fear of art: the terror of entering a magical world from which after all there may be no return.

Throughout the first half of her story Rebecca insists time and again on the circumstantial details of the narrative: the pub, the roundabout, the layby, the telephone in Ardington, 'four miles back'. It is out of such mundane materials that the shock of the ending is to be conjured. The point of no return corresponds to a remarkable gap in the narrative flow, a kind of caesura, at the moment when Rachel insists 'I've got a play to put on.' 'Her father thought for a moment. Five minutes later he had gone to find a telephone.' The distance between these two sentences, highlighted by the sudden change of tense, signifies the chasm that has opened between father and daughter. For the father, despite Rachel's imploring shout, there is nothing much to worry about, just a telephone to find. For the daughter this is the moment of crisis, the point at which she slips silently into her own fiction. By the time the father returns she is gone, even if he fails to recognize the parting.

I have always interpreted Rebecca's story as a tale of enchantment and the fear of enchantment, but it is possible to take a gentler view. Perhaps the separation is not so much between imagination and reality as between one generation and the next. When Mr Slatter goes in search of a telephone without so much as a by your leave, it is time for Rachel to set out on her own, to become herself, however eccentric or unrecognizable. And perhaps, then, her father's shake of the head and smile at the close is less a failure of recognition than a gesture of acceptance. At any rate, when this alternative interpretation was first suggested to me, I noticed that in transcribing Rebecca's manuscript I had unwittingly repunctuated the last line. I had always read it as follows: 'Mr Slatter shook his head, and smiled. "As mad as a march hare," he thought.' But a closer inspection shows that there is what looks like a full stop after the words 'As mad as a march hare' and that the word 'he' is given a capital H. How significant that full stop might be I leave for now as an open question.[8]

I have presented to you three young storytellers, each at her or his own complex point of development, discovering and inventing the world through narrative. To understand their achievement is to turn the world of education upside down. This is what Tolstoy must have meant when he gave his own astonishing account of children's writing the extravagant title 'Should we teach the peasant children how to write or should they teach us?'[9] Teachers and pupils come together as storytellers. For all their differences they are committed to a common enterprise, engaged in a common critical practice. Children have much to learn and much to be taught, but they can be taught successfully only by those who recognize their elementary artistry.

Unfortunately, the common sense that passes for educational thought at the present time has no place for children's artistry. It gives us no clues about how to provoke, sustain and challenge children's critical practice. It deals with rules rather than exceptions, measurement rather than quality. It promotes technical accomplishment irrespective of meaning or purpose. In effect it denies the significance of children's thought. So much the worse for common sense, which in present circumstances amounts to little more than philistinism, an almost compulsive desire not to understand. For many of us who spend our professional lives in the classroom, the recognition of critical practice is nevertheless just what teaching is about. That is why we have chosen to teach. That is why we still enjoy teaching. That is why it is still the greatest of all intellectual excitements to sit in a class of 5-year-olds, 10-year-olds, 15-year-olds, reading and writing and telling each other stories.

Notes

1   Paul Ricoeur, *Time and Narrative: Vol 1*, University of Chicago Press, Chicago, 1984.
2   *Ibid.*
3   Vivian Gussin Paley, *The Boy Who Would Be a Helicopter*, Harvard University Press, Cambridge, MA, 1990.
4   For an account of the origins of storytelling in infancy see also Katherine Nelson (ed.), *Narratives from the Crib*, Harvard University Press, Cambridge, MA, 1989; Jerome Bruner, *Acts of Meaning*, Harvard University Press, Cambridge, MA, 1990.
5   Vivian Gussin Paley, *Wally's Stories*, Harvard University Press, Cambridge, MA, 1981.
6   *Ibid.*
7   Walter Benjamin, *Illuminations*, ed. Hannah Arendt, Shocken Books, New York, 1969.
8   The author of *Girl Today, Hare Tomorrow* is 16 now. On completing this essay I sent her a copy. I wondered whether she still remembered the story and how she might react to my interpretation. Her reply to my letter reopens the circle of interpretation. 'I hadn't forgotten the story at all', Rebecca writes:

   nor any others I wrote at Harwell. Reading it again, however, I was struck that it was so short and find it a bit irritating. I had, and still have, such an incredibly vivid picture of the hare jumping away in the moonlight purple and silver; and my words just seem to clumsily imprison the scene. I remember at Harwell hating using reality in stories, and always tried to escape from what seemed to me boring events like 'I went to call for my friend . . .' I am prouder of so-called fantasy works than those such as *The Patient*, about being sick at school . . . Because of this, the early part of the story is uncomfortably familiar, at least to me. I think you'd probably argue that you need this factual part to contrast with the later, magical developments – and perhaps the story would be worse if it was completely alien. But because the first half is basically real memory, I find it hard to accept it in the story . . . I tried to implicate the father as merely a shadow, a reliable but uneventful figure. The point of his final shake of the head is to show his complete unconnection with the hare and his daughter. The idea that his daughter has just grown ears and leapt over a hedge never occurs to him. Whether this reflects my own view of parentage at the time, I'm not sure; more likely that is how I wanted Rachel to feel. There is almost resentment of his narrow vision, total incomprehension for fantasy, and failure to recognize his own daughter. I actually feel angry towards this stupid man as I'm writing now – how can he not see? She has left one world and left him behind, bemused but unsuspecting. You say some people think he knows about metamorphosis. They don't seem to treat the change as I do. It *is* more sinister, as you suggested. I was fascinated by 'darkness' . . . and wouldn't have wanted the metamorphosis to have been either acknowledged or a sparkly, magical thing. Incidentally, there is no full stop between ' . . . a march hare' and 'he thought', which would imply a twist such as that seen in Lydia's story. [The ms, however, does not seem to me to justify Rebecca's categorical denial.] I think it makes my story slightly tackier, though Lydia's far better. I don't think I would ever use the term 'magic' to describe what was going on. That seems to imply innocence and imagination. I wanted the change really to happen, rather than have Rachel turn into a rabbit in her mind and end the story on a limp, 'all a dream' ending – falling back to the reality I tried to escape in my stories . . . Do you think that children have the same ideas as adults, but just can't express them as well? Or maybe their naivety helps them express them better? If I had written this story last year, would it have been better or worse?'

9   Alan Pinch and Michael Armstrong (eds), *Tolstoy on Education*, Athlone Press, London, 1982.

CHAPTER 11

Finding a Voice
A Consideration of the Stories
That Girls Dictate

Brigid Smith

Earlier chapters have made strong claims for the power of narrative and the power of children's own voices. In this chapter, Brigid Smith starts from the point of view of writers who seem not to have found ways of using these two sources of power. She describes the position of some girls who are not confident writers, de-powered because they cannot 'lay out their ideas and feelings in words'. Scribing stories for these girls helped them to explore their feelings. In capturing their authentic voices through scribed stories, Brigid Smith hopes that some of the power may return to girls who may not easily be heard otherwise.

Why has it been so difficult to do this piece of writing; to find the end of a thread and wind myself into the narrative? I think because, maybe for the first time, I have stopped writing 'out there' in the quiet neutrality of education-speak and have tried to engage with a new voice. It is a voice which does not necessarily seek to please and it has come about because of a growing conviction that for women who write, and for girls learning to write, a space has to be created in which we can live an inner life that is authentic.

For many years I was unable to use the word 'I' in my journal – an experience I have found to be familiar to other women. Finding a true voice, following the hand across the page and believing in the resulting words, take courage and experience; the sense of being on show, not to say 'shown up', constrains. If I, as a professional woman working daily with pen and paper, find writing so difficult, how must the girls that I have taught, many of whom were inexperienced or novice writers, have felt about it? And what about those who were unable to write sufficiently competently to express themselves and lay out their ideas and feelings in words?

Much of the work that I have done with pupils has been concerned with helping them to find a voice by setting up the conditions in which they *have* been able to tell a story. These stories have been dictated, told orally, then used as reading texts. In this way inexperienced writers have been encouraged to 'read like a writer',[1] standing in the common ground between composer and reader and finding out for themselves where the meaning of a text lies. The Japanese poet Akemi Tachibana writes:

> What a delight it is
> When skimming through the pages
> Of a book, I discover
> A man written of there
> Who is just like me.[2]

and Margaret Meek[3] suggests that we go to books to find ourselves, to read the story of our own lives, and that this is a powerful motivation for reading. People need to find themselves in the books that they read. Where could the inexperienced writers I worked with find themselves in their reading texts? If they were girls, what did they find of themselves in the books that they read, and was the voice that they were hearing a real voice?

I received a story in the post some time ago from one of the girls whom I had worked with some years earlier. Debbie, now in Year 8, writes a story that is called 'The Talking Car', although it begins with a description of trouble in school:

> One day I went into tutor and Mr. Williams said to me, 'Mrs. Arthur said you have been a very naughty girl so your mother has to come in.'
> I said, 'What have I done wrong?'
> 'You have been hitting everyone over the shopping arcade and having fights with Perry School.'
> In an innocent way I said, 'Who told you that?'
> 'I have had phone calls from Perry School teachers because their pupils has been coming in crying and I have seen you over there many of times.'
> I went home and that night I told my Mum . . . she didn't look that pleased.
> Every so often I saw her eye-brows drop and look at me.

This sounds like an authentic voice. Many teachers will recognize this sort of story – but Debbie has made it her own in the telling. 'I saw her eye-brows drop and look at me.'

After this realistic beginning she shifts the narrator's voice to the detached, third person, past tense narrative of the familiar 'magical' story:

> I went to bed that night and I dreamt of a talking car. I am going to tell
> you the story . . . One day in a small village there lived a little girl . . . she
> was a nice girl. When she was twenty her Mum bought her a car. I mean
> not a normal car, but one with flashy lights and all the good gear . . .
> sometimes I used to wish I had a car like that.

Again her own voice re-enters the story with 'I mean' and 'sometimes I
used to wish', nudging the reader in a way that makes the language
engage the reader in a collusion with the author. Tannen calls this
involvement focused text,[4] and it is one of the ways in which authors
can reach out from a text and reveal themselves to the reader, involving
them in the emotions and plot of the story. 'The Talking Car' continues
with Debbie being invited for a ride in the car, which talks to its
passengers. She is frightened and says: 'I would rather walk than go in
that talking car', but once she gets used to it she agrees to go out in it
that night. Debbie goes to the pub, is persuaded to drink Vodka:

> I felt really ill.
> I kept falling over and being sick.
> We went home.

On the way home 'a massive lorry went into us' and she ends up in
hospital 'in this special container called a coma'. It seems that what
Debbie has to tell the reader, in her true voice but safely contained
within a magical narrative, is about her anxieties as she grows up in a
confusing world. Writing this story allows her to make public and
accessible, in an acceptable form, her real-life experiences. She knows
that stories can carry messages and that you can extend and fictionalize
real-life situations in a safe way, and she has learned this through
dictating and reading her own stories as a way into learning to read.

One of the important aspects of becoming a reader is that it enables
us to engage safely, and yet courageously, with fears, anxieties, hopes
and sadnesses, life and death, through stories and particularly mythic
stories. Applebee underlined the need for extended fictions in which
readers can address issues in their own lives; the children in his research
told stories in which they distanced themselves from difficult happenings
by creating naughty characters who do unacceptable things.[5] It seems
obvious that children who are unable to read and write are doubly
disadvantaged. They are not able to find themselves in a book and to
engage vicariously with emotions through their reading, neither can
they 'write out' their anxieties in the way in which experienced writers
can use diaries, fiction or poetry to express the nearly inexpressible and
to distance themselves while exploring real-life feelings.

For some time I have been interested in exploring this extended
fictionalizing in the dictated stories of inexperienced readers and
writers. In particular I wanted to reflect on the possibility that girls, and

especially girls who find it difficult to express their opinions and ideas, might find a way to do this through dictated stories. In the world of school some children's voices can be difficult to hear; perhaps the voices of girls like Debbie, who are not successful in an academic way, may be particularly muted. Valerie Walkerdine in *Schoolgirl Fictions* focuses on the way in which schools, and especially primary schools with their majority of women teachers, perpetuate the idea of 'good, nice, helpful girls, guardians of moral order, keeper of the rules'.[6] What does this mean for someone like Debbie, who wants to express her sense of herself in ways that do not conform to this stereotype? Where is the space in which to challenge the status quo safely, to break the rules? Walkerdine suggests that even clever girls find it difficult to explore their ideas or to find a voice in the classroom, and that they may choose to show their cleverness in writing rather than orally because it is not open to public scrutiny or dispute. If *these* girls need to write in order to express their ideas and feelings safely, how much more may girls who are perceived as having special educational needs be without a voice? Such girls are often overdependent in their learned helplessness, hard to motivate, passive and yet toughly resistant to attempts to engage them with learning.

The experience of enabling girls to become composers by scribing their stories suggests to me that this may be a way that they can find an authentic voice. In their stories it seems that they can both try out their own voices as authors and also create alternative fictions for themselves as readers. As Walkerdine writes: 'If we want to understand the productions of girls as subjects and the production of alternatives for girls, we must pay attention to desire and fantasy.'[7]

In another exploration of young girls' fictionalizing Steedman considers the way in which a group of 8-year-olds write out their future role as mothers and wives, and she points out their acute consciousness of the oppressive nature of such roles and expectation that they will none the less eventually co-operate.[8] However, through their story, they also clearly question and debate these expectations and give themselves space to consider the question of non-conformity.

Walkerdine asks: 'Good girls are not alway good but how and where is their naughtiness lived out?'[9] I am in correspondence with a young writer, Louisa, aged 5, who suggests a solution in a story dictated to her mother and sent to me:

> Once upon a time there was a girl who left her brains at school and when she came home from school her mum said, 'Could you go to bed because it's time to go to bed.'
> And she didn't go to bed. All she did was lie on the settee and watched television . . .

Next day she went to school. And her teacher said, 'I told you to make the playhouse tidy but you didn't.'

Then the teacher said, 'You must have left your brains at home.'

It seems that girls can be naughty – but only if they dissociate themselves in some ways from the acts of naughtiness.

Many of the stories dictated by girls I have worked with are domestic or circumscribed in their titles and intentions, but sometimes these domestic contexts mask brave explorations of other possible fictions. Cheryl, aged 11, wrote a long story called 'The Otter Family', whose main characters: 'live by the sea. There is a Mum and Dad and three baby otters. There is Peepee, Sweep and Neepee who are three years old.' Her choice of names may, in itself, constitute an act of defiance directed at school proprieties! Although the otters live in a hole, 'lined with leaves and grass so it is safe and comfortable and warm for the babies', it is not long before: 'the babies got on the ice and ice skated but to us it looked like they was slipping. They were screaming and laughing', and after that they are found 'mucking around on machines', 'starting to fight' 'and they start to swim up river'. After an absence of three months they go to a Dolphinarium where there is a 'bear that burped and farted' before they return home to go 'to the islands to settle and have families of their own'. Away from home they are able to 'muck around' and behave in an adventurous way, uninhibited by the need to conform or to behave well. In the end, though, there is a domestic reprise and reorientation; when you settle down, real life and real work begin.

Steedman talks about the 'war in the nursery', and some of the dictated stories certainly suggest a mother–daughter conflict. Sarah was quite a timid and passive girl, but in her story 'Birthday Ghost' the behaviour of the mother is quite disturbing, when she returns as a ghost to steal her own baby's birthday toys. In fact, looking more closely at the eleven ghost stories that Sarah dictated, I find that she created havoc everywhere. All her ghosts are anarchic – they steal lollies, splash in pools, frighten people and are not averse to some real violence here and there. Her first and last chapters, however, are domestic and detailed, a description of transformed but ordinary life:

> Henry Jones lives in an invisible house in the middle of a field in Kingsland at number 36 . . .
> On the last day of their holiday they went to the pub for a quick pint until half past twelve because they had to take the presents to their wives and had to get back on the plane.

Through these ghosts, carefully created by a variety of accidents and disasters, Sarah has found a space in which to express strong feelings of anger, revenge and chaos.

Angela Carter in her introduction to *The Virago Book of Fairy*

Tales reiterates the fact that goodness is to do with order, obedience, rationality and co-operation, but she also suggests that fairy-tales are 'over-generous with the truth rather than economical' and reminds us that television 'soaps' are modern fairy-tales.[10] Sarah's stories, with their detail of place and their precise characterization, have something in common with a soap opera, although distanced by the magic of the ghost device. The 'fairy-tale' context of ghosts and unearthly or impossible happenings allows her to go deeper into the truth of her feelings and to create more chaos than a normal fiction would allow.

There are two more points that might usefully be made about fairy-tales – that they empower and that they make people fearful. As writers like Debbie and Sarah compose their stories, they discover that the extended fictions of fairy stories allow the exploration of the subversive in action, and they are able to take control, to exercise power and to consider alternative behaviours. They also discover that in a story difficult issues can be addressed in a safe and unthreatening way. The 'wicked stepmother', an icon from a time when early death was prevalent and such a figure would be frequent in a family, may, for example, allow modern children to explore safely the anxious feelings that are roused by parental separation and remarriage. The other familiar fairy-tale icons of woods and wolves, the encoded 'warnings' about child abuse, molestation and possibly cannibalism in early communities, seem to have lasted and are often used by young girls in their stories. I was surprised to find how frequently 'the dark, dark woods', the 'shadowy woods', and woods with traps, holes, enticements and ghosts figure in the stories that girls dictated.

Both Anna, aged 9, and Kelly, also aged 9, start their stories in the wood, but on the edge, an edge embroidered by the domestic: 'Anna, Kelly and Natalie went out to the woods to pick blackberries. Their Mum wanted to make some blackberry pie', writes Anna. Kelly starts in a similar pattern: 'Once upon a time there was me and my sister walked in the woods to pick blackberries because mum wants to cook blackberry pie for dinner.' Their stories continue, though, in a markedly different way, showing the possibility for exploring inner fears and outer situations which dictating a story allows. Anna continues to compose a typical ghost story – full of 'Thump, thump, thump' made by ghosts who 'knocked all the trees down as they came through them' and ending with the girls, after much screaming and being scared, running safely home. Anna's story has a knock-about feel to it – rather like the ubiquitous 'Then I woke up and found it was all a dream' which so many young writers use to round off their stories.

On the other hand Kelly's story, already written in the first person narrative, describes a much more alarming situation:

> My sister found a trap and the trap was covered with a net with leaves
> over it. I accidently fell in it and my sister tried to get me out with a rope

but she couldn't get me out because she was too heavy.
  So she fell in with me.

A man appears in the trap, her sister eats from a forbidden cupboard where an apple has a caterpillar in it and marmite sandwiches, and then she gets fat. The man cannot get them out and Kelly herself eventually resolves the situation. 'I put my sister on my shoulders to get her up because she was too small. And I got up by the ladder. After that he took us home.'

Kelly's second story explores the theme of the 'spying wolves' who are eventually caught in a trap and then 'the woodcutter came and chopped them in the trap'. It may be only in the safety of the wood, in the form of the conflict and eventual overcoming of the wolf, that Kelly can begin to come to terms with her feelings and her self; it is the place she has created in which to explore things she may not consciously be able to address. It is the privilege of the writer to have this world to explore. It would be wrong therefore to get entangled in the undergrowth of psychological analysis.

Cheryl and Sarah, like Debbie, later produced stories which continued the exploration of inner feelings and outer contexts. On one occasion they worked with a teacher to produce a dictated book which was written by all three of them. A joint story made it possible to incorporate vocabulary and syntax that was more complex, and while it still built on the composers' own voice, it reached out into the more formal language of printed text. Their story is concerned with motherhood, authority and 'good behaviour'. It begins:

> Once upon a time there was a deep, dark forest, it was so deep and dark that when you stood in the middle of it, it was very quiet and shadowy and when you looked up you could hardly see the sky.

The girls introduce a girl into the story who has the same name as the teacher, and who: 'looks like a witch . . . The woodchopper was very sorry for the ugly girl.' The woodchopper takes this girl home and she has twins: two girls called Sarah and Cheryl! Here the relationship of teacher/authority is reversed. The teacher/girl is to be pitied because she is ugly but then, again exploring the relationship between them, she becomes the mother/authority for the twins, both representing closeness and affection on the one hand and ultimately becoming the target for the twin's rebellion and rejection as they grow up on the other. The story ends with a description of mud-bomb fights in the park when the authors' voices revert to their own reactions to their own 'mums'. Did they go through the dark, dark woods in order to enter their own selves, selves now transformed into the dominant, unco-operative and critical actors in the story?

Debbie, Cheryl and Sarah, like their younger counterparts Louisa, Anna and Kelly, know that in the world of story anything is possible and that what is frightening, confused or contradictory in their lives can be safely addressed here. Magic, and the symbols of magic and myth, allow writers to signal the world of the real through the world of the unreal. In this rite of passage it may be possible for some children to find their voice to express their wish to be in control, to dominate and to call attention to their needs, fears and hopes. Authentic voices come clearly from these texts, voices which may not be easily heard in any other way. 'Giving a voice' to non-reading, non-writing girls enables them to reflect on texts, to reread, to 'write like a reader', and at the same time to address important issues as they grow up into young women. The end of the thread is ready to hand.

Notes

I would like to thank Isobel Urquhart, who was the class teacher of Debbie, Sarah and Cheryl and whose current research is also exploring extended fictions in children's dictated stories.

1   Frank Smith, *Essays into Literacy*, Heinemann, London, 1983.
2   Akemi Tachibana, from 'Poems of Solitary Delights', trans. A. Thwaite and G. Bownas, in *The Penguin Book of Japanese Verse*, Penguin, Harmondsworth, 1964.
3   Margaret Meek, 'Prolegomena for a study of children's literature', in M. Benton (ed.), *Approaches to Children's Literature*, Southampton University, Department of Education, Southampton, 1980.
4   Deborah Tannen, 'Relative focus on involvement in oral and written discourse', in D. Owen and N. Torrance and A. Hildyard (eds), *Literacy, Language and Learning*, Cambridge University Press, Cambridge, 1985.
5   Arthur Applebee, *The Child's Concept of Story*, University of Chicago Press, Chicago, 1985.
6   Valerie Walkerdine, *Schoolgirl Fictions*, Verso, London, 1990.
7   *Ibid.*
8   Carolyn Steedman, *The Tidy House*, Virago, London, 1982.
9   Walkerdine, *Schoolgirl Fictions*.
10 Angela Carter, *The Virago Book of Fairy Tales*, Virago, London, 1989.

CHAPTER 12

'It's Only a Story, Isn't It?'
Creativity and Commitment in Writing for Children

Robert Leeson

In this challenging chapter, Robert Leeson examines the power of the writer. Stories themselves are powerful and the story-maker has to accept both the praise and the responsibility for the power unleashed by story. Tracing the ambivalent relationship between 'the scribe and the powers that be', Robert Leeson looks at didacticism in books for children, following a move from assertion of values to assumption of those values in story. 'A story will always be more than a story', and writers, he argues, cannot claim exemption from the political implications of the assumptions underlying the stories they tell.

In 1980, just after publication of the first of a series of books linked with the phenomenal *Grange Hill* TV series, I travelled to a town 'somewhere in England', as we used to say in the Second World War, for a book event.[1] The organizer invited me to have supper with her family and there were some 12 to 15 people at the long table – sons, daughters, in-laws – and at the head sat her husband, a newly retired police superintendent. Before we reached the main course he launched into a frontal attack on *Grange Hill* – responsible in his eyes for bad behaviour in the young generation. Everyone else sat in horrified silence, wondering if a row would break out. I chose to listen politely, hoping he would get it off his chest and we could then return to less explosive topics. But he pressed on. *Grange Hill* was the source of the crime wave. It ought not to be on TV, in books. It was not allowed in his home. The tirade was cut short only when the youngest person present, a 15-year-old boy, had the nerve to say: 'Dad, it's only a story, isn't it?'

Since then, I have often thought of that moment. I was grateful to the lad for his assertion that the writer had a welcome, traditional role as bringer of entertainment. Yet I had to admit the superintendent was right – not that *Grange Hill* caused the crime wave (which goes back farther than 1978) but that the writer has another traditional role – influencing, arousing, changing and challenging outlooks. Ever since the alphabet was first invented and used to record grain stocks and their distribution, the scribe has had an ambivalent relationship with the powers that be. It is no use writers saying their function is just to entertain. The dictionary definition of 'entertain' includes 'treat, receive, hold the attention and thoughts of, receive and take into consideration, keep and hold in the mind', among other things – a larger brief than transient amusement.

Traditionally the storyteller recognized the larger role. The skald (bard) who first recited the opening lines of *Beowulf* paused for an apparent aside ('That was a *good* king'). He was sending a signal, and both rulers and ruled knew he was. When the ruler of medieval Khorusan told his favourite storyteller that a new tale would win him land, castles, life-long tax-free income and the position of Grand Wazir, and failure would mean he could say farewell to his family, His Majesty may have been an exacting lover of style, but he knew also what the story did for and to its audience. 'O wise and subtle one, you have taught me many lessons', said another king of Shahrazad, on the thousand and first night. She embarked on her marathon not (as is sometimes said) to save her own life. As she told her anxious father, her aim was to wean the king from his murderous paranoia and thus save her fellow women.

It is not only a story, is it?

It is no use my accepting the applause of audiences of pupils and teachers one day, and on the next whingeing when a Divisional HMI tells me, 'You are alienating the child from the parent, the pupil from the teacher.' It is no good saying: 'What, me sir?' For the HMI, the superintendent, and King Shahryar were each in their way restating a basic fact – writers matter. Writers change people's perception of the world, and help change the world itself. And this applies particularly to those who write for children, transmitting society's heritage to the next generation. Not all voices raised want to censor, control, or silence. Some want to enlist writers in causes, or urge them to look again at how their writing reflects the world we live in. Writers have never lacked advice, and over the past two or three decades writers for children have been at the heart of the debate, sometimes stormy, over issues like racism, sexism and class bias. Now it seems we have a backlash against the 'politically correct'. Stephanie Nettell, for example, tells us that at the 1992 *Guardian* Children's Book Award discussions, where all the judges are writers, there was a pile of rejected books, 'victims of a ferocious rebellion against novels too obviously out to open children's eyes to the problems of society and human relationships, producing correct-thinking documentaries rather than literature'.[2]

There are other signs that teachers, librarians and parents (never mind those who thought the debate was all a Communist plot) are worried that the passion for guidelines may have overwhelmed the tender plant of creativity. Well, writers and the story are not all that delicate. But after the clamour there seems to be a pause for thought about where we all are. Is it the reactionary 1990s following the radical 1970s? Or is it the imagination breaking free from didactic commit-ment, a pendulum swing back to normality? No, I think something more complex and interesting is going on. Our 1970s–90s *Sturm und Drang* years seem at first like a speeded-up version of the century of children's literature from the 1780s to the 1880s. This earlier period (also one of profound technological and social change) brought to centre stage a distinctive group of people. Edward III would have called them 'the middling sort'; Queen Victoria called them 'the middle class'. Philosopher James Mill said they 'gave the nation its character'.[3]

Lacking as yet power, either by numbers or wealth, they were conscious of the crucial role of education – by the book. With their eyes on the future, they wanted an appropriate body of fiction and non-fiction for their children. John Newbery, the famous bookseller of the day, offered them books which would 'infallibly make Tommy a good boy and Polly a good girl'.[4] For ideological reasons they wanted to replace the existing oral tradition, the 'vain fantasies' as they called them of the folk-tale (told in the nursery by young servants freshly come from the villages), with meaningful stories, in books. Tom Thumb and Jack the Giant Killer were to go, because in the contemporary judgement:

> These ill-consorted, artless lies
> Our British youth shall now despise.[5]

Or as Lady Eleanor Fenn wrote in 1783, middle-class children should not receive 'their first notions from the most illiterate persons'.[6] It was a campaign to change the story or its impact on the young generation as inevitable and as deliberate in its way as the drive against the 'isms' two hundred years later.

In the year Eleanor Fenn was writing, Thomas Day began work on the seminal story *Sandford and Merton*, about the civilizing of a spoiled rich brat. Social rank, said Day, was essential, but it was a duty not a privilege, and those who held it should show 'they regretted the necessity of their elevation'.[7] The many authors who followed Day were not equally genial and their output was often grim, humourless and hardly entertaining in any sense of the word. This applied often to radical as much as to conservative writing. 'I do not see', wrote Ernest Jones, the Chartist leader, 'why truth should always be dressed in stern and repulsive garb. The more attractive you make her, the more easily she will progress.'[8] Eventually there was a reaction.

In the 1840s, when Thomas Hughes wrote *Tom Brown's Schooldays* (another pioneering book), he said it should be 'a real novel for boys, not didactic like *Sandford and Merton*, written in the right spirit, but distinctly aiming at being amusing'.[9] It has been fashionable (on one side of our twentieth-century debate) to see this earlier transitional period as one in which fantasy triumphed over the didactic impulse, giving birth to a Golden Age of 'pure' literature. Late nineteenth-century books like *Treasure Island*[10] (with its 'lordly disregard for the moralists') and *Alice's Adventures in Wonderland*[11] with its apparent absence of meaning, are often cited to prove the point. But I would assert that *Treasure Island* is in one way memorable because of its moral core. Young Puritan Jim Hawkins repudiates Livesey's assurance that a promise given to a blackguard does not count with the assertion that his word is his bond. And the Duchess slyly tells Alice: 'There's a moral there if you know how to find it.'[12] Carroll is encouraging his young heroine (and reader) to look sceptically at everything taught – people do not always mean what they say. Alice ends by upsetting the whole pack of cards – as subversive in its subliminal way as Stevenson's rattling good yarn is morally bracing.

Charles Dickens was emphatic that the fairy-tale 'taught forbearance, courtesy, consideration for the poor and aged, kind treatment of animals, love of nature, abhorrence of tyranny and brute force'.[13] Few contemporaries would have challenged him on this – the issue was not what children's books were about, but how they should be written. Alexander Strachan, magazine editor, defined the children's literature of the 1870s as one in which, 'the spirit of divine obligation and human service must be everywhere present though nowhere obtruded'.[14] What we see here is the evolution of the literature from the stage of assertion of its principles to that of assumption of its values.

George MacDonald, the great Victorian fantasy writer, declared that fairy-tales were not allegories. He said wryly that it was almost impossible to write an allegory which was not a weariness of the spirit.[15] But the link between outer and inner reality was real.

'The natural world has laws, but they themselves suggest laws of other kinds and a man may, if he pleases, invent a little world with its own laws'.[16] In his autobiographical *Surprised by Joy*, C. S. Lewis describes his childhood habit of creating and populating mind-worlds, which served him well when he came to write the Narnia books.[17] There in the Narnia chronicles you have a piece of religious didacticism woven into a story which has charmed millions of unsuspecting young readers. George MacDonald could (time-lag apart) have been describing the Narnia books when he wrote: 'While without doubt for instance that I was actively regarding a scene of activity, I might at the same time be aware that I was perusing a metaphysical argument.'[18] Without the inner core of meaning the artistic work is not memorable. But until that meaning has the force of an assumption rather than an assertion, it is difficult for the artistic design to be memorably realized.

The trouble with assumptions is that they are based upon shifting sands. Society, the outer world of human beings is in constant flux. Thomas Hughes, founder of the school story, believed that the British Empire (and, by extension, his way of life) would last forever. So did my junior school headmistress before the Second World War. She would point to the map and say: 'See, our country is the centre of the world.'[19] At secondary school, however, a geography teacher showed us how, on the globe, every country is at the centre. The assumptions of the literature of the Victorians (which persisted for the first half of our century) – that one country, or one race, or one class, or one gender, for that matter, shall be seen as the epicentre of human life and the epitome of art – could not continue.

Let me take the most striking – even grotesque – example of a literary assumption – that 95 per cent of schools and pupils did not exist ('In England, all boys go to public school', said Tom Brown).[20] For more than a century the school story maintained – if I may put it so – this fiction. In the 1970s, change overtook the literature. This was not due to any aesthetic considerations. Pure aesthetic criticism never changed anything. Indeed conventional critics continued to review school stories '*sui generis*', which is Latin for 'I know this is rubbish but I happen to like it.'

In the 1960s I was often told by publishers that day school pupils liked boarding school stories and that was it. Well, the assumption collapsed because of external pressure, from teachers, librarians and some writers with social inclinations, and because of television and its audience (which brings us back to *Grange Hill*). It is true that early comprehensive school stories were sometimes self-conscious, sometimes overly 'political'. But that was in the stage of assertion – the new assertion that all children counted, not just those above the literary Plimsoll Line. But can anyone say that the new school story, embracing all schoolchildren, with creators like Gene Kemp, Berlie Doherty, Jan Mark, Bernard Ashley *et al.*, is not stylistically and aesthetically a match for, if not superior to, the tired literature which existed before the 1970s? What we have now is – in a double sense – a comprehensive school story, with Jennings and Chalet School reprints at one end of the spectrum and Grange Hill at the other.

And the same may be said about the whole range of children's literature, fantasy, humour, historical, which has emerged from the past couple of decades, because what we have now is not simply a rerun of the earlier process of a century ago. Then the universalities of the old folk-tale were exchanged for the narrow particularities of one stratum of society. From our twentieth-century time of assertion into assumption, we have begun to achieve a literature which reflects the lives of *all* children, recapturing the breadth of the oral tradition and also meriting the term of 'folk'.

This has not been a comfortable time for writers, however, with pressures and demands from all sorts of well-meaning people, particularly those who expect writers to react immediately to what Shostakovitch ironically called 'just criticism'.[21] Lobbyists, enthusiasts of all kinds, do not always take account of the complex and contradictory nature of creativity, the blend of the explainable and the unexplainable, the calculated and the fortuitous, the conscious and the unconscious – the inspiration and the perspiration.

Writing arises from the interaction of the conscious and unconscious mind. The flights of fancy must be ordered and subjected to the critique of the aware mind; recorded dreams do not make sense in stories. Likewise the products of the conscious mind must be subjected to the critique of the inner one – what we know as 'sleeping on it'. Our fictional imaginary world owes its origins to real life, but indirectly, like rain which, falling on the ground, seeps through many strata, all with trace elements, before it reaches bed rock and lies, unseen, to be drawn up as water from the well. It is not, as some people appear to think, like going to the tap and filling the bucket. The unconscious mind may be more deeply political than the conscious, more deeply convinced and convincing, yet ignorant of its real-world sources, while free from the compromises and contrivances of the conscious mind. One mind deals more in assertions, the other more in assumptions.

The writer may appear to move in the wake of the social reformer, but, working at a deeper level, may achieve truths which by being timeless will always be ahead of the field. Writers, like anyone else, will not be pushed around. But neither should they hide from the world, nor claim exemption from its laws and rules. If we are willing to take the land, castles, tax-free income and Wazir's turban, then we have to risk the alternatives. Praise, reward, pressure and demands alike remind us we have a special place in the world, as writers. A story will always be more than a story and it will always elude attempts to pin it down completely.

In my book, *The Last Genie*, sequel to *The Third Class Genie* and *Genie on the Loose*, Alec the hero embarks on a time-space journey, to save his old friend the genie Abu Salem.[22] To do this he engages in a riddle contest with Dahnash the Prince of Darkness. This is won when Alec asks:

'What has no legs but travels swifter than a horse? What has no body but lives in many cities at once? What makes us laugh and cry in the same

moment? What costs nothing yet enriches all? What lasts but a short time, but endures for ever? What is easily forgotten but always remembered? What seems to lie but always tells the truth? What takes the poor wife from her cooking pot and the king from his council chamber? He who brings it, leaves it behind and takes it away with him. What is it?'
I leave the answer to you.

Notes

1   Robert Leeson, *Grange Hill Rules OK*, BBC and Fontana Lions, 1980; *Grange Hill Goes Wild*, BBC and Fontana Lions, 1980; *Grange Hill for Sale*, BBC and Fontana Lions, 1981; *Grange Hill Home and Away*, BBC and Fontana Lions, 1982.
2   Stephanie Nettell, *The Bookseller*, 13 March 1992.
3   James Mill, *Westminster Review*, 1826 quoted in Brian Simon, *Studies in the History of Education, 1780–1870*, 1960.
4   John Newbury, quoted in F.J. Harvey Darton, *Children's Books in England*, Cambridge University Press, 1932.
5   Niky Rathbone, *Mirth Without Mischief: An Introduction to the Parker Collection of Early Children's Books and Games*, The Library Association, London, 1982.
6   Eric Quayle, *Early Children's Books*, David and Charles, Newton Abbot, 1983.
7   Thomas Day, *Sandford and Merton*, 1783–9.
8   Ernest Jones, quoted in Martha Vicinus, *The Industrial Muse*, Croom Helm, 1974.
9   Thomas Hughes, quoted in Edward C. Mack and W.H.G. Armitage, *Thomas Hughes: The Life of the Author of 'Tom Brown's Schooldays'*, 1952.
10   Robert Louis Stevenson, *Treasure Island*, 1883.
11   Lewis Carroll, *Alice's Adventures in Wonderland*, 1865.
12   *Ibid.*
13   Charles Dickens, *Household Words*, 1 October 1853.
14   Alexander Strachan, *Bad Literature for the Young*, first published 1875, *Signal Reprint*, 20 May 1976.
15   George MacDonald, *The Fantastic Imagination*, first published 1908, *Signal Reprint*, 16 January 1975.
16   C.S. Lewis, *The Chronicles of Narnia* in seven volumes, Geoffrey Bles, London, 1950–56.
17   C.S. Lewis, *Surprised by Joy: the Story of My Early Life*, Geoffrey Bles, London, 1955.
18   MacDonald, *The Fantastic Imagination*.
19   Thomas Hughes, quoted in Patrick Howarth, *Play Up and Play the Game*, Eyre/Methuen, London, 1973.
20   Thomas Hughes, *Tom Brown's Schooldays*, 1857.
21   Dmitri Shostakovich, dedicatory note on his Fifth Symphony, 1938.
22   *Third Class Genie*, 1973; *Genie on the Loose*, 1984; *The Last Genie*, 1993.

Eaten Father, Eaten Mother

Ben Haggarty

Accompanied by the sound of a rolling drum, Ben Haggerty asks a member of the audience,
   'How does a fairy-tale begin?' The reply is 'Once upon a time'.
   'Are you sure? Just once?'
   'Yes, just once upon a time.'
   'Good. Well then . . .'

Once upon a time, not twice upon a time, not three times upon a time, just once, once and never again there was, and there was not . . . a kingdom – and it was Red. Everything in that kingdom was Red! Red! Red! Hot, baked clay. There was a king – and he was the Red King and there was a queen, and she was the Red Queen. And the Red King and his Red Queen had three sons. The eldest son was a fine son. The second son was a fine son – but the third son – well, they weren't too sure about him – you see, from the day of his birth to beyond his eighteenth birthday not one sound had ever passed between his lips or through his throat. In the eyes of his parents the boy was dumb – he was a fool, he was mute. He was shame upon the family. They ignored him. They bullied him. They neglected him. They even forgot his eighteenth birthday.

And one of the reasons they forgot his eighteenth birthday was because there had been another birth that day. An extraordinary thing had happened. The queen had given birth to a baby girl.

'Oh! a girl, a daughter,' said the king. 'She will grow up to be a princess that I can fuss over and spoil.'

The queen said, 'Ah, she will grow up to be almost as beautiful as me,' and the two eldest brothers, they said, 'A little sister to look after and protect.'

And the youngest son, he said . . . he said nothing.

150

A strange thing happened, that night security must have been very lax, because a thief got into the castle. Somehow the thief got into the kitchen, ripped open the larder door and ate all the royal food and smashed half the royal plates. The king was furious. He spoke to the captain of the guard.

'Captain of the guard! You and your men are not doing their duty! Double the guard.'

The next night the guard was doubled, but somehow that thief got in – in to the kitchen, opened up the larder door, ate all the new food that had been bought and smashed the other half of the plates. The king was furious.

'Triple the guard!'

The guard was tripled but the third night the same thing happened – food gone, plates smashed.

'Post a sentry on the door!'

A warrior woman with a great spear, she was there – ooof, strong! But the following morning she was found sound asleep.

'She's no good! Put another warrior there!'

Another warrior was put there, but the following morning he was found sound asleep, too. Food gone – plates broken. Another warrior put there – but he too was sound asleep. Eventually the king said to the captain of the guards,

'You do it yourself! Show them how to work.'

But he too fell asleep. Food gone – plates broken. Finally the king was furious and he turned to his eldest son and said,

'Show them how to guard a door. Here, take my sword.'

And he gave it to the eldest son. The eldest son sat all night with his father's sword. But the following morning, what had happened? Food gone – plates broken.

'You're no son of mine!' He turned to the second son. 'If you succeed in guarding this door you will inherit my crown. Take my sword.'

So the second son was there, but he too fell asleep. So who could he put in front of that door?

The third son came and stood before his father. The king hesitated – but then offered him his sword. The son wouldn't take it. Instead he went to his mother's room and from her chest of drawers took out her sewing basket. He opened the sewing basket and took out the pin cushion. He removed all the pins and took four long iron needles and pushed them through the little cushion. Then he went and sat in front of the door, resting his head on the cushion, with the four long needles just pricking the back of his skull. He wasn't going to sleep!

Nine o'clock came, and went. Ten o'clock came, and went. Eleven o'clock came, and went. Then somewhere in the distance a bell sounded midnight and, when the twelfth chime faded to quiet, from somewhere deep inside the castle, came a strange sound – a music . . . and with it a strong desire to sleep. His head fell back – he got a sharp jab! Again his head was heavy, two times, three times . . . suddenly with a fourth jab he was more awake than he had ever been in his life. He was going to find the source of this noise. So he left the kitchen. He went down the corridors. He went up a flight of stairs. He turned left into the corridor that led to his mother's room – the door was open. He stared in.

That little baby sister of his – she was floating up from her cot. Her head went up. Her feet went down. The coverlet that was on her fell back into the cot. Slowly she did one somersault in the air; she did two somersaults in the air; she did three somersaults in the air. And then *there she was!!* Huge and fat and naked, with teeth like iron axe blades and fingernails like razor blades and with a great shriek – *Yeeuch!!* She went flying past his head. *Yeeuch!!* – down the corridor. *Yeeuch!* down the stairs. *Yeeuch!!* along the corridor. *Yell!* into the kitchen. She ripped open the larder door and *yuch! yuch! yuch!* she stuffed all the food down into her face! And then *smash! smash! smash!* – she smashed all the plates. *Yeeuch!* – she flew back to her room. She did one somersault, two somersaults, three somersaults . . . shrank and fell back quietly to sleep in her cot. The youngest son was standing there his mouth open, his jaw dropped. And he was still there when the cock crowed to bring on the dawn.

The king woke up and saw his son. The king said, 'What have you seen?'

The boy said, 'What have I seen? What have I not seen?'

The king said, 'You just spoke! – what have you seen?'

The boy said, 'What have I seen . . .? What have I not seen . . .? Father', he said, 'give me a horse.'

The queen woke up 'Our boy is speaking! He has never spoken before!'

'Father', he said, 'give me a horse.'

'He has never asked us for anything before, you'd better do as he says.'

And with that the father took the boy down to the stables. There, early in the morning, the boy selected a beautiful, fine grey mare. The father saddled it for the boy and the boy was up there and out into the court yard. The father looked at the boy and said, 'Where are you going?'

And the boy said, 'Where am I going? I'm going to get married.'

'Well, if you're going to get married then you need some money,' and the king disappeared and came back with a stone box full of gold. 'Here, take this.'

The boy took it. Then he looked at his father, then he looked at the castle and *Whoosh* – he rode straight out of the courtyard. Down through the streets of the city, and out through the city wall, out through the fields that were all around the city.

It was still very early in the morning. There was hardly anyone about
. . . smoke rising from breakfast fires. He didn't need this where he was
going. He didn't need money. He saw a well and stopped the horse and
got off. He took the stone box, took three paces to the west of the well
and buried the gold there. Then he got back on the horse and he rode,
and he rode, and he rode for the whole of that day. Then, when it was
getting dark, he said to himself, 'I'm not going to sleep.' So he rode for
the whole night. Then he rode for the whole of the next day, and said,
'I'm not going to sleep.' So he rode for the whole of the next night. He
rode for the whole of the week, and he rode for the whole of the next
week. He rode for the whole of the month, and he rode for the whole of
the next month. He rode for the whole of the year. He rode for a year
and a day . . . until he came to a huge forest.

At the edge of the forest there was a hut, and sitting on a bench
outside the hut was a beautiful woman, the most beautiful woman you
can imagine. And she looked up and she said, 'You look tired.'

He said, 'I am tired. I've just ridden for a year and a day.'

She said, 'Then, get off your horse and spend the night with me.'

He looked at her and she was very beautiful and he said, 'Maybe I
will.' As he was getting off the horse, she stood up and he noticed that
in her hand she had a small silver penknife attached to her belt with a
small chain. Between her fingers was a small piece of wood and she just
whittled it away to nothing.

'Come indoors.'

Whether he slept with her that night or just slept that night, I do not
know – the story doesn't say, but the following morning he was up
early and he was saddling the horse and he was away. She said, 'Wait,
wait, where are you going?'

He said, 'I'm just going.'

She said, 'No, stay – I like you, please stay. Where are you going in
such a rush?'

He said, 'Where am I going? Where am I going? I will tell you where I
am going. I am going to find a place where there is no death.'

She said, 'Then get off your horse because it's here with me.'

He said, 'How do you mean – here?'

She said, 'You saw what happened last night. Each evening I go to
one of these trees, I break off a twig, I whittle it down into shavings, I
blow it away. Only when I have whittled down the whole of this forest
will old age and death take me.'

He looked at the forest, and it was huge, then he looked at her. 'Even
so one day this forest will all be gone and if I were to marry you, old age
and death would take you, and then old age and death would take me.
I'm sorry, I'm not able to stay here.' With that he rode straight through
the forest and when he came to the other side he stopped and listened –
and it's just as well he did, because this is what he heard:

> Eaten father.
> Eaten mother.
> Eaten both your elder brothers.
> Now it's time for you!

No it isn't . . .

And he rode. And he rode, and he rode, and he rode. And he rode for the whole of that day, and he rode for the whole of that night, and he rode for the whole of the next day, and he rode for the whole of the next night, and he rode for the whole of the week, and he rode for the whole of the next week. He rode for the whole of the month. He rode for the whole of the next month. He rode for the whole of the year. He rode for a year and a day. Until he came to a huge mountain and there there was a hut and sitting outside on a bench was a beautiful woman and she said, 'You look tired.'

He said, 'I am.'

She said, 'Why don't you stop for the night?'

And he looked at her and said, 'Maybe I will.' As he was getting off his horse, he noticed a little black bird with a yellow beak landed on her finger and she took from her pocket a small silver spoon attached to a chain and went to the side of the mountain and stuck it in and fed that bird three granules of granite. The bird flew away. They went indoors.

Whether he slept with her that night or just slept, I do not know – the story doesn't say. The following morning he was saddling the horse and she was saying, 'Where are you going?'

He said, 'Where am I going? I am going to find a place where there is no death.'

'Then get off your horse because it's here with me.'

He said, 'How here?'

She said, 'You saw what happened. Each evening that bird comes. Each evening I feed it a teaspoon full of this mountain. Only when the whole mountain has been fed to the bird will old age and death take me.'

He looked at her and he looked at the bird, and he said, 'Even so, one day this mountain will be gone. If I was to marry you old age and death would take you and old age and death would take me and I want to be where there is no death.' With that he rode to the top of the mountain – and he stopped and he turned and he listened – and it's just as well he did because this is what he heard:

> Eaten father.
> Eaten mother.
> Eaten both your elder brothers.
> Now it's time for you!

No it isn't . . .

He rode down the other side of the mountain. And he rode. And he rode. And he rode, and he rode, and he rode. And he rode for the whole of that day, and he rode for the whole of that night, and he rode for the whole of the next day, and he rode for the whole of the next night, and he rode for the whole of the week, and he rode for the whole of the next week. He didn't sleep. He rode for the whole of the month and he rode for the whole of the next month. He rode for the whole of the year. He rode for a year and a day, until he couldn't ride any more. He couldn't because he had come to the edge of the world – and what is the edge of the world? The sea. He couldn't go any further so he went along the beach, and he came to a hut, and sitting outside on a bench was, guess who? Another beautiful woman. And she said, 'You look tired.'

He said, 'I am tired.'

She said, 'Why don't you stop for the night?'

And he looked at her and said, 'Maybe I will.'

As he was getting off his horse, he noticed that she stood up and went and looked along the edge of the gently lapping waves and then she took out a teaspoon, bent down and fed a teaspoon of the sea to a tiny fish.

Whether he slept with her that night or just slept, I do not know – the story doesn't say. The following morning he was saddling up his horse and she was saying, 'Where are you going?'

And he said, 'I've got to go.'

She said, 'But I like you – please stay here.'

He said, 'No, I've got to go.'

She said, 'Where is it you've got to go?'

He said, 'I'm looking for a place where there is no death.'

She said, 'Then it is here, at the edge of the world – it's here, get off your horse.'

He said, 'How?'

She said, 'You saw what I did. Each evening I feed that fish a teaspoon of the sea. Only when the whole ocean has been fed to the fish will old age and death take me.'

He said, 'Even so, one day it will be gone. If I married you old age and death would take you and old age and death would take me.'

She said, 'But there is nowhere else for you to go.'

He said, 'I don't care, I'm going.'

And he rode along the beach, and he stopped and turned and he listened . . . and it's just as well he did because what he heard was:

> Eaten father,
> Eaten mother.
> Eaten both your elder brothers.
> Now it's time for you!

No it isn't . . .

He said, 'Horse, my fine mare, you have ridden well this far, you have ridden well. Can you swim?' Without hesitation she lunged into the sea and she swam. And she swam. And she swam, and she swam, and she swam, and she swam, and she swam, and she swam. And she swam for the whole of that day, and she swam for the whole of that night, and she swam for the whole of the next day, and she swam for the whole of the next night, and she swam for the whole of the week, she swam for the whole of the next week, she swam for the whole of the month and she swam for the whole of the next month, she swam for a year. She swam for a year and a day and, at last, her hoofs were there, on the farthest shore. Now the boy – he'd had his first chance to speak, and now it was the horse's turn. She said, 'You've ridden me well this far, but the farthest and hardest part of the journey lies ahead. Ahead is the plain of regret. If we stop or hesitate here, even for a moment, we're doomed, but in the saddle you'll find a whip. Beat yourself twelve times with it and beat me twenty-four times – don't hestitate.'

The boy took the whip and he beat himself and he beat the horse and he went across the plain of regret – and suddenly there was a lush green valley ahead of him with fruits, green fruits, sweet smells, flowers and buzzing bees.

The horse said, 'This is worse. This is the valley of grief. Beat yourself twenty-four times. Beat me forty-eight times.'

So he beat himself and he beat the horse and he galloped across the lush green valley of grief until there was a clatter and a clang, and now the horse was climbing over a mountain made of pure copper. When they had crossed that, there was a mountain of pure silver, and when they had crossed that there was a mountain made of pure gold.

At the place where the three mountains, gold, silver and copper, met, there was a hut, but there was no bench, there was just an empty doorway. And the one on the horse stopped. A voice said, "Who are you?'

And he said, 'I'm the one who is trying to cross the world, looking for a place where there is no death.'

'Then you've found it.'

'How?' he said.

The voice said, 'I am the Lord of the Wind. I was here before the world was created. I'll be here long after the world is destroyed. In this place there is no death.'

'We'll see about that', said the one on the horse and he rode to the top of the mountain made of copper. He turned and he listened. What did he hear? . . . The wind. So he turned and he rode to the top of the mountain made of silver. What did he hear? . . . The wind. So he turned and he rode to the top of the mountain made of gold. He turned and listened and he heard nothing but the wind. So back to the hut he went and he said, 'Can I stay in this place?'

'Yes,' said the voice. 'Stay here, hunt in these mountains, but whatever you do don't go into the valley of grief or on to the plain of regret.'

So the boy unsaddled the grey mare and he hunted in those mountains and he stayed there for a very, very, very, long time . . .

But then one day he was walking by the lush green valley of grief and there were trees and flowers and lush red fruits, and one of them looked so sweet – it was just out of reach. It was a hot day and he wanted it, and he reached for it, and he stretched. As he reached for it, a slight movement of wind moved the branch. He stumbled into the grass. As he did that the fruit came away in his hand. He bit it. But it was bitter and suddenly welling out of his heart, like a waterfall in his chest, were tears, streaming down his face, and he was sitting down.

'What is this I'm feeling?' And then in his mind's eye, he saw visions of his mother and his father and his two elder brothers. Even though most of his life they had bullied him and ignored him, they were his kith and his kin and more than anything else he wanted to see them. He wandered across the valley of grief and onto a dusty plain – and on to the plain of regret. And in his mind's eye he saw some one else and suddenly he regretted one thing more than anything else . . . '*I must warn them about my baby sister!*'

With that he ran back and he got the saddle and he saddled the mare and said, 'We're off' and with that they rode.

But a voice said, 'Where are you going?'

'I'm going home.'

'Where is home?'

'It's the City of the Red King.'

'The City of the Red King? The City of the Red King is gone.'

'What do you mean it's gone?'

'You've been here a very long time.'

'So!'

'The City of the Red King is long gone. In that place now they just grow watermelons.'

'Watermelons? I don't believe you. How do you know?'

'I am the wind and I was blowing there only this afternoon.'

'Watermelons? On my father's city? I don't believe it.'

And with that he rode. And he rode. And he rode, and he rode, and he rode. And he rode across an enormous desert of dust. In the distance he saw a hut. He rode up to the hut. He stopped and there, sitting on a bench was an old, old, old, old woman. She looked up and she said, 'It's you. You've come back? I waited for you but it's too late now.'

He looked down and he saw that in her hand there was a teaspoon and in a tiny little puddle of water was the fish. She scooped up the water and fed it to the fish. The fish closed its lips and the scales fell off the fish, then the flesh fell off the fish, the bones crumbled to dust and the wind blew it away. She looked at him and then the spark was gone from her eyes and she slumped forward and her hair fell off and she crumbled into bones and dust and the wind blew her away.

And the one with the horse, he said, 'Watermelons! In my father's city? I don't believe it.' And he rode. And he rode. And he rode and he rode and he rode. And he rode across more desert until he came to a second hut. It was the same. Another old woman was there. She said, 'I waited for you. Why were you so long? It's too late.'

And he looked and already on her finger was the little bird. She took up the last three granules of granite and fed them to the bird. The bird fell off, dead. The feathers fell off the bird, the flesh fell off, the bones crumbled to dust and were blown away. She too crumbled to dust and was blown away. He said, 'No! Not on my father's city.'

And he rode until he found another hut and there was the third old, old woman and she said, 'Why were you so long? It's too late.'

Between her fingers was less than half a matchstick of wood that she whittled away. She blew the wood away. She blew the flesh from her fingers. She crumbled to dust . . .

'Not on my father's city!' And he rode, and he rode, and he rode, and he rode, and he rode . . . and he came to an enormous field of watermelons. As the mare went slowly across, great green fruits broke open under her hooves – red inside. He looked around and saw an old man. He rode up to him, and said, 'Hey you, tell me which way to the City of the Red King.'

'Who?'

'The Red King – my father.'

'The Red King? The only Red King I've ever heard of is in stories, fairy-tales that my grandfather used to tell me.'

'Where is the City of the Red King?'

'There's no such thing.'

'There was once a city here. Where do you get your water from?'

The old man said, 'The well.'

'Is it far from here?'

'No, not really.'

'Take me to the well.'

They went to the well and the boy got off the horse. 'I'll prove to you that once there was a Red City here and once there was a Red King – it's true. Can I borrow your spade?'

The boy took three paces to the west of the well. He said, 'I'll prove it,' and he dug. And he dug, and he dug, and he dug, and he dug. He dug a very deep hole and then suddenly he hit something and on his knees he pulled out the stone box. 'Here,' he said, 'I'll prove it. That's a picture of my father there.'

The old man had never seen gold in his life and it was soft and dull and glowing. He bit it and his teeth made a mark. The old man said, 'Where did you get it from?'

And the boy began to tell the story.

He was so engrossed in telling the story to the old man, that he didn't notice that when he picked up the very last coin something small and white went . . . flip – up into the air. It turned round once, it turned round twice, it turned round three times and there she was. Gross and fat and naked with teeth like iron axe blades and fingernails like razor blades, sitting there, towering above the boy. She said, 'If only you could have waited but one day more. I, who am your death, would have died, but because you took that fruit you returned and all I have to say is . . . I've

> Eaten father.
> Eaten mother.
> Eaten both your elder brothers.
> Now it's time for you!

And she ate up the boy.

And she ate up the horse.

And she vanished.

And as for the farmer, he stumbled towards the village made of mud and sticks where the beggars lived. He started throwing the gold coins out, saying to each person, 'Take this and pray for my soul. Take this and pray for my soul. Take these and pray for my soul.'

And they said, 'Old man, old man what's the matter? What have you seen?'

And he said, 'What have I seen? *What have I not seen?*'

Notes

Adapted from four East European traditional tales.

PART III

Beyond the Word

Beyond words are other words written by talented authors of the past and present with a story to tell. Then there are the unspoken words, the pictures that say something different from the printed words, and the words that together form 'memorable speech', which is poetry. In the closing part of the book, four writers show us just what words can do and explore the secret places where there are gaps between words. What cannot be written about in adult literature is passed over in silence: children's literature is a place where strong feelings between children and parents can be written about and, indeed, illustrated.

Literature is composed of these 'other words'. Ben Haggarty's dramatic story reminds us how extraordinary ordinary words can be and powerfully claims a place for the oral tradition as literature. Victor Watson shows what a fine line there is between what is written for and about children. The neat juxtaposition of his title, 'Children's literature and literature's children', invites the reader to consider the very basis of children in fiction, as well as fiction *for* children. He also makes us aware of an imaginative chasm at the heart of the Victorian novel: few writers seemed able or willing to write naturally about affection and respect between parents and children. Sentimentality about and authority over children were there in abundance, but it took writers for children, mostly women, to begin writing honestly and tenderly about love (and loss and difficulty) within families. In fact, Victor Watson even suggests that within the everyday discourse of novels for children, writers started to heal the breach between the generations.

Anthony Browne is also interested in probing layers of significance in his portrayal of relationships within families, recognizing the communication gap that can sometimes exist. His texts are often deceptively simple but, counterpointed with illustrations, provoke readers to find

161

new meanings, complex undertones and jarring recognitions. He has brought a new dimension to the genre of picture books. Many of his books explore loneliness, fragmentation, confusion, and unhappiness as it is experienced by children who all too often suffer in silence. Browne's adults are rarely cruel, but they find it hard to express warmth and experience closeness with their children. His powerful artwork echoes the disturbance in lives fractured by divorce, separation, sexism, the birth of a new baby, with all its ambiguities, puzzles, questions and transformations. The difficulties are sometimes healed by animals, like Gorilla, who find an easy rapport with Browne's child characters. The fact that Anthony Browne does often deal with painful aspects of the human condition is tempered by a glorious sense of humour, visually expressed.

Fred Sedgwick's concern is the gap between poetic language and everyday words, 'the music of the ordinary' as he calls it. He is passionate about the power of poetry to transform lives, but wants to remove its pretensions. And in a scathing attack on the mechanistic, élitist, testing mentality which dominates the thinking about English teaching at present, Sedgwick asks for the unthinkable – time in the curriculum for children to explore their obsessions. He reminds us that real education is risky, open-ended, untidy and essentially humane. The pivotal point in his chapter is a teacher responding to a poem written by a child, not as a tester or judge, but as an interested reader with a positive, yet tentative, suggestion to make. 'We are searching,' as Sedgwick says, 'for those moments when the imagination glimmers, and is not snuffed.' Quite so.

Jill Paton Walsh once said that writing for children is a way of loving them. In her chapter we not only see a caring and responsible author at work: we gain insights into the workings of the creative art of writing. Childhood incidents, half-remembered fragments of her past, historical events and her own unique imagination are woven together with consummate skill into a vivid investigation of where her inspiration comes from. In a finely observed account, Jill Paton Walsh shows how history (personal and communal), memory and imagination fuse together to make literature. The prose and the passion, indeed: what better place to end?

CHAPTER 13

Children's Literature and Literature's Children

Victor Watson

'The history of children's fiction is inseparable from the history of childhood in fiction.' In a highly original chapter, Victor Watson considers how constructions of childhood have been reflected in literature, from Tom Thumb's Folio *of the 1760s to Wordsworth's poetry, from Dorothy Wordsworth's journal to the ending of* The Railway Children. *In tracing this compelling history, Victor Watson discovered an empty space within adult fiction: there were no genuine or persuasive accounts of love between parents and children in Victorian novels and, indeed, precious little since. Victor Watson goes on to suggest that children's authors have breached that gap by making affection between adults and children a central concern. He takes the reader on an exciting journey whose landscape includes the history of children in our culture, as well as their books.*

Children's literature does not have its own history apart from the thought of the times; it has no momentum and no tradition in its own separate sequence. At every point in their past, children's books have been caught up in the great imaginative and cultural upheavals of history. In particular, they assume the central significance and 'specialness' of children in our culture.

Ours is a culture preoccupied with childhood. It is my purpose in this chapter to argue that children's literature registers that centrality, confirms it and provides for it. Mainstream adult literature, on the other hand, has hardly addressed it at all. What distinguishes children's books from adult books about childhood is not that they are easier or more optimistic, nor that the subject-matter is more sheltered, nor that they are truncated fictions which stop when the characters enter adulthood. I believe that children's literature in the United Kingdom has defined for itself an important imaginative role which adult literature has shown little interest in assuming.

In Hugh Scott's *The Haunted Sand*, this short conversation takes place between Frisby and her mother about the mother's second husband:

> 'Darren said murder.'
>
> 'I don't think it was murder. Though you were nearly murdered when you came in with your coat . . .' Mother drank her tea. 'I expect I'll remember in the bath, or during the night, when there's nobody to tell.'
>
> 'Your George will be home tomorrow.'
>
> 'Yes.' Mother smiled. Her gaze drifted around the kitchen and Frisby knew she was thinking about her husband; seeing through the kitchen walls with their tall cupboards, to the other rooms, quaintly grand, and the views north, of curved fields; and to the front, houses built this century, red brick and flat gardens.
>
> 'You do like him?' Mother's eyes warmed suddenly on Frisby.
>
> 'It's been two years!' said Frisby.
>
> 'But you do?'
>
> 'You know I do. And you love him a lot, don't you?'
>
> Mother nodded.
>
> 'Better than Daddy?'
>
> 'Better?' sighed Mother. 'That's not a question you should ask. There's no real answer. Different. But, oh, so good! We change, Frisby.'[1]

It is a feature of Scott's narratives that the parents are almost as involved as the child characters in the strange, often supernatural, events he writes about. And the children and the parents talk to each other. As in this extract, parent and child (except for the mother's irritation about the muddy coat) talk and listen to one another, directly and comfortably, as equals, seeking to understand.

It is an unremarkable piece of writing – except for the fact that such converstions occur infrequently in children's fiction and hardly ever in adult fiction. There are numerous fictional scenes which concern themselves with parental hierarchies of authority, cruelty or neglect; and there are countless fictional examples of parents and children *failing* to understand one another. But I challenge the reader to call to mind two or three episodes in adult fiction in which parent and child are convincingly portrayed – without irony – talking and listening to one another, affectionately, and taking each other seriously as equals in mutual and loving respect.

Our culture has not always been preoccupied with children. It is becoming apparent that there occurred around the end of the eighteenth century a gigantic cultural shift which Edward Shorter has described as a 'revolution in maternal love'.[2] Shorter believes that there is a well-documented body of research which indicates that – at all social levels – children were beaten into silence when they cried, left unattended for hours in filthy swaddling clothes, and subjected to various practices arising from ignorance of hygiene and child-rearing. There are difficulties with this reading of the history of the family. One is the complexity of the social and economic factors which influenced the treatment of infants; another is the impossibility of precise dating; yet another is Shorter's sources. Nevertheless, there seems little doubt that – at a time which closely coincided with what we know as the Romantic period – there occurred a slow and incalculable cultural shift in which adults sought a new significance in children, and believed that this significance could be found only through an increase in parental love and tenderness. Linda Pollock – more cautiously – suggests that parents became 'more ostentatiously concerned with the state of childhood.'[3] This development probably had its origins in those God-fearing Puritan families of the seventeenth century, was handed down in less austere forms within the Dissenting tradition, and finally became socially acceptable approximately two hundred years ago.

It seems increasingly clear that during the Romantic period children were brought in from the cold and placed at the centre of family life. Before that, although there had been in eighteenth-century England an increasingly affectionate interest in children, writers assumed that there were unbridgeable differences between children and adults; and they were seen primarily as *differences of scale*. Children were regarded affectionately but warily, and with a repeated emphasis on their smallness. They were seen as small people in need of small stories in

TOM THUMB's

F O L I O;

OR, A NEW

PENNY PLAY-THING

FOR

LITTLE GIANTS.

To which is prefixed,

An ABSTRACT of

The LIFE of Mr. THUMB,

AND

An Hiftorical ACCOUNT of the

WONDERFUL DEEDS he performed.

Together with

Some ANECDOTES refpecting

GRUMBO the Great GIANT.

LONDON:

Printed for the People of all Nations; and fold by T. CARNAN, Succeffor to Mr. J. NEWBERY, in St. Paul's Church-Yard, 1776.

[Price One Penny.]

small books, with small chapters, small type and small woodcuts. Stories of smallness were particularly popular, and it is no coincidence that one of John Newbery's most successful publications was *Tom Thumb's Folio*.[4] The title page's mock-heroic playing with ideas of big and small, and upper- and lower-case type, is characteristic of the time. Swift had inadvertently supported this insistence on differences of scale by providing a vocabulary: children were frequently referred to as Lilliputians (there was a magazine called *The Lilliputian Magazine*),[5] or conversely they were described as resembling Gulliver in the land of the Giants.

To 'discover children' means to discover new responsibilities, to celebrate new forms of loving, and to establish a new emotional basis for the family. It also means discovering the remembered – or forgotten – child in yourself. When in 1802 Wordsworth made the extraordinary suggestion that the child is father of the man, it was this shift in cultural perspectives that he was registering. For him, the child's ambiguous state of fatherhood is incommunicable and short-lived – and of great significance. Here is the poem in full:

> My heart leaps up when I behold
> A rainbow in the sky:
> So was it when my life began;
> So is it now I am a man;
> So be it when I shall grow old,
> Or let me die!
> The Child is father of the Man;
> And I could wish my days to be
> Bound each to each by natural piety.[6]

The poem's mysterious assertions have attracted a great deal of critical attention. I find equally interesting the anxiety barely concealed in the last two lines. The problem for Romantic thinking was this: how is it possible to understand the *gradual* progression from child to adult if there is an *absolute* difference between the two states? It is epistemologically baffling. How can the days which link the child with the adult be 'bound each to each'? And in what way 'bound' – like slaves roped together? Or as in book-binding, with each page 'bound' to the next? If it was the latter, perhaps we could say that the Victorian novelists took the hint and resolved the problem through narrative.

Wordworth's lines quoted above were written on 26 March 1802. About six weeks earlier, on 14 February, his sister Dorothy had written this passage in her journal:

> After dinner a little before sunset I walked out. About 20 yards above
> glowworm Rock I met a Carman, a Highlander I suppose, with 4 carts,

the first 3 belonging to himself, the last evidently to a man and his family who had joined company with him and who I guessed to be Potters. The carman was cheering his horses and talking to a little lass about 10 years of age who seemed to make him her companion. She ran to the Wall and took up a large stone to support the wheel of one of his carts and ran on before with it in her arms to be ready for him. She was a beautiful creature and there was something uncommonly impressive in the lightness and joyousness of her manner. Her business seemed to be all pleasure – pleasure in her own motions – and the man looked at her as if he too was pleased and spoke to her in the same tone as he spoke to his horses. There was a wildness in her whole figure, not the wildness of a Mountain lass but a *Road* lass, a traveller from her Birth, who had wanted neither food nor clothes. Her Mother followed the last cart with a lovely child, perhaps about a year old, at her Back and a good-looking girl about 15 years old walked beside her. All the children were like the mother. She had a very fresh complexion, but she was blown with tagging up the hill with the steepness of the hill and the Bairn that she carried. Her husband was helping the horse to drag the cart up by pushing it with his Shoulder. I got tea when I reached home and read German till about 9 o'clock.[7]

This homely description has a rare and unpretentiously appealing authenticity. The differences between the two pieces of writing are striking. William's child is solitary, a single responsive Self in a natural landscape; Dorothy's child is a social being, comfortably negotiating complex family relationships. William's child is an Idea; Dorothy's is an objective reality lovingly observed. William's poem is composed in a language which assumes a public reception; Dorothy's vigorous passage is written in the personal language of a private journal. (There is a related question: if Dorothy call tell us in the 'real language' of women how her heart leapt up when she beheld this child, why is it that William's poem is Literature and Dorothy's journal is marginalia?)

At about this time, coinciding roughly with the Romantic period, there was the new cult of nursery rhymes. The Opies have taught us that many of the rhymes are of great antiquity and many had originally no specific connection with children. They were transmitted orally, as far as we know, and in the middle of the eighteenth century there were only a few published collections. But by the 1820s there was a flood of them, and anthologies of nursery rhymes had come to be seen as an essential part of middle-class infancy. According to the Opies,[8] the first recorded use of the term 'nursery rhyme' was in 1824.

British and American nursery rhymes are as much an expression of Romanticism as *The Prelude*, the novels of Scott, or the paintings of Constable. It is not their existence, but their being defined as *nursery* rhymes which is significant, for when these unruly and zanily rhythmic miniature narratives were collected from oral traditions and published for parents and nurses, they exerted a different kind of influence and had a new familial significance. Although there are no definitive versions, collectively they possess the unobtrusive authority of a great Romantic text. They are a literary canon for babies, a crazy and wise national curriculum with its own built-in programmes of play. A cult of nursery rhymes could develop only in a culture which valued adult–child intimacy. When lullabies, counting rhymes, lap rhymes and fingerplay rhymes were anthologized together, it was implicitly assumed that parents and nurses were willing to enter into states of intimate and loving play with babies. Nursery rhymes are interactive, physical and dramatic. Toes are counted, stomachs are tickled, hands are clapped. They assume and require that adults and children should *welcome each other* into new and special relationships.

But you cannot play pat-a-cake with a swaddled infant; and it is no coincidence that the practice of swaddling was increasingly questioned. In 1817 an influential work was published called *The New Female Instructor, or Guide to Domestic Happiness*.[9] The anonymous (but probably male) author covered every aspect of a young woman's life, from courtship to cookery. There is a long and thorough section on infant rearing from which we can learn a great deal about contemporary parenting. It is significant that the work, in its section on infant dress, makes no mention of swaddling clothes, but is content to recommend comfortable, loose garments; from which we can probably assume that, at least among the literate classes, the practice of swaddling had long been discontinued. The same writer, quoting Rousseau in support of his argument, is vehement in his attack on the contemporary practice of putting children out to wet nurses.

When mothers took to breast-feeding their own babies, a new intimacy was created at the heart of family life. This state of intimacy was regarded by Wordsworth as an essential formative condition for later growth, and from 1799 in the various versions of *The Prelude* he speculated upon it, notably in the famous passage which includes the lines:

> . . . blest the babe
> Nursed in his mother's arms, the babe who sleeps
> Upon his mother's breast, who, when his soul
> Claims manifest kindred with an earthly soul,
> Does gather passion from his mother's eye.
>
> . . . that first time
> In which, a babe, by intercourse of touch
> I held mute dialogues with my mother's heart.[10]

William's gentle reference to 'mute dialogues' with his mother's heart suggests that he thought of this intimacy as essentially *silent*; it was simultaneously both eloquent and inarticulate.

For two centuries books for children have found their ambiguous meanings inside this paradox. The history of children's books has to do with the struggle to find a voice to express an absence, a loss, a distance between parents and children. It had been a matter of little significance when children had been brought up mostly by servants, but became urgent in the nineteenth century when parents were beginning to have more direct relationships with their children. I believe that Victorian parents were seized by a sense of the importance of children, but beset by a lack of language, a failure of vision. William Wordsworth's 'mute dialogues' reflected this difficulty. Nursery rhymes, on the other hand, were less cautious; they required a more robust dialogue, and rhymes like 'This little piggy' involved a more energetic intercourse of touch than William had in mind. And it may be that it was the nursery rhymes – because they provided an interactive dynamic in which loving is made possible through shared play – that first invited mothers (and perhaps some fathers) to talk to and play with very young children.

The Prelude was not published until after the poet's death in 1850, and by then the English novel was already turning its attention to children. In 1814 the opening chapters of Jane Austen's *Mansfield Park*[11] had firmly kept the small Fanny Price in her narrative place, obliging the reader to view this shy and frightened child as her cousin Edmund views her – generously but *distantly*.

It was Dickens who gave the great Victorian reading public its first nudge towards a serious interest in children. *Oliver Twist* (1837–8) was the first work of fiction with a child as its central character – but Oliver is presented externally; he is object, not subject, a locus of pity, pathos and social indignation.[12] Little Nell in *The Old Curiosity Shop* (1840–1) is a more powerful realization than Oliver but, for all that, she is a sentimentalized and idealized child-object.[13]

The most symptomatically revealing of Dickens' early work is *Dombey and Son* (1847–8), in which the young Paul's mother dies in childbirth, the father is remote and egotistically incapable of loving the new baby except from an austere distance, and the women who care for his needs are presented by Dickens as ridiculous.[14] Although this novel is concerned with almost every conceivable variety of love, the 'absence' at its heart is mother-being-with-her-child; Dickens makes this absence the subject of the text – the absence of a parent's love in the lives of Paul and Florence Dombey. But that absence is also what Dickens could not write about. *Dombey and Son* defines a vacuum; it articulates a central silence and confirms my thesis that Victorian fiction lacked a rhetoric for describing authentic interplay between parent and child.

Supposing the adjective 'Wordsworthian' derived from the work of Dorothy instead of William, what would it describe? Certainly a resistance to literary pretentiousness; little of the egotistical, and nothing at all of the sublime; an easy and colloquial language able to convey feeling and drama in a form hardly distinguishable from chat. Something like this, perhaps:

> There was no possibility of taking a walk that day . . . I was glad of it: I never liked long walks, especially on chilly afternoons; dreadful to me was the coming home in the raw twilight, with nipped fingers and toes.

These were the opening words of a new novel by someone called Currer Bell.[15]

When *Jane Eyre* was published in 1847 Victorian readers recognized that this was a new kind of writing. No one had written about childhood in this way before. A fictional child was making a space for herself in the English novel – a small enough space, no more than a window-seat, a refuge from the bleakness that pressed upon her on both sides.

> A small breakfast-room adjoined the dining-room. I slipped in there. It contained a bookcase: I soon possessed myself of a volume, taking care that it should be one stored with pictures. I mounted into the window-seat: gathering up my feet, I sat cross-legged, like a Turk; and, having drawn the red moreen curtain nearly close, I was shrined in double retirement.
>
> Folds of scarlet drapery shut in my view to the right hand; to the left were the clear panes of glass, protecting but not separating me from the drear November day. At intervals, while turning over the leaves of my book, I studied the aspect of that winter afternoon. Afar, it offered a pale blank of mist and cloud; near, a scene of wet lawn and storm-beat shrub, with ceaseless rain sweeping away wildly before a long and lamentable blast.[16]

The extraordinary innovativeness of this account has specifically to do with language. Dickens had described the infant Paul Dombey climbing upstairs: 'These ceremonies passed, Cornelia led Paul up stairs to the top of the house; which was rather a slow journey, on account of Paul being obliged to land both feet on every stair, before he mounted another.'[17] The semicolon indicates a change of key, a pause in readiness for the joke – a kindly joke, but one assuming the perspective of an amused adult. But when Jane tells us she 'mounted' into the window-seat and 'sat cross-legged, like a Turk' hidden by the curtains, she is half-consciously and dramatically invoking and *acting out* an exotic, *Arabian Nights* escape. The impulses of her private imagination are determining the musculature of the language. Dickens' observation is precisely that – an 'observation'; it falls into two parts: observation and joke. There is no such division in Charlotte Brontë's sentence because the language of fabulous story arises from *within* Jane's needs and is inseparable from everything she feels. The 'I' of the narrative is simultaneously the child Jane was and the intelligent adult she grew into, so that the reader is both inside her and alongside her. This is dramatic, but not theatrical; we 'see', but we are not just spectators.

The opening chapters of *Jane Eyre* provided the imaginative antecedent of what was subsequently to be referred to as 'children's literature'. It was not those legions of hack writers who had been producing didactic books for children since the Puritans; it was not even John Newbery — he founded a trade, not a literature; it was certainly not Hannah More and the writers of the Religious Tract Society — for they wrote in the belief that moral texts were directly imprinted on receptive minds. We know that children do not read like that; so did Charlotte Brontë. She established connections which have interested writers ever since — between loneliness and solitary reading; between children and pictures; between girls and enclosed spaces.

The history of children's fiction is inseparable from the history of childhood in fiction. This was especially so in the middle of the nineteenth century when the mainstream novel turned its attention to childhood. Dickens was greatly influenced by *Jane Eyre*, and in *David Copperfield*,[18] *Hard Times*[19] and *Great Expectations*[20] he was able to place himself in a closer and more passionate imaginative stance alongside his child characters.

Children were being allowed to speak in the English novel — or, more precisely, adult narrators were being allowed to speak with the remembered voices of childhood, an apparent acknowledgement of the William-Wordsworthian notion of the child within the adult. Childhood was born into articulate meaning when Jane Eyre climbed into her window-seat — but it was born *dispossessed and parentless*. Victorian fictional children were allowed to have voices — but not riches, or understanding parents. They were invariably in search of sanctuary — from poverty or cruelty, from a morality which saw children as sinners, and, in particular, from silly mothers and uncomprehending fathers. Jane Austen was responsible for what seems to have developed into a kind of fictional habit, an imaginative predilection for well-meaning but inadequate parents rich in comic and pathetic possibilities. Her Mr and Mrs Bennett[21] cast long shadows across the nineteenth-century novel, extending to Maggie Tulliver's parents in *The Mill on the Floss* (1860).[22] A year later, in *Silas Marner*, George Eliot placed little Eppie at the heart of a fairy-tale about wealth and poverty — and the denial of parenthood. Godfrey Cass does acknowledge that he is Eppie's father — but only when she has grown into a young woman.[23]

This is a puzzle. If childhood occupied a central place in the Victorian family, why did it invariably occupy a solitary or orphaned place in Victorian fiction? The domestic loving intercourse between parent and child which, according to the social historians, must have occurred in thousands of families was resolutely ignored, or perhaps even resisted, by the great popular novelists of the day. If there were men and women whose hearts were warmed by children in the way Dorothy Wordsworth's had been by the traveller child, why was there no testimony in the great fiction of the day? Why was parenthood invariably either sentimentalized, ridiculed, presented as inadequate, altogether absent, or – as in the work of Henry James – manipulative and egotistical? Does this imaginative gap in the fiction of the period reflect some kind of embarrassment at the heart of Victorian parenting? Was it perhaps because they were uncertain about what a fulfilling parent–child relationship might be?

Victorian families were the victims of two powerful but conflicting imperatives. One, deriving from Romanticism, required them to love their children as special and vulnerable innocents able to evoke a deep and poignant delight in sensitive and loving parents; the other, deriving from old Puritan habits of thought, directed them to regard their children as unregenerate sinners, and authorized wretched programmes of severity and restraint. The language of the latter was firm and unambiguous, but the language of the former was private, uncertain and marginalized, so that the parental dilemma could not be articulated, let alone resolved. The voices that warned of original sin were everywhere to be heard; but where were the voices that spoke of original innocence?

Where, in any of the great Victorian fictions, is there a convincing and authentic account of a loving and trusting relationship between parent and child?

In the nineteenth century, children's fiction was concerned with children who had dealings with adults in positions of authority – nurses, governesses, teachers, magistrates, clergymen or commanding officers. Here too – as in the adult novel – there were no varieties of rhetoric for describing what Dickens called 'natural affection and gentle intercourse'[24] between parents and children. The authoritarian voices of parenting were everywhere represented in the stream of didactic books sanctioned by the many wings of the Sunday School Movement. But the voices of *loving* parenthood remained silent.

Then, in this silence, was heard the voice of Alice – kind, composed, sensible and forthright.

Lewis Carroll was not a parent. Like all those bachelor uncles and bachelor friends who seem to have been such popular visitors to Victorian nurseries, he was not troubled by the parental dilemma I have described. He did not have to fret himself about Alice Liddell's moral condition and was free to be lovingly inventive and playfully respectful.

But he could say nothing about parenting, and there is no room in his fiction for those William-Wordsworthian speculations about a private continuity from child to adult. His two stories imply not a continuity but a disastrous disruption between the kind and intelligent little girl and the cruel and stupid adults she encounters. It is inconceivable that the Queen of Hearts was ever a little girl like Alice. His two stories draw ironic attention to the *breach* between children and adults, the incommunicable incomprehensibility of each generation to the other.

Lewis Carroll in his fiction did not resolve this dilemma of silence (though he may, of course, have resolved it personally in his relationship with the real Alice). But after (and perhaps because of) *Alice*,[25] it became possible for writers to use children's books to express adult needs. And these needs invariably had to do with parental love. There seems to have been an unacknowledged compulsion – a kind of imaginative obsession – which drew some writers of children's fiction to focus upon the unspoken theme of family disruption, this breach in parent–child intimacy. The best children's writers went further than writing about it – *they magically healed it*, and they did so with such storyteller's tact that readers hardly notice that a so-called child's book is powered by such an adult longing. Take *The Railway Children*. It begins with the loss of the father, and ends with his recovery. Its chapters are composed like short stories held together by the children's longing to have their father back. Bobbie, the eldest, discovers that he has been unjustly imprisoned, and it is she who goes to the station, unaware that her father has been freed. It is clear from the way Nesbit stages this incident that it is the climax of the novel – not a resolution of the unknown, but a *climax of the desired*, a consummation that has been devoutly wished by characters and readers alike. And the readerly satisfaction which is made available is so intense – so long awaited through fourteen chapters – that the unlikeliness of the whole episode is simply of no significance.

> Only three people got out of the 11.54. The first was a countrywoman with two baskety boxes full of live chickens who stuck their russet heads out anxiously through the wicker bars; the second was Miss Peckitt, the grocer's wife's cousin, with a tin box and three brown-paper parcels; and the third –
> 'Oh! my Daddy, my Daddy!' That scream went like a knife into the heart of everyone in the train, and people put their heads out of the windows to see a tall pale man with lips set in a thin close line, and a little girl clinging to him with arms and legs, while his arms went tightly round her.[26]

There is an unobtrusive artifice here, working for a mixture of the magical and the everyday, with an emphasis on the prosaic as a setting for the intense. It is Dorothy-Wordsworthian in its language – she would have felt at home with the baskety boxes, the grocer's wife's cousin with her brown paper parcels, and that uncomfortable simile of the knife.

The use of unpretentious language to convey significant experience is not just a stylistic choice; it has the effect of allowing *unpretentious characters to be significant*. It acknowledges an entitlement.

It is that entitlement which links E. Nesbit's children's books with

Dorothy Wordsworth's account of the traveller child within her family, and with Charlotte Brontë's account of young Jane without hers. Frances Hodgson Burnet's *The Secret Garden*[27] and *A Little Princess*,[28] Louisa May Alcott's *Little Women*,[29] and Philippa Pearce's *The Way to Sattin Shore*[30] are also concerned with the magical and fabulous restoration of fathers to unhappy children. Both the language and the message of these books constitute a discreet *cri de coeur* for recognition of this familial need which the great public voices of adult literature had failed to represent.

Adult literature is not obliged to be interested in childhood, and parents do not have to understand their children. But children have to understand adults because they live in a world controlled by them and they are living their lives forward, towards their own adulthood. Adulthood surrounds them and awaits them.

The recognition of this – and the transformation of the actual need into varieties of narrative longing – has been the achievement of our best children's writers. I would not want to claim that there has been an alternative tradition of marginalized women's writings linking Dorothy Wordsworth with E. Nesbit. It was not so much a tradition as a *persistence* – by means of which writers (mostly women) edged into literature their language and their perceptions of the significance of familial feelings and needs. Perhaps such perceptions have been recorded in thousands of private and unpublished writings. But they made their tentative way into literature by a side door, so to speak – by books written for children.

Notes

I would like to express my gratitude to Mary Nathan, a former student, for her interest and help while I was writing this chapter.

1   Hugh Scott, *The Haunted Sand*, Walker Books, London, 1991.
2   Edward Shorter, *The Making of the Modern Family*, Collins, London, 1976.
3   Linda A. Pollock, *Forgotten Children*, Cambridge University Press, Cambridge, 1983.
4   John Newbery and Thomas Carnan, *Tom Thumb's Folio*, first published 1768.
5   John Newbery, *The Lilliputian Magazine*, London , 1751–2.
6   E. de Selincourt (ed.), *The Poetical Works of William Wordsworth*, Clarendon Press, Oxford, 1940.
7   Mary Moorman (ed.), *Journals of Dorothy Wordsworth*, Oxford University Press, Oxford, 1971.
8   Iona and Peter Opie, *The Oxford Dictionary of Nursery Rhymes*, Clarendon Press, Oxford, 1951.

9   Anonymous, *The New Female Instructor, or Young Woman's Guide to Domestic Happiness*, London, 1817.
10   William Wordsworth, *The Two-Part Prelude*, first published 1799.
11   Jane Austen, *Mansfield Park*, first published 1814.
12   Charles Dickens, *Oliver Twist*, first published 1837–8.
13   Charles Dickens, *The Old Curiosity Shop*, first published 1840–1.
14   Charles Dickens, *Dombey and Son*, first published 1847–8.
15   (Currer Bell) Charlotte Brontë, *Jane Eyre*, first published 1847.
16   *Ibid.*
17   Dickens, *Dombey and Son*.
18   Charles Dickens, *David Copperfield*, first published 1849–50.
19   Charles Dickens, *Hard Times*, first published 1854.
20   Charles Dickens, *Great Expectations*, first published 1860–1.
21   Jane Austen, *Pride and Prejudice*, first published 1813.
22   George Eliot, *The Mill on the Floss*, first published 1860.
23   George Eliot, *Silas Marner*, first published 1861.
24   Charles Dickens, *Little Dorrit*, first published 1857–8.
25   Lewis Carroll, *Alice's Adventures in Wonderland*, first published 1865.
26   E. Nesbit, *The Railway Children*, first published 1906.
27   Frances Hodgson Burnett, *The Secret Garden*, first published 1911.
28   Frances Hodgson Burnett, *A Little Princess*, first published 1905.
29   Louisa May Alcott, *Little Women*, first published 1868.
30   Philippa Pearce, *The Way to Sattin Shore*, Kestrel, London, 1983.

CHAPTER 14

Making Picture Books

Anthony Browne

This chapter is based on the talk Anthony Browne gave at the conference, where he discussed the genesis of some of his ideas and how he goes about 'making picture books'. It was fascinating to learn that the author of Gorilla *and* The Tunnel *had once worked at different times as a medical artist and for a firm associated with rather sentimental birthday cards! Both experiences taught him disciplines and forms which proved useful, but it is as a children's illustrator and writer that Anthony Browne excels. He is extremely popular with a large young readership and with many adults who share books with children. A new Anthony Browne picture book is an event of note. This edited transcript offers some insights into how this gifted illustrator works.*

The title of this talk, I notice, is 'Making picture books' – now whether I gave it that title, or whether Victor did, I am not sure, but I think it's a very apt title because that's the way I think of it.

Although I write and illustrate books, I don't think of it as writing a story and then illustrating it, or indeed, illustrating some pictures and then writing a story around it – those are the worst ways to do a book. The two things come very much together for me.

What I am going to talk about mostly is a question I am asked when I go into schools. Whether this question comes directly from children, or whether it is put into the children's minds by teachers, I'm not sure, but apart from 'Why do you like gorillas so much?' and 'How much do you earn?' the most popular question is 'Where do you get your ideas from?' This is a question I have tried to answer in various ways, in various schools, never really coming up with a good answer. I can't actually remember where many of the ideas came from – they sort of percolate up to the surface and force themselves out.

My first picture book was never published. I approached several publishers of children's books. I eventually got an interview at Hamish Hamilton and an editor said, 'Well, have a go at a picture book.' So I went and looked in libraries and saw what I could find in those days, which was mostly books by Brian Wildsmith and John Burningham. What I saw was lots of white paper, bright colours and animals in the jungle. So I sort of 'wrote' a story about a young elephant that gets lost in the jungle and can't find its way out. He asks a crocodile, but the crocodile is too cross. He asks a gorilla but the gorilla is too grumpy. He asks various animals, and none of them can help him. He eventually asks a little mouse who climbs up on his back. The elephant thinks the mouse can't possibly help him because he is so small, but the mouse helps him out of the jungle. I did the whole thing – I didn't think how many pages there should be, what size the book should be, how a book works at all. I just wrote the story and then illustrated it.

Because I was working on thick card in those days I thought when I took it to the publisher I should make it look like a book, so I stuck each page onto the back of another one, so it was like a page, and I put them all together and staggered in with this foot-thick book to the man at Hamish Hamilton. He looked at it and handed me on to another editor called Julia MacRae, who was the head of children's books at Hamish Hamilton in those days. She is still my editor, and one of the luckiest moves I ever made was to go along to Hamish Hamilton and be introduced to Julia MacRae. She has really taught me a lot about picture books and how they work.

I had left art college with very little ability at all. I really couldn't have been employed at anything. I became a medical illustrator eventually. Then I left and did lots of little things, like advertising work and greetings cards. I really wasn't very good at it. I was a rotten student at art college and I really wasn't very good in the advertising world or with greetings cards, but I got better as time went on. I was asked to draw a picture illustrating the inside of a caravan – it was for a black and white advert, for caravan furniture, in a newspaper. I had to draw a happy family in the caravan all having fun; mother, father, daughter and son. No matter how I drew these characters, I couldn't make them look happy – they all looked as if some terrible tension was going on. I really couldn't transcend that happiness barrier. I had earned a good living being a medical illustrator, but when I became freelance I was thrown out onto the streets, as it were, and had to earn some money. I worked for Gordon Fraser, who was an old-fashioned patron. He was a very useful person to meet – he taught me to do commercial cards and taught me how to make a living painting happy pictures. He also allowed me to experiment with more realistic pictures and funny pictures – so I was learning a lot about different techniques, different styles and started thinking a bit about who I was doing them for.

When I was passed on to Julia MacRae with the story of the elephant who was lost in the jungle, she discussed the idea of doing a dummy and making pencil drawings and working the thing out with the editor. I wrote a book, or developed a book really, called *Go and Open the Door*. It was based on a series of doors. It was a door-shaped book and the front cover was a door and the first page was a door, and you opened the door and outside, maybe, there's a magic mirror, or a blue orange. I had lots and lots of surreal images beyond these doors – so every other page was a door – dead boring really. I was trying to find new ways of painting a door every other page. So not much plot, but one or two ideas in there. With one picture, which was very much based on Magritte, Julia said, 'Here's the boy – why don't we imagine what it would be like in that world he is looking at, in the mirror world – imagine he steps through the mirror and finds what appears like normal life but isn't quite.' This idea didn't really come from *Through the Looking Glass*, which is how it might appear, seeing this book. It came from my old friend Magritte and became *Through the Magic Mirror*.

My second book was called *A Walk in the Park*. The original idea for this came from when I was at art college. Most of the time at art college we were doing things that I had no connection with at all – I did graphic design at Leeds and we were designing logos for non-existent firms and doing a lot of typography and things that I thought were incredibly boring. I spent a lot of time in the life class, just drawing models and eventually drawing the inside of bodies, which is what led on to medical illustration. One of the projects we were given was to come up with an idea for a children's book. I came up with the idea of two dogs and two owners – a middle-class owner and a middle-class dog, and a working-class owner and a working-class dog who met in the park, and the dogs mixed and the adults didn't. It didn't actually amount to much, and I couldn't draw a dog. I could have drawn a realistic dog, but I was trying to do a Brian Wildsmith/John Burningham sort of dog and it just ended up grotesque. So I was a terrible failure at art college. Nobody would ever have guessed that I could have done children's books – least of all myself.

Nevertheless, years later, I resurrected the idea of the dogs and the owners in the park and this became *A Walk in the Park*. Julia MacRae suggested that I might introduce children into the story as it's a children's book, which I thought was a good idea, and I went ahead with the story. I try to pretend that the details in the background were consciously trying to reflect the imagination of the child – that the parents were very cold and dogmatic and dressed in their armour, their overcoats and so on – but the children take off their overcoats, their armour, and they play together and copy the dogs and play together as the dogs do without any barrier between them. So I am trying to suggest that Robin Hood, and the tree that becomes a foot, and the man

walking the tomato, and various other things were a conscious decision
on my part to reflect the children's minds. But I don't actually think
they were. I think in those days I just included these things in the
background, partly to interest me and partly because I felt insecure
about the very simple nature of the story. Man, daughter and dog go for
a walk in the park; woman, son and dog go for a walk in the park; the
dogs play together; gradually the children do; the parents don't; the
children are taken home. I thought this was not very substantial, so I
was trying to interest both myself and the potential child who was
going to look at this book by putting these funny things in the
background. Now I think, at least I hope, that when I put jokes or
details of surrealistic stuff in the background I try to make it have a
point, I try to give it relevance in the story.

I started to use words in a conscious way in this book. For instance,
when Mr Smith and Smudge let Albert off the lead I used very basic,
down-to-earth words and sentences, whereas when Mrs Smyth and her
son Charles detach the lead from Victoria's collar, I use the language in
a different way, tentatively, and not particularly well, but nevertheless I
was starting to think about the words for the first time.

Bear Hunt was my third book, and the idea for this came from the
first sales conference I had gone to at Hamish Hamilton after
publishing *Through the Magic Mirror* and *A Walk in the Park*. I was
cornered by two salesmen who told me that they thought I was on some
kind of ego-trip with my books, and their kids didn't understand them
at all, and who was I doing it for anyway, and why couldn't I do
something more like the Mr Men books? So this was my attempt to do

a commercial book, which hasn't been as commercial, I think, probably hasn't sold as many copies as *A Walk in the Park* – but nevertheless was an attempt. It was going back, in a way, to my elephant in the jungle. I thought commercial books probably have very bright colours, jungles and animals, and although I think it was more than that, I still use this character. I don't think there will be any more bear books, but whenever I go into schools I draw a bear and I get the kids to come out and make up a story around the Bear. I usually say that I am going to use these ideas in a book, and I have on a couple of occasions – so Bear has the magic pencil and draws his way out. Even then I couldn't leave the background alone – I was painting things going on in the background which I can't think had any significance at that stage. I think really I was just trying to make the book more interesting in this particular case.

By that time I had illustrated *Hansel and Gretel*, which was a sort of a dark treatment of a dark story, and so I was still in that dark period and I did a sort of dark bear book which, I think, wasn't what either the publishers or some parents had in mind. In fact one or two people complained to me that their children were frightened by Bear, because I think they had been expecting it to be light and airy and easy, and it wasn't.

When I come up with an idea and talk it over with Julia, I can tell by the amount of enthusiasm what she thinks about it. She has never actually yet said, 'I don't like this idea', or, 'I don't think it will work', or, 'It won't sell', or 'This isn't good enough', but I can tell that she isn't as enthusiastic as she has been in the past. She asked me if there was a childhood fairy-tale that I remembered from the past, and I said 'Hansel and Gretel', and went back home and did just one picture, and that was it. And at one stage I must have made a decision to paint them in contemporary clothing, but I don't remember thinking, 'I will make this story more relevant to children today by bringing it up to date.' It didn't work like that at all – that's just how it came out. Julia was shocked, but told me to go ahead.

This was a watershed book for me, because it was the first book I had illustrated that I hadn't actually written myself. I felt more vulnerable, which I always do when I am illustrating somebody else's text. I felt I was going to be judged just as an illustrator. Somehow when I'm doing both, it's a bit like being an all-round cricketer – if you can bat and bowl people are amazed. You don't have to be particularly good at either, but because you can do both you can get away with an awful lot, and I sometimes feel like that about writing and illustrating children's books. I don't feel quite as vulnerable when I'm illustrating my own things. So I found myself becoming more self-conscious on this book and deciding, before I started, how I was going to treat it. I decided I didn't want to do a pretty book, because it's not a pretty story, and all the other versions I had seen of 'Hansel and Gretel' were set in very beautiful forests with very beautiful peasant clothing and beautiful interiors – even though it was a story of poverty.

I decided also that there were going to be certain themes in the book – and one of them is of prison, of cages, of bars. So right on the title page I decided to introduce the idea of bars with a bird being caged. The other theme in the story is birds; birds occur constantly through the book. As they are walking through the forest for the first time Hansel keeps dawdling, dropping stones, and his father challenges him. He says he's just waving goodbye to his pet dove which is on the chimney – so that is the first bird. The second birds are the ones that eat up all the bread. The third bird is the one they encounter when they are totally

lost in the forest and it's the bird that leads them to the gingerbread house. The fourth bird is the one on the final return home; it's the white duck that takes them back over the water.

The idea of bars I introduced right at the beginning. The picture shows the woodcutter's cottage and the trees behind the house are painted to look a little like the bars of a cage. The door, which is later locked, I have shown having bars on the window. I then decided on the idea of bars on the chairs, the striped dress of Gretel and the shirt of Hansel and the father's striped shirt – and even the doll on the floor had got a striped dress. There is more feeling of bars on the striped pillow case and the bed head later. When Hansel is trapped inside, when he can't get out to get the white stones, the trees become made of metal. And, of course, he's literally locked in a cage by the witch. Again trees which look less like trees and more like cage bars.

The third visual theme I wanted to introduce into the story was the idea of transformation – the idea of one thing changing into another. I wanted to suggest here that the stepmother, in the eyes of the children at least, is the same person as the witch. So her shadow behind her, when taken in conjunction with the gap in the curtains, gives the feeling of a witch. This black triangular shape is echoed in the spire of the church and the shadow on the chest of drawers. Even the mousehole is a black triangle, and something on top of the wardrobe may, or may

not, be a witch's hat. The first time the parents made their way back from the forest, I wanted to show this connection between the step-mother and the witch, so I show her at the window with the reflection of the trees in the background, and the first time you see the witch she is in the same position – again using that black triangle. More transform-ation – the witch's hand, in shadow, becomes a serpent when she is testing Hansel's finger to see if he is fat enough to eat yet. Again, more transformation, the tree beyond the well is a hand saying 'Stop! No further'. Gretel can't get away. The base of the tree has been transformed into what looks like dead birds.

The final transformation is of the house when they return home. The bars of the trees have gone – the bars from the windows are fainter and I used completely different colours in this picture. The hardest picture

of all to paint was the final return home, when the stepmother has died, according to the story. I tried drawing and painting this in different ways – I wanted to show the expressions of delight on the children's faces as they came home. No matter how I drew the expressions on the faces, it looked exaggerated – it looked like a still from a silent film somehow. As soon as I start putting heightened emotion, particularly on children's faces, it looks overemphatic – over-dramatized. So my eventual solution was not to show any of the faces at all, but to show them joined together as if they are one being – one body. And there's a new shoot growing in the plant pot and Arnold Bocklin's 'Isle of the Dead' on the windowsill – which probably won't mean anything to anybody really. I often use paintings on the wall to try and tell another aspect of the story – I hope this isn't seen as 'winking over the child's shoulder' – sharing a joke or some reference with the adult. I think as long as the images work in the context of the story, it's just another layer.

I had done an illustration of a gorilla for a birthday card some years before. When I originally designed it, Gordon Fraser said he liked the design, but who could it possibly be sent to. *King Kong* was another influence on *Gorilla* – it is a film that I still like very much. I am trying to write a version of *King Kong* for the future and to illustrate it. So there are two ideas coming together – the idea of a great big macho gorilla needing the comfort of a teddy bear, and a seemingly fierce creature and the relationship with a young woman – as in *King Kong*. In the book *Gorilla* there are different sorts of gorillas. There are the gorillas in Hannah's head because she's obsessed by gorillas. She reads books about gorillas, she watches programmes about gorillas, draws pictures of gorillas – she thinks about gorillas all the time, and on the night of her birthday she goes to bed tingling with excitement because her father has promised her a real gorilla. The second gorilla is the toy gorilla that her father gives her, which she is disappointed with and throws onto the floor in the middle of the night along with her other toys, but, of course, something amazing happens. She meets this gorilla of the night, which may be her father, may be a dream, or maybe it's how she would like her father to be – although it looks terrifying, she actually isn't scared of it. The other gorillas are the real ones they see in the zoo – he takes her to the zoo and they have this night-time adventure.

This is an example of me using a visual language which would tell part of a story that the words don't tell – I talk a lot about this, as if I

was calculatingly doing it at the time, but I honestly can't remember how much this happened by accident and how much was deliberate. I contrasted two meal scenes, Hannah with her father at breakfast and later on in the night Hannah and the gorilla having a meal in the café. I was trying to show the relationship between Hannah and her father and Hannah and the gorilla in ways that the words didn't, because the words just said something like, 'Hannah's father didn't have time to take her to the zoo.' Right away I exaggerated the perspective to widen the gap between the two of them. There's a low eye-point – so we are looking up at the father, showing the fact that he is the top of the hierarchy. I used very geometric shapes – squares, triangles, hard edges, sharp angles – everything is neat and tidy, cold, clinical. I used blues, whites and greys – cold colours – on everything apart from Hannah. Everything is smooth, hard – there is no real texture there. In the meal with the gorilla it is the same point of view, but I flattened the perspective so the gorilla is nearer to us and to Hannah. Everything is textured. You can imagine feeling things, touching things, tasting things. Hardly anything, apart from the table cloth, is geometric. The colours are all warm reds and browns. Again, all the words say here is 'Hannah said "I'm hungry", "OK" said gorilla "Let's eat".' So the picture is saying more.

I developed the idea of a picture telling a different story to the words in a book called *The Visitors Who Came to Stay*, which was written by a friend of mine, Annalena McAfee, who presented me with what seemed like a non-idea for a picture book. I thought I couldn't do it. I knew she was a good writer, but it didn't seem I could illustrate the idea she came up with because nothing happened – it was just about a girl's feelings really, about a girl who lived alone with her father. The father brought in a new friend, a woman friend with a son, who moved in for a while. The little girl got jealous, told her father, and the visitors went away again. I couldn't think how to illustrate it. If it had been presented to me as most stories are presented to illustrators by publishers, just as a bare text for the illustrator to illustrate – never to meet the author or to discuss it with them – then I couldn't have done it. Because I know Annalena we developed the book together, more as if we were the same

person, writing and illustrating it together. She could make suggestions about the pictures and I could make suggestions about the words.

One of the things I was pleased with was the idea of the pictures and the text seeming to tell a very different story. Annalena was writing about the father and the daughter living together in their own little cosy world. Everything very routine, everything very ordered, a kind of 'Listen with Mother' text. Each morning Dad got Katie off to school and made a packed lunch, etc. With the text I'd paint a very realistic cosy picture of the boiled egg she was eating and on the page opposite I tried to show that things were not quite what they seemed, so she is actually imprisoned in here. There is no catch on the window to get out,

the regimented brickwork is holding her in, the sunlight doesn't quite reach her (those significant bars again), and there is the burglar alarm above her head. Every weekend she goes to see her mother, who lives in another town, and again everything is ordered and routine. Her dad accompanies her there and she packs her nightie and her teddy bear, but again I am trying to show something else; that where they are is winter, and grey and ominous blacks and winter trees, but beyond the bridge there is a hint of something else. Because I live near the sea and Annalena lives near the sea, at some stage we decided to use the seaside as a background to this to represent the two different sides of the story.

So when Katie and her father are living together their very ordered and secure little life, we decided to show the seaside out of season – in winter – cold, grey and windswept but sort of beautiful in its way too. In the summer, when the visitors come, we use it to represent when the actual visitors in the story came, and so I get a chance here to use lots of jokes. Lots of surrealism, lots of seaside postcard jokes, and I had a lot of fun with this picture.

Willy the Wimp came straight after *The Visitors Who Came to Stay* and was a welcome relief. *Visitors* had been a very difficult book to do for all sorts of reasons; *Willy* was very quick, very light and very easy.

The idea for this one came from one or two sources really. One was, to a certain extent, my own childhood. I was a small boy and my father was a big man – he was very physical, he was a professional boxer for part of his life, he was a soldier, he played rugby. He was also gentle, and he painted and wrote poems for my brother and me. He encouraged my brother and me to be physical too, so we lifted weights and played rugby and boxed and so on, and I always wanted to impress him, so I was very influenced by the Charles Atlas adverts. I also remember hearing Geoffrey Moorehouse talking about a trip he made across the Sahara Desert. He wrote a book about it. He very nearly died, he ran out of food and water miles from anywhere and he really thought he was going to die. In the interview he was asked if this had changed him in any way and he said it had: now, when he walks through a crowded street and somebody bumps into him, he doesn't say sorry – which is what Willie does. Every time he walks down a street and somebody bumps into him he says, 'I'm sorry.' When the suburban gorilla gang bully him, he again apologizes as they thump him. They call him Willy the Wimp. He hates that name but one night he's sitting at home reading his comic and he sees the original Charles Atlas advert, or something similar, sends off for the course, goes jogging, does special exercises, goes on a special diet, learns how to box, goes to aerobics and even, feeling a bit silly, he goes to body-building classes. He takes up weight-lifting until he looks in the mirror and he likes what he sees. He walks down the street with a new self-confidence. He sees the gorilla gang bullying Millie. They run, and he is rewarded.

That was a book that got me into quite a lot of trouble, because I was accused of racism for one thing, sexism for another, which to a certain extent I could understand, as the only female in the story is a kind of token, silly female. But worst of all I was accused of transvestism, because this female gorilla is obviously a transvestite apparently! As those criticisms all came from the same source, I didn't take them too seriously. There is a lot of seriousness in Willy, but I wanted to make it a very light and funny book, and I think it is the funniest book I have done. It certainly is one of the most popular books with kids. I get more letters about Willy books than all my other books added together. My favourite one was from a boy in Australia – which was addressed to Willy the Wimp. He said, 'Dear Willy, you don't have to be big and strong, but just watch where you're going.' Because I wanted to make it light and funny, I used lots of different techniques. I think this relates back to the greetings cards. Until then I had used fairly strict confines for my pictures, they tended to be in boxes – a little box on the left with some text and a big picture on the right. With this book I used sequence pictures, circular pictures, I used pictures which bled all over the page, I used bits which were seemingly torn out of a magazine – lots and lots of different shapes of pictures to keep the story light. I used lots of different paints. I used ink, crayon, watercolour – lots of different techniques just to keep the thing light and airy.

Alice in Wonderland is the book that I felt, and still do feel, the most vulnerable about. Not only was I illustrating somebody else's text, but I was illustrating one of the best books ever written for children. The book was illustrated brilliantly the first time, by John Tenniel. Everybody in Britain thinks of *Alice in Wonderland* through the imagery of Tenniel or Disney. I was also aware that it had been illustrated over one hundred times since Tenniel. My reaction on hearing that someone else was going to illustrate it would have been, 'Do we need another one?' I was in one of those periods when a book that I had been working on wasn't quite ready, and Julia suggested there might be a longer text that I could illustrate and made various suggestions, none of which I wanted to do. *Alice in Wonderland* was the one I chose, partly because it was a book that I remember very vividly from my own childhood, partly because of its surreal nature. I thought that the idea of surrealism and Alice meeting would be the perfect combination. Some of the sequences – the transformations in the book – I hadn't seen done as sequence pictures: the baby turning into the pig, which I found incredibly difficult to do, and the Cheshire cat disappearing. Sometimes in the book, where the most bizarre happenings are, I used the same technique as when I was a medical illustrator, although I would have said that I couldn't imagine two careers further apart than a medical illustrator and a children's illustrator. You had to be accurate, but it also had to be realistic and yet not realistic at the same time, because an operation didn't actually look like that. We had to clean everything up as medical illustrators – clean everything up and show what was hidden behind other things, show what people would expect it to look like. Veins and arteries, for instance, had to be in different colours – even though in the actual body they look very similar. I learned really about telling the story of the operation in pictures. So to show the bizarre or grotesque things happening in Alice, I used the same technique.

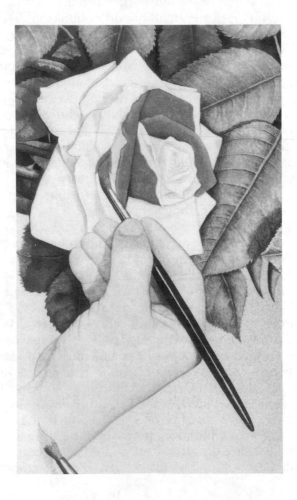

One of the things I discovered about illustrating a long novel was that there were pictures I had to paint that I wouldn't have been particularly attracted to paint. For instance, Alice on the ground crying isn't a picture I would have been interested in painting, but because it was a long novel, there had to be pictures at certain pages in the book. So I found myself having to invent reasons for illustrating something. I didn't just want to illustrate Alice crying. I wanted to play the same sort of games that Lewis Carroll was playing. I wanted to give the reader some kind of involvement in the picture, so there were puzzle pictures and 'spot the difference' pictures, hidden pictures, and visual puns which I used a lot to try and echo Lewis Carroll's visual puns. More shades of Magritte. If the gardeners were painting the roses red, maybe I could show my own hand being painted by my paintbrush! How do you paint a bowl of green pea soup and make it look interesting? Again, more visual puns, the lobster quadrille, a real starfish in the sky, crocodile rock, a cat fish, a sea-horse and a real jellyfish with a spoon.

One of the main problems was getting round Tenniel's imagery. His duchess is the way I always thought of a duchess – and influenced the way a lot of people have illustrated *Alice* ever since. I tried to get round it by thinking about the duchess and what she was and what she was like, and if she had a baby which turned into a pig, what did that make her? So I tried to show the 'piggy' aspects of her – the bow in her hair which looked like pig's ears; the nostrils like a snout; she is dressed in pink; there are sausages round the apron of the cook. I think of the Mad Hatter as having top hat with a 10/6 tag in it. Again, I tried to get round the Tenniel image by thinking of the aspect of him being mad – by splitting his face into half happy and half sad. When I painted the final artwork, I introduced jokes and visual puns in the sandwiches and the cake. Although I did feel vulnerable illustrating *Alice*, because of the feeling of 'challenging' Tenniel, it is such a wonderful book that it can stand any amount of interpretation. I console myself with the fact that of all the hundreds of pictures Tenniel did for both *Alice* books, Lewis Carroll was only happy with one illustration – and that was Humpty Dumpty, apparently.

The last illustration for the book that I did was Alice falling down the rabbit hole. With every other illustration I worked consecutively through the book, and this was a scene which I deliberately avoided, because it was described so well in the book it didn't need somebody coming along and showing you what it looked like. But a picture was needed here in practical terms. By then I was totally immersed in Wonderland myself, so when I originally roughed out this picture I drew Alice as she was going to be and I drew the shelves – but I didn't know what was going to be on them. As I actually painted the picture I started off at the top and meandered down, almost putting in anything that came into my head but that had relevance to the story – even

though it may have been illogical relevance – a bit like a dream. So as she is falling down, she is wondering about what it would be like to come out in Australia where people walk upside down. So I did a little blackboard, as if she may be dreaming about her geography lessons at school, with a picture of Australia – upside down. There are things which relate vaguely to the story – keys, teapot, pig. For instance, she is thinking about her pet cat, Dinah, as she is falling down again and she wonders if cats eat bats. So I showed a pet cat's bowl with Dinah written on and a cricket bat in it. She is trying to remember her geography lessons, and I used a map that was drawn by the surrealists in the 1930s. They redrew the world with the size of each country as important as they felt it to the surrealist movement – so England actually doesn't exist.

Changes is an unusual book for me. I'd made a lot of books with odd things going on in the background. What I wanted to happen was the odd things to take up a life and develop stories of their own. I started off with this transitional idea of something hard-edged and mechanical – like an electrical kettle – changing into something furry and real and warm-blooded – like a cat. I was fascinated by the half-way stage, where there was half a kettle and half a cat. I spent a lot of time trying to think of a story which wasn't just a fantasy. I was talking to friends who had a 9-year-old daughter. The mother had become pregnant and the girl burst into tears when she was told, she was upset for a long time – in fact right up until the baby was born. So this gave me the idea of how the things might be changing in the boy's head. Normally I make a story board when doing a book. With this book I couldn't do it, because I knew things were going to change. I knew how the story started and I knew how it finished, but I didn't know how I was going to get from one end to the other. I had to paint each picture and develop the story with each one. It felt very risky and as a result the book was very enjoyable to do, because I didn't know if the thing was going to be 32 pages or 64 pages or indeed 73 pages. I included lots of clues in the book as to what was really going on. So on the television screen I had a cuckoo, and then a pink cuckoo's egg, laid in a nest of sparrow's eggs, and the mother sparrow feeds the chick; and there's a pig in the family photograph on top of the television. A stork comes out of the football. At the end of the book all is made clear. 'Hello love,' said Mum. 'This is your sister.' So that's what the changes are all about.

Zoo is my new book. I have been wanting to do a story about a zoo for a long time, since *Gorilla*. One of the spreads in *Gorilla* presented animals behind bars, which was different in flavour from the rest of the book. *Zoo* naturally followed on from this. *Zoo* is very realistic – the division of the page as a way of suggesting bars and also enclosing the

chimpanzee in the page so the page becomes the cage. I didn't want to do a book about animals escaping from the zoo – I felt that had been done before. I think all this stems from my days at art college. I had studied a lot of animal behaviour and I did a series of drawings and paintings using quotes from animal behaviourists and illustrating them with human behaviour. I wanted to write this story from a child's point of view – showing there is, maybe, not as much difference between the animals in captivity in the zoo and this particular family.

But there were masses of cars on the road and it took ages to get there. After a while Harry and I got really bored. So we had a fight. Harry started crying and Dad told me off. It's not fair, he never tells Harry off, it's always *my* fault.

'What kind of jam do you get stuck in?' said Dad.

'Don't know,' said Harry.

'A traffic jam!' roared Dad.

Everyone laughed except Mum and Harry and me.

When we finally got there Dad *had* to have a row with the woman in the ticket booth. He tried to say that Harry was only four, and should get in half-price. (He's five-and-a-half actually.)

'Daylight robbery!' Dad snarled.

Finally we found the gorillas. They were really funny. Of course Dad had to do his King Kong impersonations, but luckily we were the only ones there. Then it was time to go home. In the car mum asked us what was the best bit of the day. I said it was the burger and chips and Harry said the monkey hats. Dad said that the best bit of the day was going home and asked her what was for dinner. 'I don't think the zoo really is for animals', said Mum, 'I think it's for people.'

That night I had a very strange dream.

Do you think animals have dreams?

CHAPTER 15

The Only Lemon in a Bowl of Planets

On Children, Their Poems and Their Obsessions

Fred Sedgwick

In a splendidly provocative chapter, Fred Sedgwick, who is both poet and teacher himself, gives a passionate and compassionate airing to his own strong views about poetry and children. He is convinced that children must be powerfully engaged, obsessed even, with the subject matter of their poetry if they are to write with conviction and flair. He provides some delightful examples of what children can write when they are inspired. And he reminds us of the tact and delicacy that teachers require when dealing with the making of poetry by young writers.

Poetry starts at a disadvantage . . . it is either numinous . . . or an object of comic derision.[1]

Poetry! oh! as to poetry, I foreswore *that*, and I think everybody else should foreswear it, together with pink ribbons.[2]

A poet asked me once in conversation: 'You're a writer . . . what's your obsession?' Thirteen years later, 12-year-old Hazel Flack, of Brandeston Hall School in Suffolk, wrote a poem under my influence – but indirectly under the influence of that poet, and his remark. More importantly, she wrote the poem under the influence of an obsession:

Making Jewellery

Eyepins, earclips, shiny, new
beads are my favourite,
rose red, grass green, any colour will do.
Bugles come in any shade but only one shape.
They're tiny, fiddly, hard to handle and small.

199

Eyepins, earclips, shiny, new.
Christmas is the best time to buy
when all the clips are cheap
and in the shops there's unusual beads
with glistery streaks.

I adore to see beads spread out
like leaves in fall.
I thread beads onto the wire.
Eyepins, earclips, shiny, new,
turquoise, magenta, any colour will do.

I must have satisfaction before I clip off the wire.
Bending the wire is the hardest bit.
The long-nose pliers smell of metal
and they're greasy in the middle.
My hands are hot and sweaty
trying to get the loop just right.

Eyepins, earclips, shiny, new,
blues and yellows, any colour will do.

It is the careful choice of words, I think, that make it magical in a small way. First, there are the nouns, some of them obscure to the non-specialist: bugles, eyepins, earclips, long-nose pliers. So often this kind of material is dismissed as 'jargon', as though every passion does not have its lexicon. As a motor mechanic, my late friend Robin traded in words like cam-shaft, carburettor and air cooler. For relaxation, he read motor vehicle manuals, relishing the delicious specialist words. Few of us dismiss the names of parts of our body – heart, muscle, ligament – as jargon when our doctor uses them, and as teachers we frequently accept, rightly or wrongly, terms like reading age, IQ and attainment target. We would help children to learn about their lives, their obsession and their language if we were less dismissive about their jargon, the words of 'all trades, their gear and tackle and trim'.[3]

Then (to return to Hazel's poem) there are the adjectives, especially the colours, but also the tactile words: rose red, grass green, fiddly, glistery, greasy, sweaty. And finally, there are the verbs. For most writers, not just children, these are the hardest things. So writers of all ages soften their attempts at the main, the vigorous, *doing*, part of a sentence, by making verbs present participle (–ing) or by putting them off until another adjective arrives. This is because a main verb *does* it, owns up, makes action implicit, commits the writer: 'jumped' – there, you've done it. 'Jumping', by contrast, is still provisional, and it is easier on our souls to remain provisional rather than committed.

Here, in Hazel's poem, after the care with detail, we get the sudden expansive, frank 'adore', followed immediately by a return to detail: 'I thread beads onto the wire'. There is also the repetition, and, partly as a result of that, the rhyme. The poem I'd shown her was my 'Apple Poem', which I had written under the influence of an interest in, if not obsession with, English apples, and some study of the *Reader's Digest Cookery Book of the Year*, which has lovely watercolour paintings of different apples:

The Apple Poem

> George Cave, James Grieve,
> Miller's Seedling, Laxton's Fortune,
> Scarlet Pimpernel;
> any one of, any one of,
> you'll do very well.

Crisp even-coloured
reddish-brown skin –
Egremont Russet,
body crisp and firm –
soldiers make one terrifying
last November visit.

Thick-skinned
Worcester Pearmain,
pale-green yellow
dipped in crimson –
Autumn's here, the
year's skin's sallow.

> George Cave, James Grieve,
> Miller's Seedling, Laxton's Fortune,
> Scarlet Pimpernel;
> any one of, any one of,
> you'll do very well.

Yellow-reddish-green
Cox's Orange Pippin,
skin flushed with gold,
aromatic favourite –
keep dreaded Dr Suit
away from my child.

> Discovery, Crispin,
> Laxton Superb,
> palest lemon skin,
> marked with muted red –
> what shall we cuddle this
> winter Baby in?

> George Cave, James Grieve,
> Miller's Seedling, Laxton's Fortune,
> Scarlet Pimpernel;
> any one of, any one of,
> you'll do very well.

Both these poems are concerned, successfully or not, with the magic, the music, of the ordinary. George Herbert is the best example of this that comes to mind: there are many ways of sweeping a room, and some of them make 'that and th'action fine' and so represent 'The famous stone / That turneth all to gold'.[4] All this is preferable to the self-consciously numinous, the search for the awe-inspiring, the mysterious, the sense of the presence of divinity. Indeed, it might well be that the searcher after the everyday might stumble on God quicker than the searcher for the numinous.

Anyway, through whatever filters I had insisted on – that poet, my poem – a girl's obsession shines through. And this chapter is about obsessions: about how one's obsessions are the only subject for any serious artist; about how young people's obsessions constitute a powerful way into teaching those young people to write poems – or to make pictures, or drama, or dance, or music.

Poetry still has a battle to fight. Hannah More's observation quoted above could be echoed a thousand times, had one the patience: teachers emerge in satirical mood from a poetry course, for example: 'Oh there's a fire extinguisher/a daffodil/my Ford Sierra – let's write a poem about it' ('the object of comic derision'). There is often a hint of the feyness of poetry – those pink ribbons. It is (as Martin Amis once wrote)[5] 'a school thing, a skirt thing, a church thing'. A teacher said to me 'Poetry's my favourite . . . but after the National Curriculum I can't teach it any more . . . there isn't the time.' Whether this is true is not the point: it is enough that it is felt to be true by many teachers.

In a gloriously robust attack on poetry readings, Flann O'Brien tells a story about a man

> who found himself present by some ill chance at a verse speaking bout. Without a word he hurried outside and tore his face off. Just that. He inserted three fingers into his mouth, caught his left cheek in a frenzied grip and ripped the whole thing off. When it was found, flung in a corner under an old sink, it bore the simple dignified expression of the honest man who finds self-extinction the only course compatible with honour.[6]

'You should have been a poet', Vladimir observes. 'I was', says Estragon. [Gestures towards his rags] 'Isn't that obvious?'[7]

Well, the poet's rags aren't merely evidence of her or his poverty, but also of the low status of the art. In the National Curriculum, among other examples of non-chronological writing, there is no mention of poetry. But there is increasing pressure on children, through testing, to get grammar and punctuation right first time, which is essentially anti-poetic, and also, of course, anti-educational, because concentrating on a full stop gets in the way of thought about ourselves, or our human context, or the natural world, or, come to that, the strength and potentialities of our language.

My central contentions are: that most schooling is, at worst, an antidote to the obsessions of the pupils; that, at best, those obsessions are only grudgingly allowed into the classroom; and that writing would be more powerful if the children were licensed to use more raw material from the activities that obsess them in their time at home: sailing, horse-riding, cooking, football, television and, as here, making jewellery; that the poems come when the writer addresses what really bothers him or her. And, by extension, that is when the learning comes, too. So, in the era after the ERA, there ought to be more poetry, not less, despite what the heirs of Hannah More and Flann O'Brien's faceless man say.

The teachers at the Homerton conference that started this chapter wrote about their obsessions. They were working to a deadline, as all writers, as all artists, as all humans beings are. One offered some notes from a holiday journal (kept over three years) that she was intending to turn into poetry 'when there is time':

Egyptian smiles make me feel very British and buttoned up. One friendly guide took a group of about ten English-speaking tourists round what had been King Farouk's palace. He made it clear that Farouk had been evil, and the people were glad to be rid of him. Beaming at us, the guide held his arms out wide, and said in his clear short sentences: 'He was a very big man. This is his throne. He used to sit in it, cross-legged. It is made of solid gold.'

A crimson carpet leads up to it, and it has two lions on either arm. There are intricate decorations all over it: wreaths and shields and spears, as well as more abstract patterns of which the Egyptians are very fond.

We stared at the throne, as people do when they are told something is gold. Then the guide turned back to us, picked my son up, lifted him over the rope that is there to stop anyone getting too near – and placed him on the throne. 'Cross your legs. That is right.'

Then he bowed to the little English boy in the solid gold throne: 'My king!'

Other teachers used the idea of obsessions with their children. Laura Nowak (aged 10) of Cottenham Village College, Cambridge, wrote some notes following the instructions to 'Write down words about your obsession, about what matters to you most':

> The music plays, the baton conducts the symphony, leggiero, adagio, majestic and adante, the grave rhythm beats, the strings pizzicato, and the brass blow. the tempo moves on to semi quavers and crochets, the music is staccato and rhythmic.

This is what the teacher had called the 'wordhoard', a word best defined as Anglo-Saxon for 'database'. The first step in the writing of this poem is this brainstorming, often with a colleague writer. Then Laura wrote her first draft:

> The music plays, the baton conducts the symphony
> Leggiero, Adagio, Majestos and andante.
> The rhythm beats grandly
> Pizzicato go the strings, con motto tongue the woodwind
> The tempo changes, fast semiquavers and whole crochets
> play the orchestra, staccato and rhythmic is the music.
>
> Piano, Forte, Piano, Forte, the tempo darts about,
> A gentle slurring solo comes from the flautist
> Comes from the flautist,
> A loud but steady drumroll begins
> and ends.
> The audience ascend and clap rapidly
> while the instrumentalists bow.

Now I turn to what the teacher has written underneath this piece, because this is critical. Indeed, this is the central paragraph in this chapter. This is the educational moment, the moment when non-understanding ticks, we hope, into partial understanding. This is the moment when, if we are alert and lucky, we *teach*. This is the moment when we change from being child-minders at worst, child-trainers at second worst, to being, if only briefly, educators. This is the moment when we surrender control to a child who might be about to gain some autonomy over a part of the world with her language. This is the moment when (in spite of all the nonsense put in her way – test papers, rules about hairstyles, other petty restrictions over what she may or may not wear) she might learn something.

Perhaps we only truly educate in moments when we are educated ourselves. As a writer I am not only a teacher (I can, of course, only hope I am that) but also a learner. Writers have long accepted that they learn as they write – as Auden put it, 'How can I know what I think till I see what I say?'[8] Perhaps this is also true of teachers. How do I know what I teach till I see what I learn? Attainment targets merely comprise a cumbersome, ugly brocade to help us believe in the delivery model of education, which insists that we own knowledge and we only need to dump it, somewhat selectively, in the mind of the pupil. It is more honest to the truth of human experience that as we teach, we learn. And, conversely, as we accept ourselves as finished, educated persons, who have no higher function than delivering knowledge, we fail to teach. We merely train children in the acceptance of a view of society that is either ours, or one imposed on us, or, more likely, a complex of the two.

The problem in harnessing the power in educational moments in classrooms is that we are busy human beings, and at the lowest level we say, 'That's lovely, now draw a picture.' Maybe we have a dinner register to complete, or a playground duty to do, or an adviser to welcome, or some other educationally irrelevant activity awaiting us.

I have collected, from among the bare ticks, some examples of responses from my son's notebooks:

Very good
Try harder, please
Good, but be neater
The ending is a bit jumbled, wouldn't you agree, Daniel?

I add some of the banal things I have written on children's writing:

Very good
Ace!
Keep this standard up
A bit scruffy, I'm afraid

Laura's teacher, though, wrote: 'See if you can match the *shape* of the poem to the pace of the music.' This, as a remark to a pupil, has four advantages. It requires further purposeful thinking. It does not discourage. It does not patronize. And it owns up to the fact that the teacher does not know how the poem should finish.

Laura then wrote:

> The music plays, the baton conducts.
> Leggiero. Adagio
>   majestos and andante.
> The rhythm beats
>   gravely and largo
> Pizzicato
>   go the strings,
> Con motto
>   tongue the woodwind,
> The tempo changes, fast semi-quavers
> and whole crochets play the
> orchestra,
>   staccato
>   and rhythmic is the music.

Piano,   Piano,
    Forte,   Forte,
The tempo darts about
A gentle slurring solo comes
from the flautist.
A LOUD drum roll begins
                              and ends

          ascend and clap rapidly
The audience
While
      the
            instrumentalists
                                    bow.
      tempo
The   about.
            darts

The final draft is identical to this one, except for a few punctuation changes that may well not be deliberate.

What is the use of this work? First, it increases autonomy as we are allowed to find our own experiences valuable. This is important in Laura's case, but it is even more important when young writers are empowered to use material from areas of experience that are not always considered school-friendly, such as pop music and football and other media obsessions:

Ancients of Mu Mu
    Ancients of Mu Mu
        No 1
Everybody in the house of love
    Dance, dance,
    Jive, Jive
Pump it up . . .[9]

Second, it allows writers to draw on a vocabulary they already have, and if we have helped children to escape from the tyranny of the word-book, or the 'personal dictionary', they can use those words without worrying about whether they have spelt them right first time round. They can briefly link two disparate worlds: school and a personal passion; and this activity can only do both worlds a favour. It insists on originality, on the writer's using words that she or he has thought of, in an order that she or he then plans. It is, therefore, play, and, most powerfully, play with a material for which the writer has responsibility.

The difficulty is cliché. I received work from schools all over the country about obsessions, and almost all the children who wrote about horses talked about 'munching grass', while several lapsed into sentimental anthropomorphism about 'four-legged friends . . . whinnying and neighing, stating their point of view'. Several mentioned 'an old brown carthorse . . . daydreaming'. How do we help children avoid this kind of cliché? And why do they do it in the first place? Left to themselves, young children will produce vivid and fresh phrases. These are 5- and 6-year-old children at Parkland CP School, South Wigston, Leicestershire, talking abut jelly they have made and eaten:

> It's sticky, like red pop, like blood in a bowl, a red swimming pool, it's stretchy like a pair of pants when you stretch them, soft like a sponge, squidgy like a flannel, stretchy like elastic bands, sticky like chewing gum, squashy like doughnuts, like a balloon, it wobbles in the mouth, it's like a trampoline, it's bouncy like a bouncy castle . . . when the spoon sticks in it, make a crack in the jelly.

Something happens between this early stage, with its frank vigour ('red pop . . . blood in a bowl . . . wobbles in the mouth') and the later one at the beginning of adolescence when the vigour goes, and we hear again about horses munching, about four-legged friends whinnying and neighing, stating their points of view, as though Tex Ritter and Roy Rogers had visited these classrooms. Can it be that teachers contribute to the cliché-driven excesses in the years that follow adolescence? There is, certainly, something in the system that encourages writing that is expected, hand-me-down, correct according to some cultural definition of poetry. I have explored this question elsewhere,[10] noting that banal rhyme, high-falutin' phraseology and casual, passing quotation from previous poems all mark work by young people infected (as, of course, we all are) by this inert tradition.

Another obsession one can teach directly is ourselves. 'The magic box' is a technique many teachers use for getting children writing – but they all use it in different ways. I ask children to close their eyes and to see in their heads a box. I asked four questions about it:

- What is it made of? What kind of wood, of metal? What mysterious or strange materials?
- How big is it? 'It's as large as . . . as small as . . .'
- What colour is it?
- What is its shape? It does not have to be a cube – it can be any shape you like, however strange.

I then ask them to write, quickly, notes in answer to these questions. Children do not find this a problem: they accept the interesting fiction immediately and begin to write down extended metaphors for their own personalities. Then they answer, in a similar way, the following questions:

- How does the box open? If it opens to music, what kind of music? What other noises? What adverbs might you use to describe the way it opens?
- What is your most precious object, there inside the box?
- What impossible things are inside the box?
- The box closes. How does it close? And what are your feelings about this?

Ten-year-old Rebecca Swinn, of Denver, Downham Market, wrote:

> My box is tiny.
> Inside is me as a baby.
> My box is made of pine and pear wood.
> Around it is golden gilt.
>
> My box holds great secrets.
> As you take them out they unfold like parasols.
>
> The most impossible things are in there.
> Tiny twirling animals of different kinds dart about, touching
>   loving harmless things.
> Day and night swirl out of the box like smoke.
>
> On my box are faraway places, places no one could ever get
>   to. In my box are places further than space.
>
> The box closes, sucks everything into it, and I go to sleep.

(The original ending was 'and I die').

Aidan Chambers has said that 'the closer you get into your own nerves, the closer you get to what's universal'.[11] Writing about one's own nature, making metaphors, as here, for one's own character, is a tentative – but still surer than most – route into that knowledge about one's own nerves, and hence, the universal. To hell with, one might say, the numinous: what is needed is a closer knowledge about oneself, about one's own nerves. Know then thyself, indeed.

A less direct route to those nerves and that universal is through our perceptions of other people. Robert, who is a 9-year-old at Giles Junior School in Stevenage, wrote about his uncle in terms of the weather, plants, music, drink, furniture, television programmes, an animal, food and what would be in that person's mind in the small hours. This framework, and the original idea, comes from Sandy Brownjohn.[12] Robert wrote these notes under great pressure, and they only took about twenty minutes:

> He is a sunny day when you're inside.
> He is a daffodil glittering in the sun.

He is the music of God,
He is the drink of the angels.
He is a warm electric bed.
He is a programme about kindness.
He is a bee in a flower that fills the air with its odour.
He is the food of the trees the leaves the birds and the bees.
He's got a lot of people on his mind – the angels, the god, and
    the sun.

Vernon Scannell has said that children cannot write poems.[13] On the other hand, 'the child / is a great poet, / with an imperfect tongue / lisping perfect verses' says Bing Xin, quoted by Robert Hull.[14] Somewhere between these two unnecessary, sentimental, but predictable extremes, there are children using their language to learn about themselves, and their world; to learn, even more critically, about their relationship to that world. If, in their move from the everyday towards the numinous, in their search for the new, they verge dangerously towards over-romantic images ('the music of God . . . the drink of the angels'), that is preferable to the banality of the pencil-and-paper grammar lesson being foisted on them by current legislation.

All poetry is in some way the articulation of what is hidden. That is why it is connected with the past. That is also why it is connected with the untamed, with the risky, with earthquakes and endings. To license this articulation, children must be allowed (indeed, *all* writers must be allowed) to take their work through drafts. It counters the experience of writers to insist on a perfect first word or line, and that is why the testing used at present is uneducational in its insistence on correct use of full stops and capital letters in prose.

We are searching for those moments when the imagination glimmers, and is not snuffed; when a child writes a sentence that no one in the history of the human race has ever written before, as Leanne (aged 9) from Giles Junior School did, in her poem 'To the Sun': 'You are the only lemon in a bowl of planets'.

Eventually, long after the deadline, the teacher who had taken her son round Cairo sent me the poem she had written from her notes quoted above.

My King

We traipsed around the palace,
British and buttoned up,
and here was the bad king's throne.

The guide held wide his arms.
'This is the bad king's throne.
It is made of solid gold.

'He used to sit, cross-legged . . .'
Such clear short sentences!
A crimson carpet. Lions

raged mute on either arm
among wreaths and shields and spears.
Then the guide picked up my son,

my one certain obsession,
my one undeposable King,
and placed him on the throne

and knelt, and said 'My King!'
And I laughed through my tears,
wanting to sing. To sing.

Notes

Thanks are due to the following for their help with this chapter: Nigel Cox, H.B. Elliott, Mary Gwilliam, Sheila K. Johnson, Sue Mitchell, Mandie Morgan and Ann Roberts. Also, thanks to the following schools: Brandeston Hall School, Suffolk; Cottenham Village College, Cambridgeshire; Parkland Primary School, South Wigston, Leicestershire; Denver Primary School, Downham Market, Norfolk; and Giles Junior School, Stevenage, Hertfordshire.

1   *A Language for Life* (Bullock Report), HMSO, London, 1975.
2   Hannah More, quoted in Grevel Lindop, *The Opium-Eater: A Life of Thomas De Quincey*, Dent, London, 1981.
3   Gerard Manley Hopkins, 'Pied beauty', *Poems of Gerard Manley Hopkins*, Oxford University Press, London, 1918.
4   George Herbert, 'The elixir', *Works of George Herbert*, Oxford University Press, London, 1941.
5   Martin Amis, *The Observer*, 16 February 1986.
6   Myles na Gopaleen (Flann O'Brien), *The Best of Myles*, Picador, London, 1977.
7   Samuel Beckett, *Waiting for Godot*, Faber, London, 1956.
8   W.H. Auden, quoting E.M. Forster, *The Dyer's Hand*, Faber, London, 1962.
9   The KLF, *3 a.m. Eternal*, Album: ref 005CD, 1990.
10 Fred Sedgwick, 'The sifter's story: experiences of a poetry competition', *Cambridge Journal of Education*, 18 January 1988.
11 Aidan Chambers, quoted in Philippa Hunt and Elizabeth Plackett, 'Booktalk: an interview with Aidan Chambers', *The English Magazine*, 17 (1986).
12 Sandy Brownjohn, *Does It Have to Rhyme?*, Hodder & Stoughton, London, 1982.
13 Vernon Scannell, *A Proper Gentleman*, Robson Books, London, 1977.
14 Robert Hull, *Beyond the Poem*, Routledge, London, 1989.

CHAPTER 16

Memory, and Writing for Children Especially

Jill Paton Walsh

Jill Paton Walsh's account of her personal memories, dreams and reflections, sharpened with the writer's eye, is a tour de force. It could only have been written by a novelist at the height of her power, with considerable experience of life and literature behind her. But it is the young readers of her books who concern Jill Paton Walsh, and she speaks up eloquently for their rights and their needs. Here, indeed, is the passion and the prose.

I am going to start by offering you three small vignettes from childhood. First may I ask you to imagine a child born with an incapacitated right arm, the cause of which was not well understood in the then state of medical knowledge. The parents were told it was probably the effect of brain damage of unknown extent. Naturally they were anxious, and even more anxious when the child was very slow to learn to talk. One day when the child was nearly 3, and still had not spoken a real word, a neighbour leaned over the play-pen in which she was sitting, and said, 'What do you do all day, little girl?'

The child said, 'Today I am painting this picture, but normally I play with bricks.' This well-formed sentence caused immense relief and rejoicing in the family. To the end of her life, if the mother heard the daughter holding forth articulately about something, she would say, 'I *think* you're normal!'

Now would you imagine a child being held by the hand and led through crowded streets. Everyone is making for the harbour-side. A Salvation Army brass band is playing; there are little flags flying overhead. The child is led right out along one of the quays, and to the very edge. A number of small fishing boats are entering the harbour, and being tied up. Grandfather leans down and gives the child a basket of flower petals – everyone has paper confetti and flower petals – they are throwing handfuls down onto the decks of the boats, and people are cheering. The child throws her petals as hard as she can, but they all fall into the murky water between the weedy wet side of the quay, and the stern of the boat.

Bear with me while I offer you a third vignette. A child is getting up in the morning very early, in a house overlooking the shore. The child puts on sandals, and goes out, in her nightdress. She walks through the garden, and opens a gate to a cliff-path. She goes down the path to the beach, and finds it wonderful – swept clean by the tide, and left without a single footprint on it. A line of seaweed and sea wrack marks the limit of the now falling tide. The child runs around on the beach, and comes suddenly upon a dead body, lying face down in the sand. The body has one shoe missing. It is locked down in sand smoothed all round it, the way large pebbles often are; its hair and clothes, and the one eye visible in the profile of the embedded face, are full of sand, and the scour of the water that has placed it and left it has marked the beach around it with a system of drainage channels, lightly indented, a logic of flow round its complex shape. The child stares, but does not touch. She goes home by and by, and does not tell anybody what she has seen; of course she would get into trouble if the adults knew she had been roaming around alone at five in the morning.

As you will have guessed, all three mental pictures are pictures of my own childhood. But they differ one from another in important ways. The first story – the 'normally I play with bricks' one – is something of which I have not the smallest shadow of recollection. I have no idea who the neighbour was, what the playpen looked like, in which room or house it happened, or exactly when. It is simply something I have been told about myself. I have been told it often; my parents liked it as a story. I suppose it is true, and that it is about me rather than one of my brothers; but I don't know. I quite like it as a story myself, and I can see with adult hindsight and knowledge what it is about it that we all like, and why it seems to the family, including myself, significant rather than trivial. It is about somebody triumphantly confounding a low expectation of their abilities. The child who normally played with bricks was being shaped into someone who later ignored the teachers who thought a scholarship to Oxford out of reach – later refused to heed advice that getting books published was almost impossible – and so on. This story in effect is one of the factors in a personal legend which has constructed my adult personality. I still can't remember it.

The second story – the one about the child throwing petals at a boat, and missing – is something that I really do remember. I can tell you a lot about it. But oddly, those adults who took me, didn't – they are dead now – remember that I was ever there. They remembered the occasion all right – simply for them, the fact that they had me with them was not important enough to lodge in their minds. I can date this memory precisely – June 1940; over fifty years ago. In June 1940 I was 3 years and 2 months old. The boats were in the harbour of St Ives in Cornwall, returning from Dunkirk. They had been part of the little flotilla of boats which had rescued the British Expeditionary Forces from the beaches across the Channel. This time I'm very certain that I can remember it. My grandfather's story of the day could just have included me – though it didn't – but surely would not have included that picture of the handful of petals and paper fragments landing on the water, and floating away. Surely I was the only one who would have noticed that my particular handful had gone astray and was floating, along with a bottle, bottom up, bobbing in the seaweedy fringe of the bottom step.

What has happened here, I suppose, is that at some stage I have stitched together a memory of throwing petals in the water with someone else's account of the boats coming home from Dunkirk. I don't think I could say that I remember the boats coming home from Dunkirk; that sounds as though I remember having known that that was what was happening. Whereas in truth I have this brilliant visual memory of flags, and the band, and the falling petals . . . and I could be quite wrong. It could be that I chucked my petals on some other occasion altogether.

This second story lies on the intersection of history and memory; it contains public events and a private impression woven inseparably together. In principle many other people could verify most of it; but a small fragment of it – the floating petals – is wholly individual to me, and belongs to the private interior landscape of a single individual. Large tracts of human lives are like this – composed of eccentric individual views of public events, sometimes public events of historic importance. The oddity of such intersections can itself become a matter of interest to people, as it is in the extensive modern oral folklore theme, 'Where were you when President Kennedy died?'

Can we now consider the third vignette, the drowned man on the sands. Among many memories of my early childhood, that one has to a very high degree the qualities described by Wordsworth in his 'Ode. Intimations of Immortality'. That 'visionary gleam' shines from every detail of the memory, which is indeed apparelled in celestial light in my mind's eye. But whereas I know that I don't remember the first story, and I know that I do remember the second, I have not the faintest idea whether or not I remember the third. It is something that might easily have happened. I lived in a house above a beach; it was wartime, it is a rocky coast, torn by storms. Once again I can supply more information round the edges of the picture; French trawlermen hated paying the harbour dues, and would shelter in St Ives bay by anchoring offshore.

Then the wind would veer northwesterly, and their boats would drag anchor, and go onto the rocks. Nothing about what I remember so clearly is impossible, or even unlikely. The trouble is that in the story the child went alone to the beach, and returned alone and told nobody. That I remember it as clearly as if I was making it up now. That perhaps I sat overhearing the adults saying that a man had been washed up on the beach, and imagined it, and am now remembering the imagination. Certainly that stuff about harbour dues, and no love lost between Cornish and French trawlermen, is adult knowledge; something I overheard . . . and then too, the image of myself in a nightdress, walking on the printless sands, has a quality more like dream than reality. I think it is the literary quality of the memory that makes me suspicious of it, the detail and the beauty in which it comes to mind. Of all three stories this one brings about, also, the sharpest sense of dissociation from the earlier self. Why wasn't I upset? Why did I mind it so much less than I remember minding missing the deck with a handful of confetti? Hadn't I any heart? Any sense? Well, no it seems not. There it was among the weed and the driftwood, and the cuttlefish bones, and I looked at it with innocent attention, and went home. Lastly I am suspicious of it because of a fourth thing I can remember with uncanny vividness; I remember being shut into a red bedroom as a punishment – an unjust punishment – for some small act of defiance, and going nearly out of my mind with terror. This memory too has a literary quality; naturally. For what I am remembering this time is a reading, when I was very young, of Charlotte Brontë's *Jane Eyre*.

I would like now to compare three kinds of writing for children – I always mean to say writing fiction for children; of telling them the naked facts I have no experience – to the three kinds of personal memory I have just described.

The first example – the story of the little girl who normally played with bricks – is told to serve a clear purpose. It is part of the acculturation of the child, in this case into the value-system of the family, in ways which I outlined to you. Although it is told about the child, it is not part of her personal experience, and it functions as a form of pressure on the emerging personality. It says, 'You are like this', and therefore, 'Be like this'. It would be easy to supply family stories which say, 'You are like this', and therefore, 'Stop being like this'. A very large amount of the literature written for children is bent on their acculturation in this way. It tells them things about themselves which they need telling. It offers them figures to identify with, and tells them how to be, if they want to be like these others. It used to tell them that England had a great empire, and they were English and therefore naturally brave and superior; longer ago it used to tell them that they were born steeped in original sin, and therefore damned if they did not achieve heroic levels of virtue and repentance; it used to tell any girl that she was not brave and superior, even if English, but no good at anything much, and best if meek and domestic.

Much the most interesting and often the most eloquent parts of the acculturation messages in fiction are those of which the author was not conscious, and perhaps not guilty; they were simply the bedrock assumptions of the time, and interesting precisely because of that. Any work of literature contains messages which the author did not consciously articulate; children's literature is not different from other literature in this way, but it has to be said that children's literature *is* more apt to be overburdened with conscious messages also. The urge to educate, inform and control young readers is so strong that many people cannot imagine any other reason why one would write for them.

It is relatively easy to forswear the deliberate didacticism which has often in both past and present loaded the reading matter offered to children with a dead weight of instruction. But of its nature it is harder – indeed impossible – to forswear the messages of which the author is unconscious. No doubt my own work and that of my contemporaries is disfigured by beliefs which will come later to be seen as malign, but what these beliefs are is knowable only with hindsight. There are also beliefs, condemned as bourgeois-liberal by certain critics, especially those who flourished in the 1970s, of which the author – this author anyway – does not repent; which get into the work of fiction because they are personal beliefs of the author which the author when challenged would stand by and defend. Such a belief in my case would be faith in the value of each individual personality, a belief in the importance of literature, on the grounds that literature nourishes the growth of individuals towards autonomy.

In spite of the picture drawn by certain modern critical schools of thought, societies do not really simply exhale literary work without the agency of authors; but societies do in one way or another control what is published and circulated and accepted as literature. Particularly, a society influences, or controls what counts as suitable for children.

The very existence of a separate publishing list for children's books implies that extra or different demands are to be made of children's books. In my relatively brief working life of some twenty-nine years, there have been broadly three changes of the climate of opinion influencing not what can be written, but what can successfully be published for children. When I first established myself as a writer in the mid-1960s, children's books were flourishing. The numbers of children were rising with the post-war baby bulge. Libraries and schools were reasonably well funded. Teachers and librarians were chiefly concerned with achieving high levels of literacy and low levels of television-watching, and for both purposes they required that books should be enjoyable to read. A very narrow literary orthodoxy on adult fiction lists, in Britain at least, ruled out most experimental writing and fantasy, insisting on a rigid naturalism, and consigning science fiction and historical novels to inferior genres. Talented authors escaped in droves to the richer and more varied fields offered by writing for children; the most exciting and the freshest writers I could find to follow and attempt to emulate were children's writers, and the fact that this lovely flowery field attracted almost no critical attention was part of the sense of freedom. You could do almost anything with a children's book that did not involve using swear-words in the text. Then gradually people began to notice how good some of this writing was; reviews appeared regularly in conspicuous places, and very shortly following on the notion that children's books might be literature came a virulent moral censoriousness, a demand for social relevance, and very widespread attacks on astonished authors for the alleged sexism and racism of their unconscious assumptions. The primary demand on children's books switched from being that they should tempt children to read, to being that they should inculcate approved attitudes.

If the attitudes in question had really been uncontroversial, or had been a true consensus of a large majority, then such a campaign could hardly have failed to transform children's books from a branch of art, however minor, to a branch of indoctrination. In different guise, the Religious Tract Society would have ridden again. But the views of the new pressure groups were not a majority opinion. The campaign has faded, and the atmosphere it created has been replaced by a ruthlessly commercial one. The cutting of public funds for children's books, falling numbers of children as a result of a downturn in the birthrate, and the desperate state of the publishing industry combine to favour mass-market books for the young, and to make it harder than ever to survive as a writer of would-be literature for them. It takes a certain versatility and a quantity of luck to survive in such rapidly changing conditions. Children, it seems to me, are the only stable factor in the situation, unchangeably various and unpredictable as they are.

It is possible to represent oneself as a smuggler; as a person not engaged in the acculturation of children, but concerned only to produce good things for them to read, and doing so by sleight of hand, managing to meet the external demands of publishers and reviewers and educators and the market while all the time transmitting a value-free, non-doctrinaire, disinterested story. Possible, but naive. Although I believe very forcefully that one must never use a work of fiction for consciously didactic purpose, because it ruins it, and produces bad art, this conscious forswearing is not sufficient, because of the powerful part in the creative process played by unconscious factors. In choosing what seems story-like to tell, in shaping what seems like a good ending, in following what consequences unfold from the acts of characters, in bestowing or withholding love from those characters, in portraying how the world is, always, of course, respecting what seems to oneself to be the truth of things, an author conveys a view of the world.

Such patterning of the vision offered by a book is more influential than the deliberate message-giving of the consciously controllable part of the story. My parents surely did not intend to brainwash me when they told the brick story. They would have thought of it as true – something that really happened. But in selecting that from millions of other things that also happened, and by telling it with such amusement and satisfaction, they did in fact convey to me very strongly their pleasure in the hope of having a cocksure child who triumphed over low expectations. What you mean by telling a story and what you do by telling it are not the same.

My Dunkirk memory should be compared to writing historical novels. Historical telling concentrates on public events; historical fiction includes private consciousness. The private consciousness – the inner experiences, thoughts and feelings, of the characters as public events impinge on them – has to be invented; nevertheless, because anybody who has actually lived through a public event, like the return of boats from Dunkirk, will remember a mixture of the inner and the outer happenings, as I remember a public celebration and a private disappointment at my poor aim, a narration which supplies a private element in an account of an historical event will have more credibility to the majority of readers, especially young ones. It will replicate in a greater degree the immediacy of a real experience. The difference in immediacy is very great; I am sure that I was present at the Dunkirk party because I can remember a private aspect of it; otherwise I might think it was a memory reconstructed from adult talk. Only the very sophisticated reader, the adult historian, who will be aware that part of the narration must necessarily be invented, will find it less authoritative than an account which deals only in public events. In telling children a story about something in the past, I aim therefore at an account which mixes public and private perspectives so as to imitate memory. Invention supplies what the public record does not contain. The interaction of public and private life is likely to be a frontier of continuous interest in any human life. Taking a story of a past event, and making private what is known only as a public event, is a way of representing an important aspect of life to a reader.

Which brings me to my third example. Did I ever see the body of a drowned man on the smooth sands of a beach in the early morning? Or did I dream that, or make it up? Even if I did actually see it, it belongs to the realm of entirely private experience, for nobody could ever have confirmed it to me. I was alone. And with this we have come to an example of a central purpose of writing fiction – to accomplish the making public of what is private; to confide in the reader; and by doing so to reassure them that their own inner landscapes of mind and heart are neither an aberration nor a chimera, but that others experience similar phenomena, others are similarly possessed. The writing and reading of fiction legitimates the inner world, and children have as much need of this kind of befriending as any others.

In fact, perhaps they need it more. In spite of the Romantics, children live in an adult world which pays little regard to childhood, among people many of whom have forgotten their own early lives in large stretches, and who do not retrospectively think highly of themselves when young. Both nature and the adults around them drive children to grow as rapidly as possible into adult life. The portrayal of states of childhood as having permanent value may help their self-esteem along the way.

It really doesn't matter now whether I saw, dreamed, or imagined the drowned seaman; that image of death as a kind of high-tide-mark on a tranquil shore has been with me all my life. It has had an effect on me all my life.

I would like to finish by making a distinction which has been lying ready to be made all through this talk, but which I have not yet touched on. That is a distinction between memory and recollection.

Memory is an all-purpose and often a short-term sort of thing. We use it for the most part for managing the present – for finding our reading glasses, and remembering our name for putting on forms; for realizing that we owe our brother a letter, and that we are out of coffee beans. Recollection, however, involves bringing past states of mind into the view of a present state of mind; childhood recollected is an event in an adult life. It enriches adult perception, and perhaps, with luck, makes it communicable to children; it does not – it certainly should not – cancel, undermine, or demolish an adult view. But the association of recollection with elegiac feeling, or with the elegy-and-water that we call nostalgia, is very strong.

Many writers for children in both the last century and the present one recollected childhood with passionate nostalgia, as a lost golden age, and held up to their readers a mirror in which they were supposed to see their own innocence and happiness. *Little Women*, and *The Wind in the Willows, Little Lord Fauntleroy, Winnie-the-Pooh*, and *The Moffats* . . . there are innumerable examples. One might compare *Through the Looking Glass*, in which childhood is pictured to the reader as an unsullied pool of natural good sense in a world of lunatics; a gentle flattery of reader by author; or the image of childhood as misery and displacement to be triumphed over which orginated in a blacking factory and indelibly marked the characters and the stories of Charles Dickens.

It would be possible, and interesting, to analyse dozens of different images of childhood in recollection colouring the fiction of adult writers, but the point I am making is simpler. It is that one does not recollect the present. That is why, as Virginia Woolf pointed out, the present is so much less vivid than the past; one's emotions have not yet had time to expand and take it in. One does not recollect the present, and for the *readers* of children's books childhood is the present. The superimposition of childhood recollected with adult states of mind may produce literary masterpieces, but they may be like *The Go-Between*, or *High Wind in Jamaica*, not for the young.

Although the process of writing fiction, semi-autonomous, imperfectly controllable, full of involuntary internal event, strongly resembles, indeed mimics, the operations of memory, recollection of childhood is an insufficient ground in common with young readers, whose experience of childhood is not tinged with the retrospective attitudes of adults, or indeed, with any retrospective attitudes. Children do not, in my experience of them, particularly like nostalgia – why should they? Hope is their natural frame of mind. Their writers have to find ground in common with young readers in feelings and experiences which are shared by young and old.

Helping young readers understand the culture into which they were born, helping them construct a benign and enabling personal story, helping them connect the public world and the inner world are enlightened aims, and they are not limiting aims; they are consonant with a hope of producing good literature. But in pursuit of these aims memory is like fire; it is a good servant but a destructive master. It gets things going, but it casts an unsteady light.

Difficult though it is to achieve it, we must try to see the world, and portray it to children, in the light of the present day.

Index of Authors and Titles

Subject Index